GRAPPLING WITH DIVERSITY

GRAPPLING
WITH DIVERSITY

Readings on Civil Rights Pedagogy
and Critical Multiculturalism

EDITED BY

SUSAN SCHRAMM-PATE
RHONDA B. JEFFRIES

STATE UNIVERSITY OF NEW YORK PRESS

Cover art: Margaret Bourke-White (American 1904–1971), "At the Time of the Louisville Flood," 1937. Gelatin silver print. © 2007 Getty Images, All rights reserved.

Parts of 2, "A Space of Their Own: Women Educators in the New South," by Katherine Chaddock and Susan Schramm-Pate appeared in *Southern Studies: An Interdisciplinary Journal of the South* (2006).

Published by
STATE UNIVERSITY OF NEW YORK PRESS, ALBANY

© 2008 State University of New York

For information, contact State University of New York Press, Albany, NY
www.sunypress.edu

Production, Laurie Searl
Marketing, Anne M. Valentine

Library of Congress Cataloging-in-Publication Data

Grappling with diversity : readings on civil rights pedagogy and critical multiculturalism / edited by Susan Schramm-Pate, Rhonda B. Jeffries.
    p. cm.
Includes bibliographical references and index.
ISBN 978-0-7914-7327-6 (hardcover : alk. paper)
ISBN 978-0-7914-7328-3 (pbk. : alk. paper)
  1. Multicultural education—Curricula—United States. 2. Education—Curricula—United States. 3. Pluralism (Social sciences)—United States. 4. Toleration—United States. I. Schramm-Pate, Susan, 1960– II. Jeffries, Rhonda B. (Rhonda Baynes), 1965–

LC1099.3.G74 2008
370.117—dc22   2007011638

10 9 8 7 6 5 4 3 2 1

To Olivia, Remi, and Devair

CONTENTS

CONTENTS

PART II
METHODOLOGICAL AND PEDAGOGICAL CONTEXTS
CURRICULUM, CULTURE, RELEVANCE, AND PRAXIS

ACKNOWLEDGMENTS

This volume was born in 2003 in Pittsburgh, Pennsylvania, at the American Educational Studies Association (AESA)—the spawn of several good-natured debates and messy notes on cocktail napkins. Nurtured at AESA over the next two years, this baby learned to crawl in Mexico City, Mexico and then to walk in Charlottesville, Virginia. Thanks to everyone who stayed dedicated to the volume. It is your encouragement and hope that helped us most.

We would also like to thank Trisha Guy for her dedication and hard work on this volume's index.

With peace and thanks.

Susan and Rhonda

INTRODUCTION

IMAGINE NO FENCES,
NO BORDERS, NO BOUNDARIES

Susan Schramm-Pate, Richard R. Lussier,
and Rhonda B. Jeffries

Getting high school students to focus on their academic work in the face of a myriad of teenage distractions, issues, activities, and problems is difficult work for any secondary school teacher in this country. Inducing them to grapple with serious sociopolitical issues of the day that most adults would consider challenging, if not dangerous, particularly when it is so much easier to go through the banking method of teaching a subject so famously challenged by Paulo Freire a generation ago, can be more daunting still. Teaching students to think critically about the issues of the day and face discomfiting questions of social justice that might challenge their own comfort and worldview requires tact, planning, patience, and a bit of bravery—particularly in schools located in traditional or conservative areas where any challenge to the social status quo can be, and often is, fiercely resisted. As tricky as the teaching of controversial issues can be, we think it helps in any setting if the teacher can relate to, sympathize with, and enjoy the company and the folkways of the people from whose homes the students come. It also helps to come with the expectation of doing nothing more than helping students develop critical thinking skills and apply them to issues about which they had never previously thought. In short, the teacher plants seeds of thinking that eventually may germinate into positive, progressive, social action, if only on an individual scale. Since we are all human and subject to the same foibles, it is best not to thunder prophetically from the mountaintop but rather, as Isaiah once bade his listeners, to "come, let us reason together" (Isaiah 1:17). This is essential if we are to realize the potential of the public schools for building pluralist democracy one community at a time.

This volume of chapters by a diverse and distinguished group of scholars is about recognizing alternative educational sites of knowledge production. The overarching theme of the book that holds all of the chapters together involve what Homi Bhabha (1994) calls the process of cultural "hybridity," that is, an in-between space that carries the burden of the meaning of culture, curriculum, and collaboration. Each chapter constructs a sketch of how a conceptualization of "hybrid curriculum" may function within everyday classroom activities to exercise powerful positive effects on students' thinking, social development, and critical consciousness by enabling them to link authoritative and internally persuasive discourses (Bakhtin, 1981). In addition to Bhabha's work, this volume is informed by cultural studies (Carlson & Apple, 1998; Giroux & McLaren, 1994; Giroux, 2000; Trifonas, 2000), multidisciplinary scholarship (Freire, 1995; Gioseffi, 1993; Ladson-Billings, 1994; McCarthy & Crichlow, 1993; Said, 1993), and critical issues in the social studies (Ross, 1997; Stanley, 2001).

The chapters in this book address the issues and concerns of people currently invisible, silenced, and marginalized in American school curriculum and are relevant for classroom teachers and preservice teachers who want to adopt a "civil rights pedagogy." The purpose of civil rights pedagogy is to enable students to be concerned citizens and to enable them to combine theoretical and activist forces to work toward economic, social, political, and environmental justice. In the spirit of hybridity—in the crossing of borders, the creolization of identity, and the goal of achieving social change, the authors of this volume view students as a new generation of social agents who will play an important role in the twenty-first century. But in order for them to do the Gramscian counterhegemonic work it will take for them to be organic intellectuals, thinkers, and activists as such as Martin Luther King, Jr., Rosa Parks, and Paulo Freire, they will have to hear and to heed the call for social justice. Our goal is not to simply provide historical sketches of various social movements but also to theorize what each piece of history in terms of praxis and coalition building across a politics of identity and difference can offer today's educators who may wish to work within the opposition movements facing the grand battle of undemocratic policy and practice that accompanies the neoliberal agenda both nationally and globally. In short, a civil rights pedagogy prepares young people to interact in a variety of contexts with people different from themselves by illuminating the diverse worldviews of people in our nation's history who are usually omitted, marginalized, or misrepresented in mainstream academic knowledge.

Our task is to not only include the perspectives of "others" so that students understand the felt needs and realities of our nation's peoples but also to enable students to examine the origins and assumptions that underlie the mainstream framework that divides the nation into "North" and "South," "us" and "them," "rich" and "poor," "black" and "white" and to analyze alternative frameworks for understanding people and the planet—past, present, and future. Our challenge is to disrupt the binary opposition that has framed thinking about curriculum from institutionalized divisions of people and ideas to the complexity of the interaction and syncrety of the third space.

The theme of these chapters involves reconstructing curriculum around the promotion of the kind of transformative dialogue within a new "third" space that promotes the type of interdisciplinary collaboration between teachers and students that is so necessary for helping young people understand their increasingly diverse and interconnected world.

The "hybrid" space between good and evil is examined by several of the authors through an articulation of allegories and truths revolving around the dichotomous construction of the canon of American heroes and villains and the deconstruction of the "writing of the nation" (Bhabha, 1990). For example, who was Rosa Parks, and why is she considered a normalized American hero by some and a threat to the reputation of the great, late Martin Luther King, Jr., by others? And why are Appalachian people romanticized as strong, proud, and noble (witness *Andy Griffith*) and vilified as incestuous, fierce, and backward (witness *Deliverance*)? Some of the authors use the genre of film and pulp fiction to illustrate the contested "hybrid" space between fiction and reality. For example, why are urban schools continually portrayed as either places of despair (witness *Blackboard Jungle*) or places of tender hope (witness *Dangerous Minds*)?

We have grouped the chapters into two categories "Theoretical and Historical Contexts" and "Methodological and Pedagogical Contexts." While all of the chapters are unique, they all aim to enable classroom teachers and preservice teachers to engage in the critical debates and scholarship necessary to enable students to grapple with diversity. All of the authors offer implications for curricular changes through the challenges inherent in conceptualizing "hybrid" curriculum. They examine how hybridity might function within everyday classroom activities to exercise powerful positive effects on students' thinking, social development, and critical consciousness by enabling them to link authoritative and internally persuasive discourses. By promoting critical multiculturalist pedagogy within a conceptualization of "hybrid curriculum," these chapters frame current debates over subject areas versus social studies and the pressure teachers are under to transmit "national culture" (i.e., nationalism/ patriotism debates and the national social studies standards).

While the essays of Homi Bhabha in *The Location of Culture* (1994), Cameron McCarthy in *The Uses of Culture* (1998), and Edward Said (1993) in *Culture and Imperialism* may seem remote to some teachers, they are important to be aware of since they address the paradoxes of divergent, even conflicting local and global forces that are occurring at the same time, even in the same places, and the resulting hybridity of ideas, experiences, and cultures that increasingly characterize the human experience. The chapters in this volume acknowledge the complexity and uncertainty of cultural production, yet none of them flinch from seeking avenues to imagine a "hybrid" (i.e., third) space beyond dichotomy in which to lay the groundwork for a transformative ethos of schooling.

The concept of 'privilege' is also very much at play in these chapters. The authors ask, Which stories are privileged in contemporary culture? What readings are available, and whose interests are privileged by them? These authors help classroom teachers and preservice teachers face the important crux of understanding that there is no neutral reading or safe story for us to advance in our roles as cultural workers. The terrain is always shifting, and there is no easy assurance that a curriculum is antiracist, antisexist, anticlassist, antihomophobic, emancipatory, or empowering. What these chapters highlight is the need for strategic thinking in how we utilize cultural symbols and representations.

These chapters frame civil rights pedagogy though a discussion of major issues in the contemporary teaching of change and conflict and through historical civil rights movements. While each of the contributors work from specific sites and distinct theoretical and methodological traditions, they strive to use both motivating historical and contemporary examples and coherent language that asks readers to consider an understanding of "hybridity" (i.e., as a third space of resistance) as it relates to diversity and civil rights. For example, all of the chapters in this volume take signifiers of identity, such as place, gender, ethnicity, class, sexuality, and race and explore their complexity in contemporary and/or historical times. The authors conceptualize "culture" not as a static, fixed, or predetermined entity but as reflective of American society's continual movement and changing interrelationships. Moreover, each of these works presents a model for using a "hybrid" understanding of culture as a standpoint from which to theorize new pedagogies. The chapters also bring the contradictions of public and private spaces to the fore. How is public and private space negotiated? How do symbolic representations operate to reinscribe notions of public and private? How are race, class, sexuality, and gender negotiated and renegotiated through appropriations of space in the "curriculum" as private or public?

All of the authors in this volume support detracked, heterogeneously grouped, and integrated classrooms where students are challenged to explore and transverse a variety of subjects regarding class, race, gender, and sexuality. The authors also show how classrooms can be powerful spaces to debate and explore questions of identity and difference. Students are invited to engage in a safe space each day with issues of power and difference, and they are enabled to develop a capacity to revision. For the authors of this volume an intellectually and physically "safe" classroom is one where normativity is disrupted and disturbed while still giving everyone a chance to speak and be heard.

The book contains thirteen chapters and is divided into two parts: part 1 "Theoretical and Historical Contexts," and part 2 "Methodological and Pedagogical Contexts." All the contributors to this volume are committed to thinking about public education in new ways and to shedding a powerful new light on what public education could be today and in the decades ahead through both theoretical work and practical application in classrooms.

PART I
THEORETICAL AND HISTORICAL CONTEXTS: INTERSECTIONS OF RACE, CLASS, GENDER, AND SEXUAL ORIENTATION

The authors of the chapters in this section aim first and foremost to make complex theories in cultural studies, critical multiculturalism, and critical historiography *accessible* to classroom teachers and preservice teachers. Each chapter conceives of a "hybrid curriculum" set within a context of personal relevance and the ways in which knowledge is filtered through personal stories and cultural stories and the ways in which knowledge is situated in a sociopolitical-historical-economic context. The authors discuss the most contemporary theory in critical multiculturalism and critical pedagogy and are grounded in cultural studies, queer theory, race studies, and/or feminist studies. The authors also suggest some ways to shift Eurocentric, hetero, male social contexts, literatures, cultural forms, the canon, the empire, and the postcolonial to deconstruct metanarratives and advance civil rights pedagogy in American public life.

In "Remembering Rosa: Rosa Parks, Multicultural Education, and Dominant Narratives of the Civil Rights Movement in America," Carlson reveals how over the past decade or so in American education and in popular culture, a new multicultural canon of American heroes has been constructed. One of those inducted into the new multicultural canon of American heroes is the late Rosa Parks. Among other things, Carlson is interested in the rather sudden rise of Parks as an American hero. Whereas most Americans in the early 1980s had never heard of Parks, or had only a vague sense of what she did, by the early 1990s, much was being published about Parks and the Montgomery bus boycott, particularly in the genres of children's and adolescent literature. Carlson argues that while Parks' story sometimes gets told in ways that develop its radical democratic meaning, it more often gets told by incorporating it within dominant narratives of American history and by transforming Parks into a very nonthreatening, "normalized" hero (Foucault, 1979). "In recent years," he writes, "Parks' story has increasingly been told by cultural conservatives, like William Bennett, who includes Parks in his *Book of Virtues* as a universal symbol of courage, right along side the defenders of the Alamo from the Mexican 'Other.' "

Chaddock and Schramm-Pate's "A Space of Their Own: Women Educators in the New South" elaborates upon the importance of cultural performances by southern women educators in the late nineteenth and early twentieth centuries. While the women in this chapter are not in the warrior mode of trickster they nevertheless powerfully forged important educational improvements by founding new institutions, spreading access to the underserved, sprearheading state-level legislation, and developing heightened levels of community involvement. The authors make use of binary oppositions and a schema of markers in their analysis to highlight the specific contextual markers such as traditionalism and deprivation to frame an analysis of how and why women who were otherwise inexperienced and unprepared for reform leadership managed to operate with a third space to manage significant reform achievements. By pushing the boundaries of discussions of progressive education by defining the counternarratives of voices from the margins and (re)positioning southern women educators closer to the heart of American progressive educational discourses, this chapter provides a prospective that broadens our understanding of progressive education as well as the situations conducive to female reform.

Pepi Leistyna presents the past grassroots achievements of Myles Horton and the Highlander Folk School in his chapter, "Horton Hears a Who: Lessons from the Highlander Folk School in the Era of Globalization." Highlander was the educational center of the midtwentieth-century civil rights movement with such influential activists as Septima Clark, Rosa Parks, Martin Luther King, Jr., Andrew Young, and Stokeley Carmichael participating in the school's workshops. Leistyna writes, "With Myles at the helm . . . the tiny school worked to nurture curious, creative, critical individuals and diverse coalitions . . . [Folks were] dialoguing about the world and how to go about democratizing and changing it." From the start Highlander was controversial because of its curriculum and pedagogy. Rural students at the school were made aware of the workings of capitalism and organized labor, and it was a "popular training site for training union members, leaders, and organizers." Leistyna links Horton and Highlander to the contemporary globalization movement and presents ways in which we can learn from the participatory action-based research and knowledge produced there.

Tamara Powell's chapter, "Willie Lee Buffington and Faith Cabin Libraries: Doing Practical Good in a Disordered World," reveals one man's progressive work to increase literacy in the rural South. Under the Jim Crow laws of the South when formal learning was difficult for Blacks, if not impossible, Buffington managed to rally outside philanthropic forces to serve to enable a group of disenfranchised Americans to realize a level of success. Powell documents the historic Black community's involvement in its own educational uplift through basic literacy and the impact of the Faith Cabin Libraries on the State of South Carolina's rural communities.

Suellyn Henke's chapter, "Dangerous Minds: Constructing Urban Education between Hope and Despair," focuses on the film, *Dangerous Minds'* trajectory as a "hope-filled" popular commodity. Besides its standing as a film about urban schooling, Henke argues that the story of *Dangerous Minds* can be viewed as a fairly typical cultural phenomenon of postindustrial capitalism and the dispersal of meaning. First published as a nonfiction book, *Dangerous Minds* grew much larger and in the process has spread and contextualized certain "commonsense" understandings of urban education. Based on the autobiographical teaching stories of exmarine Lou Anne Johnson, an English teacher who quits after four years of teaching at "Parkmont High School," the film *Dangerous Minds* (starring Michelle Pfeiffer) first arrived for the public as a written text: *My Posse Don't Do Homework*; however, the emergence of the film simultaneously eclipsed and reinvented its own originary text. Henke deconstructs the film *Dangerous Minds* as the object of cultural criticism is an elusive and effusive spectacle, pointing the same instance to a synchronic and diachronic understanding of culture. She argues that the imagery and the aesthetic, a constant of postmodernity, injected itself as the code for the fearful allure of the "inner city" so effectively that choice to watch and to consume was never a complete option. Henke also points to two illustrative examples of the tentacle unfurling: (1) the banding across several radio listening audiences of Coolio's rap "Gangsta's Paradise"; and (2) the image of Michelle Pfeiffer standing in jeans and a leather jacket in front of representations of African American and Hispanic teenagers. In an era where meanings and symbols are put forth instantaneously, then flashed into our minds through a blitzkrieg of publicity, the battle over a title definitely has incalculable stakes, and *Dangerous Minds'* narratives are enveloped within the image of the title itself, the fragmented phrase, and the song played at a high school dance that everyone sways knowingly to in oversized jeans and "gangsta" fashions. As Henke notes, "the multitudinous strains of the endless repetitions of the representation, in many ways becomes the story itself."

Finally, in their chapter, "Queering the Body: The Politics of 'Gaydar,' " Jennifer Esposito and Benjamin Baez apply a Foucaultian analysis to the notion of "gaydar" or what they call "a silence that speaks." The body is objectified by language and the "gaydar" gaze of individuals who seek to identify other gay people. Since, as they write, "all bodies are marked by race, class, gender, and sexuality as well as a host of other markings," it is important to note that these markings are nevertheless unfixed and fluid and positioned within power relations. Following Butler (1989), the authors argue that the struggle over gay speech where the rules are continually shifted and challenged is a hybrid—an unsettlement of speech and text that directly affects the "body politic." Further they explore the idea of gender and sexuality as performative and point to gay and straight "enactments" that are complex and multidimensional. The authors infer that culture is affected through bodies and that bodies are affected through culture and that gaydar is part of this transactional process. In this sense, gaydar permits us to read a particular culture's socially constructed notion of gayness. The authors argue that understanding how both gay and straight people use (and abuse) gaydar has implications for the generating a more positive climate in schools for gay, lesbian, bisexual, and transgendered people.

SECTION TWO
METHODOLOGICAL AND PEDAGOGICAL CONTEXTS:
CURRICULUM, CULTURE, RELEVANCE, AND PRAXIS

The authors of the chapters in this section aim to demonstrate how hybrid curriculum can function within classrooms. Following a liberatory pedagogy (Freire, 1970), these chapters start with framing units within the context of personal relevance and aim to enable students to create knowledge through person stories. It is important for students to understand that cultural stories and the ways in which knowledge is constructed are always situated within a shifting sociopolitical-historical-economic context. The authors are influenced by contemporary theory in critical multiculturalism and critical pedagogy and are grounded in cultural studies, queer theory, race studies, and/or feminist studies.

Rhonda B. Jeffries' chapter, "The Impact of Trickster Performances on the Curriculum: Explorations of a White, Female, Civil Rights Activist" begins this section of the book. Jeffries describes ways in which teachers in higher education can encourage a performance approach to curriculum construction and pedagogy among pre-service and in-service teachers and administrators. Her chapter looks at curriculum in its broadest form and extends Jeffries' long-standing examination of the trickster figure. She explores the tangential performances that subtly yet deeply impact the educational landscape in every way and on every day. This chapter continues a specific exploration of the less prominent female and more specifically the white female trickster and the impact of her influence on schools in the post–civil rights era.

In "Hegemonic Representation: A Critique of the Multiplicity of Dixie," Susan Schramm-Pate argues that to understand Confederate symbols more broadly, we must broaden our understanding of cultural hybridity (new possibilities for the North and the South—bound together for better or worse). By focusing on the North/South binary, she aims to provide an intervention into the debate over Confederate symbols as the absolute "cultural property" of the South by calling attention to the radical cultural hybridity that has historically evolved within the reality of human encounters in the contemporary world and the implications of this hybridity for social studies curriculum reform. Schramm-Pate first briefly examines the current national standards for American social studies curriculum. A discussion of the North/South binary follows as well as an outline of the theoretical framework that informs the author's work on the production, effects, and pedagogical practices of hybrid curriculum. Finally, she hypothesizes how hybrid curriculum might actually function in classrooms by focusing on a rethinking of Confederate symbols and the relationships between centers and peripheries, through three bifurcated signifiers that are universally attached to the Confederate "Old South" but that originated outside of the South. They are: (1) the song "Dixie"; (2) Blackface minstrelsy; and (3) the fictional archetype "Jim Crow."

Next, Richard R. Lussier's chapter, "The World Language Other than English Program: Confronting Diversity through Reading, Writing, and Discussion," draws on his experiences as a French, Spanish, and social studies teacher in a small, rural high school in northwestern South Carolina. In his chapter he details two developments that have recently upset the applecart in this rural county: (1) the rise of more rigorous state curricular standards (complemented by a fearsome, new battery of state examinations) and (2) the advent of a large Hispanic population now estimated to be more than 11 percent of the total county population where previously there was none a scant twelve years ago. Prior to 1970, this county was entirely traditional, completely segregated, and relatively poor and uneducated compared to the rest of South Carolina, monolingual, and almost completely Protestant. When Lussier's students started complaining that they "shouldn't have to learn Spanish" since "people who come here should learn English first," he decided to make room in the curriculum for discussions that stress dealing with increasing cultural diversity in a demographically unstable school district. Lussier's chapter details the World Language Other than English Program (WLOE) that is fundamentally geared toward second-language acquisition as the primary focus of instruction. He argues that while WLOE instruction interested a plurality of the students who were delighted to learn about other cultures, a large segment (at least one-third) retreated into a sort of rural xenophobia and ended up less accepting of Hispanic culture than before. As an alternative to WLOE, the author shares the mix of pedagogical strategies including classroom discussions of cultural values, essay writing, polling, some lecture, and focus-group techniques that comprised the critical multicultural lessons that enabled this group of students to find their voices and break cultural barriers in order to better cope with the continuously steady increasing diversity within their profoundly conservative, rural, white community.

In his chapter, "The Cincinnati Freedom Center: Implications for a More Emancipatory Praxis," Adam Renner uses the newly constructed Freedom Center in Cincinnati, Ohio, as a departure point for investigating how multicultural/antiracist education/practices can be taken up in secondary social studies curriculum. Renner explores the many ironies associated with the positioning of the Freedom Center on the northern bank of the Ohio River and examines the incorporation of critical multicultural perspectives in social studies curriculums by asking, How can one discuss the Antebellum Era and the Confederacy in one's classroom in order that a more critical and multiperspectival understanding emerges? Moreover, Renner considers the potential resource that museums such as the Freedom Center offer educators who wish to infuse service learning projects into their curriculum and hypothesizes how these museums may (1) offer a location for transgressing boundaries of prejudice and (2) open up a space for more emancipatory dialog between socially different "servers" and "served."

Mary Jean Ronan Herzog's chapter, "Come and Listen to a Story: Understanding the Appalachian Hillbilly in Popular Culture," examines the phenomenon of why Appalachian people remain one of the few cultural groups in the United States for whom demeaning images are accepted in polite society. For example, diversity educators who would never cast dispersions on blacks, Mexicans, or homosexuals readily talk about rural people as "rednecks," "hillbillies," and "grits." This chapter is framed by scholarship in Appalachian studies, a hybridity of history, literature, and cultural studies. In this chapter, Herzog shares her pedagogical practices with preservice teachers as she enables them to examine the status of the hillbilly caricature in contemporary American culture from several perspectives to provide the platform for discussions of diversity. Students in her class discuss how the CBS television network's "reality" television show titled *The New Beverly Hillbillies* perpetuates Appalachian stereotypes and they study how historically, media and pop cultural accounts of the Appalachian region and its people are often stereotypically based on undocumented assertions and gross generalizations. Readings in her class include Harry Caudill's *Night Comes to the Cumberlands* (1963), Weller's *Yesterday's People* (1965), Bill Bryson's *A Walk in the Woods* (1980), and James Dickey's *Deliverance* (1972). Images of Appalachians in these works range from barbarians to people living hopelessly in the past with the future passing them by. Herzog's examination of the hillbilly caricature from these perspectives is aimed to develop a more informed understanding of a complex and diverse region and its people and challenge the easily accepted stereotypes that perpetuate negative images.

Silvia Bettez's chapter, "Stories of Women of Mixed Heritage: The Importance of Culture" centers the voices of mixed-race young women. The stories of six women who identify as "mixed" provide a way for educators to conceive of new ways to enable students to think about race, identity, and belonging. Bettez identifies herself as *mestiza*, the daughter of a Latina mother and a white father, and her ethnographic project aims to understand how women of mixed heritage negotiate their identities. All of her participants are candid about sharing their personal stories. Bettez identifies five themes including self-definition; fitting in and not fitting in; racial prejudice; privilege; and dating, marriage, and offspring. These are relevant to these participants' lives and "help set the stage for educators to assist mixed-race young women."

Laura Kent and Terri Caron's chapter, "I Can Relate to This! 'Leveling Up' Mathematics Curriculum and Instruction through Personal Relevance and Meaningful Connections," addresses some of the lessons they have learned as white women teaching in schools with predominantly African American students under the current No Child Left Behind act. From their perspective, constructing and adapting curriculum materials that honor the potential of marginalized students can be done through relevance and access to significant mathematics. Their focus is on bringing "domain specific thinking and bridging students' informal knowledge of mathematics content with formal notations and procedures to improve their opportunities to enter and succeed in courses that traditionally serve as gatekeepers to advanced degrees in mathematics, science and engineering fields."

Finally, we would like to say that we realize that *hybridity* is a buzzword in contemporary educational discourse and that it can be a difficult concept to grasp. However, thinking about a "third space" of resistance and a "third space" in which to enable students to "dialogue across differences" (Burbules & Rice, 1991) is a useful tool that may well function within everyday classroom activities to exercise powerful positive effects on students' thinking, social development, and critical consciousness. There are so many authoritative and internally persuasive discourses in curriculum that thinking about culture as a 'hybrid' may enable students to link various discursive practices and to construct meaning for themselves.

REFERENCES

Bhabha, H. K. (1994). *The location of culture.* New York: Routledge.

Bhabha, H. (Ed.). (1990). *Nation and narration.* New York: Routledge.

Burbules, N., & Rice, S. (1991). Dialogue across differences: Continuing the conversation. *Harvard Educational Review* (61)4, 393–416.

Carlson, D., & Apple, M. (Eds.). (1998). *Power/knowledge/pedagogy: The meaning of democratic education in unsettling times.* Boulder, CO: Westview.

Freire, P. (1995). *Pedagogy of hope.* New York: Continuum.

Gioseffi, D. (Ed.). (1993). *On prejudice: A global perspective.* New York: Doubleday.

Giroux, H. (2000). *Impure acts: The practical politics of cultural studies.* New York: Routledge.

Giroux, H., & McLaren, P. (Eds.). (1994). *Between borders: Pedagogy and the politics of cultural studies.* New York: Routledge.

Ladson-Billings, G. (1994). *The dreamkeepers: Successful teaching of African-American students.* San Francisco: Jossey-Bass.

McCarthy, C. (1998). *The uses of culture: Education and the limits of ethnic affiliation.* New York: Routledge.

McCarthy, C., & Crichlow, W. (Eds.) (1993). *Race, identity, and representation in education.* New York: Routledge.

Ross, E. W. (1997). *The social studies curriculum: Purposes, problems, and possibilities.* New York: State University of New York Press.

Said, E. (1993). *Culture and imperialism.* New York: Knopf.

Stanley, W. B. (2001). *Critical issues in social studies research for the 21st century.* Greenwich, CT: Information Age.

Trifonas P. (Ed.). (2000). *Revolutionary pedagogies: Cultural politics, education, and discourse of theory.* New York: Routledge.

PART I

THEORETICAL AND
HISTORICAL CONTEXTS

INTERSECTIONS OF RACE, CLASS, GENDER,
AND SEXUAL ORIENTATION

CHAPTER ONE

REMBERING ROSA

ROSA PARKS, MULTICULTURAL EDUCATION, AND DOMINANT NARRATIVES OF THE CIVIL RIGHTS MOVEMENT IN AMERICA

DENNIS CARLSON

INTRODUCTION

Rosa Parks died recently at the age of 92, just a little over a month before the fiftieth anniversary of the event that came to define her life and make her the stuff of myth—her quiet refusal to give up her seat on a bus in Montgomery, Alabama, on December 1, 1955. She was, of course, already the stuff of myth long before she died. Visitors to the Henry Ford museum near Detroit, Michigan, can sit in the same bus she rode that fateful morning. Tourists who flock through Madam Tussaud's Wax Museum on Time Square in New York City find her figure there, along with Martin Luther King, Jr.—the symbolic mother and father of the modern civil rights movement. Parks's story has been re-presented as a made-for-TV movie, and re-presented again by the rap group Outkast, whose hip hop tribute to Parks landed the group in the middle of a much-publicized lawsuit over the defaming of her image in the public eye.

In public education, Parks has emerged as an iconic, mythic figure in the discourse and practice of multicultural education. Her arrest is reenacted again and again on elementary school stages and in classrooms across the country, most often during African American History Month. And in secondary education, Parks's arrest is studied within the broader context of the civil rights movement and the Montgomery bus boycott, which typically is represented as the founding or original event in the modern civil rights movement—a crystallization of the movement at its presumed "best," before the violent sixties and the turn toward black nationalism and black power. Within this historical mythology of the civil rights movement, Parks assumes the role of Mother Courage—a shining beacon of hope that one person can change the world, that the power of conviction and quiet courage can be more powerful than all forces that stand in the way of human freedom and justice. One of the reasons why Parks's story has received so much attention within this dominant mythology of the civil rights movement is that it can be condensed down to very basic elements of time (the afternoon of December 1, 1955), space (a bus in Montgomery), and moral choice (Parks' refusal to give up her seat).

There is nothing wrong in celebrating acts of moral courage, and I believe Parks can serve as a useful mythic hero in teaching young people, and people of all ages for that matter, about the kind of courage it takes to talk back to power, to stand up for one's rights, and to do the right thing. Such traits of character are needed in a society that takes seriously commitments to social justice and human rights, and they need to be promoted in our public schools. At the same time, I believe it is the work of teachers and other public educators, at least in secondary and higher education, to "trouble" all mythologies of progress and all mythic heroes, and to help young people develop a more complex, accurate, and (I believe) democratically empowering understanding of history. I use *trouble* here in a way that is similar Judith Butler's (1990) use of the term, to refer to questioning dominant narrations and performances of historical events, and subverting the "normal" narration of history. To trouble heroes and mythological narratives of American history is to ask, Whose interests are served by these heroic tales and mythological narratives of progress? What is getting left out of history as it is condensed down to a few mythic elements? How might we renarrate history in ways that are more useful in helping reconstruct the present and build a more equitable and socially just tomorrow?

Parks's story, in its dominant and most influential forms, is very much part of a white narration or "writing of the nation," to use Homi Bhabha's (1990) term, that in its most generic form is about the development of the "American character" in the reflective image of the Enlightenment and thus of the slow but inevitable triumph of tolerance over intolerance and equality of opportunity over discrimination. But white mythology is not all of one piece, and we want to distinguish between two distinctively different "master" narratives of multiculturalism. The first of these, which I call the narrative of "normalizing" multiculturalism, maintains the Other as an Other, but distinguishes between "good" and "bad" Others—that is, "good" and "bad" blacks, "good" and "bad" women, "good" and "bad" gay people, and so on. Normalizing multiculturalism is about building sympathy for the Other in an environment of security—in which members of dominant groups do not have to worry that they will be expected to give up power or privilege or change in other ways. This, in my view, is the dominant or hegemonic discourse of multiculturalism, and it narrates the nation's past in terms of battles between virtue and evil, civilization and savagery, good people and bad people. Of course, one might argue that such a narration of history is appropriate for early childhood education. But I found it in representations of Parks targeted at other age groups as well, including adults. By transforming history into a battle between the forces of darkness and light (which take on special meaning in a racialized society such as ours), normalizing multiculturalism confirms many of the beliefs that have been associated with structures of racial inequality in America.

A second and in my view more promising narrative of the nation I call "liberal" multiculturalism. I use the word *liberal* in its "classical" sense here, to refer to the Enlightenment belief that all citizens are to be treated equitably before the law and within realms of the public so that all have an equal chance to advance themselves and pursue their own happiness. In the conservative version of this narration of the multicultural nation, differences of race, class, gender, sexual orientation, ethnicity, and so on are depicted as standing in the way of equitable treatment. Racial progress thus gets defined as moving in the direction of a "color-blind" law and public. Liberal versions of this narrative of progress emphasize the need to take group membership into account in order to "level the playing field." In place of a discourse of sympathy, liberal multiculturalism offers a discourse of tolerance for the Other within the "public," with the "private" carved out as a counterspace in which such civic obligations need not apply. Liberal multiculturalism has framed issues in education in ways that help advance democratic projects and agendas, at least in some forms. In my view, democratic multiculturalism needs to be anchored in a discourse of human rights and citizen rights, and multicultural education must be about challenging institutional structures, such as tracking and ability grouping, along with standardized proficiency testing, that stand in the way of a more real and substantial equality of opportunity in education. Nevertheless, the liberal narration of American history, and Parks's place in it, is too individualistic and legalistic in its conceptions of justice, and too contradictory in its treatment of difference, to serve as a basis for a major assault on racial inequality in America.

A third form of multiculturalism is associated with a challenge to the "master" narratives of American history. Socially reconstructive multiculturalism, as I call it, is thus subversive in many ways, and teachers who adopt this framework or perspective must, to at least some degree, teach against the grain and behind the back of the system. It depicts heroes such as Parks as produced by movements of liberation and freedom that have deep historic roots, that continue on a new terrain today, and that involve us all whether we like to admit it or not. Those privileged on one or more axes of their identity are called upon to move from sympathy and tolerance for the "Other" to forms of solidarity that involve active intervention to challenge "othering" beliefs and practices in public schools and other cultural sites. This discourse of multiculturalism politicizes the everyday "life world" and our relations with others in ways that normalizing and liberal multiculturalism do not. And it moves beyond a concern with the rights of individual citizens *qua* individuals to a concern with the individual as a member of social movements, involved in ongoing battles over power and knowledge on an everchanging playing field.

NORMALIZING MULTICULTURALISM AND ROSA THE GOOD

The French social theorist Michel Foucault (1979) argued that during the modern era, hierarchical relations of domination and subordination have been maintained and legitimated through various "normalizing" regimes—integrated sets of discourses, practices, and technologies that are used to set up oppositional identities and to position people in relation to power, as either "normal" or "abnormal." Otherness thus gets characterized in terms of being abnormal, which is to say, outside the norms of what is considered good, healthy, intelligent, and so on. Foucault also recognized that what the modern, Enlightenment era called "abnormal" or deficient, the Christian era called "weak-willed," "corrupt," and "evil"; so that what we find is continuity and discontinuity in the shift from overtly religious to overtly secular discourses of otherness and abnormality. Thus, he notes that "bad" prisoners, workers, and students in the early modern era in France were characterized in terms of a whole discourse of "latenesses, absences, interruptions of tasks . . . inattention, negligence, lack of zeal . . . impoliteness, disobedience . . . idle chatter, insolence . . . 'incorrect' attitudes, irregular gestures, lack of cleanliness, . . . impurity, indecency" (1979, p. 178). Institutional responses to this "abnormal" performance of self range from punitive to corrective. In education, deficit theories of the child and his or her culture are examples of normalizing multiculturalism.

The normalization of difference involves the construction of an abnormal other defined as "bad"—that is, intellectually deficient, incorrigible or criminal, sexually impure, and so on. At the same time, and in a somewhat contradictory manner, normalization involves defining both "good" and "bad" categories of otherness. For example, the culture of whiteness historically has distinguished between "good" and "bad" blacks, and in a related way, between "good" and "bad" whites. What are the characteristics of the "good" black in American cultural history? We would like to suggest two answers. First, nonthreatening, and second, "almost white, but not quite." In both cases, Parks's has been a representative of the "good" black person, and more particularly "good" black woman.

For example, in William Bennett's treatment of Parks in his *Book of Virtues* (1993), he removes her history, almost completely transforming her into a symbol of a "good" (i.e., nonviolent, nonthreatening, and deserving) black person, who is used to define, position, and morally condemn "bad" blacks (i.e., prone to violence against whites, ruled by a mob mentality, impulsive, and undeserving). According to Bennett's account, while Parks was inside the courthouse, "the crowd was getting restless. Some of them were carrying sawed-off shotguns, and the policemen were beginning to look worried" (p. 492). Here we have a primary trope of white fear and resentment: the impulsive, violent, nihilistic, black mob, the embodiment of the "bad" other. The community is transformed into a "powder keg" waiting to explode. This is particularly ironic given that blacks have always had more to fear from white mobs than vice versa. At any rate, Parks is represented, along with King, as one of the "good" black leaders who helped calm the explosive black crowd, who was able to steer the black "mob" away from violence and nihilism toward peaceful, nonviolent protest.

Other narrations of Parks's story repeat again and again the litany of virtue that defines her as a "good" black person and more particularly a good black woman. Certainly, there is evidence that the National Association for the Advancement of Colored People (NAACP) in Montgomery knew full well that Parks fit the white community's image of a good black person and that she was chosen for her mission precisely for that reason. She notes in her autobiography that the NAACP leadership in Montgomery had decided that the best plaintiff to challenge the segregated bus laws "would be a woman, because a woman would get more sympathy than a man. And the woman would have to be above reproach, have a good reputation, and have done nothing wrong but refuse to give up her seat" (Parks, 1992, pp. 110–11). She was, as well, a light-skinned person from a stable heterosexual marriage and in other ways "just like us but different" to whites. Homi Bhabha writes that this transformation of the Other into a reformed, recognizable other, a subject of a difference that is "almost the same, but not quite," or "almost the same but not white," is a primary discursive strategy in colonial narratives of progress (1984, p. 126). Parks was, in these terms, more deserving, more "normal," because she was light-skinned and dressed and presented herself as almost white.

Hollywood is particularly prone to normalize difference by relying upon the "good/bad," or normal/abnormal, binaries, and the made-for-TV movie *The Rosa Parks Story* (2002) is no exception. A scene that depicts Parks's education in the Montgomery Industrial School for Girls is of particular significance in this regard. The school is run by a group of white Quaker women from New York who are on a mission to help educate poor black girls in the South. Collectively, these women represent "good" whites, which also inscribes goodness in the North as opposed to the "bad" South and links "goodness" to missionary work with the poor. Significantly, the school is led by a Mrs. White (which actually happened to be her name), who the film makes into the patron saint of whiteness in its most benevolent, caring, altruistic form. One of Rosa's friends in the school, who is also a model student, tells her: "My mother thinks that Mrs. White is a saint for putting up with what she does, for keeping the school open." Many white teachers, she says, would not teach colored girls. Mrs. White, as a saint in the church of whiteness, is represented as providing Rosa the kind of foundation of good moral character she would need to be able to later take her stand. The implication is that "good" whites from the North were needed to elevate or uplift African Americans in the South so that they could be treated as equal to whites. The irony is that in this case elevation takes the form of an education that is all about learning to be subservient, about learning to cook, set tables, and mend clothes, about learning how to say "yes, ma'am" and "no, ma'am," to speak only when spoken to.

Rosa is made into a model student in the film, one who sides with her good white teachers against some of her own peers who are represented as a bad influence. The first classroom scene shows Rosa in a class being taught by one of the white teachers. One student questions why they should have to work so hard to learn to read and write when they are only going to be doing white folks' laundry when they graduate. Instead of answering the question, the teacher poses it to the class, asking if anyone can give the student a reason why they should bother to study and work so hard. Rosa raises her hand, is recognized, and rises from her seat to speak. "We bother," she says, "so we can be equal to everyone else. . . . If I put my mind to it, I can do anything I want to in this world. . . . Can't nobody take your dignity from you but you." Here Rosa places the blame for underachievement and social and economic subordination on blacks themselves, for not believing in the American dream that they can be anything they want to be. The teacher says, "May the blessed Lord help you remember what Rosa just taught you." But what is being taught here in this fabricated scene from her Hollywood life? One of the primary lessons being taught is that "bad" blacks always look to blame whites for their problems, always are complaining, whereas "good" blacks are responsible, do not complain, and believe in the American dream.

In another important scene in the film, after Parks has been arrested, her husband calls the city jail and demands that she be allowed to speak with someone. The white police officer on the other end of the line simply hangs up on him. So he calls a white friend of the NAACP, a rich local business-man, and asks him to help. When this influential white steps in to call the police, they immediately back down and release Parks. The theme that white people were involved in, and even leaders of, the civil rights movement is related to this trope of the "good" white. We find it again in an article by the progressive educator Herbert Kohl (1991). Kohl happened to be visiting an elementary school in Southern California at a time when the children were performing a dramatic reenactment of Parks' arrest and the subsequent bus boycott, as part of Black History Month. The reenactment ended, Kohl observed, with mostly white, middle class children marching around the stage carrying signs that read, "We Shall Overcome," and "Blacks and Whites Together." The student narrator of the reenactment concluded by saying that the Montgomery Bus Boycott was finally resolved by "people coming together to protest peacefully for justice" (Kohl, 1991, p. 36). Afterward, Kohl spoke with the teacher who organized this event to point out that the drama misrepresented the civil rights struggle as interracial, with whites taking a leadership role in ending discrimination and Jim Crow laws. The teacher's response was that perhaps the play "took some liberties with history" but it was presented as part of an effort to bring black and white children in the school together and reduce conflict. The teacher feared that if the play were presented as blacks against whites it might lead to more racial strife in the classroom. Kohl disagreed, arguing that by dramatizing the bus boycott as an organized movement by the African American community in Montgomery, "it might lead all the children to recognize and appreciate the strength oppressed people can show when confronting their oppressors" (p. 37).

It is the case that some whites assumed leadership roles in the civil rights movement, and some whites marched side by side with blacks. For example, the Southern Poverty Law Center, a group of primarily white, northern lawyers played an important role in working with the NAACP to challenge Jim Crow laws in the South; and both Parks and King had spent time in the summer of 1955 at Highlander Academy in Monteagle, Tennessee, where they worked with Myles Horton and other white Appalachians to prepare for the coming battle. As the black feminist scholar Patricia Hill Collins (2000, p. 37) has argued, the empowerment movement of black people in the United States always has had some support from white "race traitors," those willing to question their own racial privilege and side with the oppressed. At the same time, this has not been the primary history of whiteness in American, even in the "enlightened" North. Even the term *race traitor* suggests that whites have engaged in policing each other so that someone who is too sympathetic to the cause of black people in America, or who dares to march with them, must be willing to endure a certain level of ostracism. The point I want to make here is that by overemphasizing the importance of influential white people in Parks's upbringing and in "saving" her from jail, *The Rosa Parks Story* not only distorts history but also recycles a paternalistic "feel-good" narrative of whiteness, with good whites stepping in to rescue blacks.

Framed within a normalizing narrative of multiculturalism, Parks's story is reduced to a morality tale, although a highly racialized morality tale, one that links "good" whites and "good" blacks (the latter represented as almost white but not quite) in a common battle against intolerance and "bad" behavior. Though it may have made strategic sense for the NAACP leadership in Montgomery to look for a symbol of the normal and the good to test the segregation laws, the result was to affirm a normal/abnormal binary that historically has been used to separate "deserving" minorities from "undeserving ones" (like unwed teenage mothers). Parks even played into this narration of her story to some extent in her later years. In two books authored by Parks in the 1990s, *Quiet Strength* (1994) and *Dear Mrs. Parks* (1996), she writes to black youth in particular; and the message is clearly that in order for African American youth to succeed, they will need to avoid "bad" influences and role models and keep on the straight and narrow path of "good" behavior. Her response begins to sound very much like that of Bennett, with a strong emphasis on character education and the teaching of moral virtues and self-discipline for black youth, so that they can—like their white counterparts—pull themselves up by their own bootstraps.

It is perhaps understandable, then, that as Parks has been transformed into a "positive" role model for black youth, a symbol of good manners, politeness, and self-discipline, many black Americans, particularly those identified with hip hop culture, have begun to question and trouble the dominant myth of Rosa Parks. In 2002, the same year that *The Rosa Parks Story* won an Emmy for best made-for-TV movie of the year, the movie *Barbershop* was released. In that film, one character, played by Cedric the Entertainer, tells the other black men in the barbershop that Parks was merely tired rather than heroic and that she and the NAACP were too timid and meek. In elements of the black community represented in *Barbershop* the viewer gets a glimpse into a frustration that runs deep, that for all the talk of progress and the great victories of the civil rights movement, blacks are still second-class citizens in America and need more assertive leaders. Parks was angered by this reference to her in the film and subsequently refused to show up to receive a black achievement award because she would have to share the stage with Cedric. Then there was Parks's highly publicized lawsuit against the rap group Outkast in the last few years of her life, in which she claimed their song "Rosa Park" defamed her good name. All of this had the effect of tarnishing her reputation with those she most sought to influence. To her credit, Parks did express resentment at times over the fact that African Americans had to be so "well-behaved" in order to be accepted as equals. In her autobiography she wrote that she never quite forgave southern whites for supporting a racial order in which black people "had to be smiling and polite no matter how rudely you were treated" (1992, p. 107).

Normalizing multiculturalism is aimed at making the other more acceptable to members of dominant identity groups, and as I have argued, it does this by distinguishing between "good" and "bad" minorities. Sentiment is thus invoked, in the form of sympathy, for "good" minorities such as Parks. She is, for example, often represented as a bit hunched over, a somewhat elderly woman (although in fact she was only forty-two at the time of her arrest), who was just tired after a long day of work and wanted to get home. By 1968, Murray Schumach could write in the *New York Times* that "from a protest begun over a Negro woman's tired feet, Dr. King began his public career" (p. 25). Parks spent much of her life trying to set the record straight about her supposed tiredness. In her autobiography she wrote that if she was tired, it was "tired of being pushed around" (1992, p. 2). There is a world of difference between "tired feet" and "tired of being pushed around," yet in many if not most accounts of Parks's life, the emphasis has been on her tired feet, for that invites sympathy for a "good" black woman who only wanted to sit down. Parks's occupation, as a seamstress, also invites sympathy and makes her seem less threatening to whites. In the movie, *The Rosa Parks Story*, we see her literally on her knees, mending the seams of the dresses of rich white women in a big department store in downtown Montgomery and being told by her white, male boss that she is doing such a good job that he wants her to work longer hours. She dutifully agrees, the model of the noncomplaining, hard-working, docile, subordinate black woman, who is no threat to middle-class white male authority.

Some progressives have endorsed forms of normalizing multiculturalism from a pragmatic standpoint. Given that the revolution has been put off indefinitely—so this argument goes—minorities need to encourage sympathy for their plight among members of dominant groups if they want to reduce bigotry and prejudice, and this means presenting themselves as nonthreatening and just like "normal" folks. The philosopher and social critic Richard Rorty provides a good example of this type of argument. In the essay "Human Rights, Rationality, and Sentimentality" (1998), Rorty begins by asserting that progressives should not put too much trust in reason to overcome prejudice and bigotry, for the world does not change primarily through appeals to what is most rational. Instead of relying so much on reason to promote social justice and fight discrimination, or trying to convince people rationally that prejudice and bigotry is wrong, Rorty argues that progressives need to return to sentiment, and more particularly to a multiculturalism that promotes sympathy and security among members of the dominant culture through stories—"the sort of long, sad, sentimental story that begins, 'Because this is what it is like to be in her situation.' " Such stories, he claims, "have induced us, the rich, safe, powerful people, to tolerate and even to cherish powerless people—people whose appearance or habits or beliefs at first seemed an insult to our own moral identity, our sense of the limits of permissible human variation" (p. 185). By sympathy, he means "the sorts of reactions . . . that whites in the United States had more of after reading *Uncle Tom's Cabin* than before" (p. 180). This is, of course, an ironic choice as an exemplar of the kind of sympathetic stories we should be using to teach tolerance for the Other. For the character of Uncle Tom in Harriet Beecher Stowe's novel became a symbol of the "good" obedient, submissive, dependent, nonthreatening African American. To the extent that Parks is also represented this way, she too risks being transformed into a modern version of Uncle Tom, someone integrated within a patronizing and condescending narrative of whiteness. Rorty acknowledges that "if we hand our hopes for moral progress over to sentiment, we are in effect handing them over to condescension" and relying on those with power to change because they feel sorry for those who have been the victims of power (p. 181). But he sees no other option given current realities. Given the continuation of inequalities of power and privilege in America, appeals to sentiment "work" better than appeals to reason, at least for those who have power and privilege; and sympathy may encourage them to treat the Other more like a real human being—again, just like a "normal" person, only different. I would agree that sympathy texts have some role to play in a multicultural curriculum, but only if sympathy can be linked with solidarity rather than condescension and pity.

LIBERAL MULTICULTURALISM AND CITIZEN ROSA

Another multicultural discourse and narration of the nation's history, and one I believe holds more democratic promise, may be associated with liberal political theory and philosophy. Nevertheless, I also am skeptical of this discourse and narrative, both for failing to live up to its claims and for accepting a minimalist or weak understanding of the public and the rights of citizens. The primary tropes in liberal multiculturalism are "citizen," "public," "public good," "rights," "state," and "law," and while all liberal political philosophy has been organized around these tropes, there are significant differences among differing strands of liberalism in terms of what these tropes mean or should mean in practice. I want to distinguish between a "weak" or minimalist form of liberal multiculturalism, which has played a large part in framing Parks's story, and a "strong" form of liberal multiculturalism that understands the public and the citizen as constituted through civic discourse and collective action.

Locke has been particularly influential in framing weak forms of liberal democracy in America through his notions of natural liberty and the equality of all human beings; the rights to life, liberty, and the pursuit of happiness; government by the consent of the governed in pursuit of the public good; a limited role for the state; and the rule of law (see Tarcov, 1996). The role of the state is limited to the protection of the rights of all citizens to pursue their private self-interests and maximize their own freedom as individuals. The public is thus defined as a sphere or space of interaction by individuals as free citizens, joining in voluntary associations as they wish, or going about their own business, and allowing others to go about their's. The public good is associated with the maintenance of laws and codes of civility that regulate how people interact with each other when they are in the public so that each is treated with respect as an equal, free citizen. In this minimalist form of liberal multiculturalism, public transportation assumes a heightened importance as a signifier of the public, and the public good, for public transportation is a space where citizens interact like ships that pass in the night, occupying a common ground for a stop or two, and relating to one another (hopefully) with a certain politeness and civility, which takes the form of tolerance of difference.

Perhaps it should not be surprising, then, to find that two of the most important United States Supreme Court decisions affecting the civil rights of African Americans were based on very similar cases involving public transportation. The Supreme Court's 1956 decision in support of Parks's right to a seat on a public bus was used as an occasion to strike down all remaining Jim Crow laws in the South, just as the 1896 decision against Plessy's right to a seat on a public train was used to sanction "separate but equal" public facilities. So the latter decision reversed the former, and the liberal conception of citizen rights expanded somewhat in the process. The *Plessy versus Ferguson* case involved a thirty-year-old colored shoemaker named Homer Plessy who was jailed for sitting in the "white" car of the East Louisiana Railroad. Plessy was only one-eighth black and seven-eighths white but under Louisiana law was defined as black and thus required to sit in the "colored" car. Plessy argued that the Separate Car Act violated the Thirteenth Amendment (that abolished slavery) and Fourteenth Amendment (equality before the law). The United States Supreme Court sided with the Louisiana State Court in rejecting Plessy's argument. Speaking for a seven-person majority, Justice Henry Brown laid out what would become the guiding principles of liberal democratic theory in the Jim Crow South. He argued that "a statute which implies merely a legal distinction between the white and colored races . . . has no tendency to destroy the legal equality of the two races." Furthermore, the Fourteenth Amendment, he wrote, "could not have been intended to abolish distinctions based upon color, or to enforce social, as distinguished from political equality, or commingling of the two races upon terms unsatisfactory to either."

The lone dissenter, Justice John Harlan, set the stage for the eventual overturning of the Plessy decision when he wrote: "Our Constitution is color-blind, and neither knows nor tolerates classes among citizens" and that this decision would encourage aggression, "more or less brutal and irritating, upon the admitted rights of colored citizens." The decision by the NAACP to fight Jim Crow laws through the public bus system in Montgomery was thus perhaps not coincidental. It was in many ways a retrial of Plessy's case, but this time with a different outcome. And it is perhaps not coincidental either that the public bus is one of the key players in Parks's story. In Bennett's account, for example, we learn that Rosa and her husband woke each morning "to the familiar sound of a City Lines bus pulling up to a stop across the road." The green and white bus stands at the stop for more than a minute as black and white workers climb aboard, on their way to work. And each evening, the bus brings them back to their homes and families again—back to a "private" world. So the way people behave on buses is linked in Bennett's text to the way they supposedly relate, or should relate, as workers once they get off the bus. Both the bus and the workplace are public places, where norms of civility and tolerance prevail. After the boycott begins, according to Bennett's account, "empty buses bounced around for everyone to see" (p. 491), visible symbols of the collapse of public life. It is thus also not coincidental, perhaps, that public schools were desegregated through court-ordered busing. The battle to desegregate public education was represented and understood very much in the way that the struggle to desegregate public buses was represented and understood. The desegregation of public education was aimed at providing all young people, regardless of race, the same rights to a seat in a public school classroom that they had to a seat on a public bus.

As public spaces, the bus, train, and subway do have some characteristics that are democratic, and in my view worth emulating in other spheres of the public. People uncomfortable with class, race, ethnic, and other cultural differences often actively avoid public transportation, for passengers on buses, trains, and subways face each other as equals for the most part, regardless of their race, class, gender, sexual orientation, age, and so forth. No one likes to give up her seat, since the norms of public life in a bus are, first come, first served. Exceptions tend to get made, and sometimes collectively enforced by the passengers, for the elderly and the disabled. Otherwise, each person has equal rights to a seat on the bus. This trope of a "seat on the bus" has, of course, become part of most Americans' taken-for-granted understanding of their rights and obligations as citizens since the Montgomery bus boycott. A popular freedom song from the 1960s, often sung on buses on their way to demonstrations or voter registration drives in the South, included the refrain: "If you miss me from the back of the bus; And you can't find me nowhere/ Come on over to the front of the bus/ And I'll be riding up there." In the movie *Philadelphia* (1993) a gay man is fired from his job because he has AIDS. His mother remarks to his lawyer: "I didn't raise my kids to sit in the back of the bus." In a 1989 *New York Times* letter to the editor about wheelchair lifts on public buses, the writer concluded that handicapped people receive "far less dignified treatment even than that once afforded Rosa Parks, with a seat in the back of the bus" (Johnson, 1989). In a 1985 article about a woman who filed suit against Xerox corporation because the company told her she was too overweight to be hired, the woman referred to herself as the "the Rosa Parks of fat people" and said she was inspired by Parks's "refusal to sit at the back of a bus" (Margolick, 1985). A 1984 *New York Times* story about women in the civil rights movement noted that "black men found themselves dealing with women who were not willing to take a back seat" (Gaynor, 1984). And in an essay written the day after Parks's death, a *New York Times* reporter visited the Henry Ford Museum near Detroit, Michigan, where the bus that carried Parks is on display. An African American woman, who was visiting the museum, is quoted as saying: "If it wasn't for her [Parks], I would still be riding on the back of that bus" (Davey, 2005). What all of these references have in common is a use of the image of "a seat on the bus" to assert the rights of full citizenship, and by implication the right not to be treated as a second-class citizen.

From the perspective of liberal multiculturalism, members of dominant groups do not have to sympathize with those less privileged, or even associate with them in their "private" lives. But they do have to tolerate various Others in public spaces. Thus, tolerance rather than sympathy is the primary virtue in liberal multiculturalism—a virtue Parks spent much of her later life promoting. In her last few years, she lent her name to a "Wall of Tolerance" monument in a museum in Montgomery, Alabama, sponsored the Southern Poverty Law Center. People visiting the monument are encouraged to make a "declaration of tolerance" that concludes: "I pledge to have respect for people whose abilities, beliefs, culture, race, sexual identity or other characteristics are different from my own." This is certainly commendable, and it pushes the discourse of tolerance and citizen rights, and of a seat on the bus, to encompass an ever-expanding array of marginalized and disempowered groups. At the same time, and by doing so, it reveals the limits of liberal multiculturalism—namely, an inability to conceive of the rights and responsibilities of citizens, and the public sphere, in more expansive terms that move beyond mere tolerance of the Other.

In fact, liberal multiculturalism may not be able to take progressives much farther on its own, for its project is nearing completion. Indeed, if the liberal project was to establish a "color-blind" law, while that might have been an important advancement over Jim Crow laws, it has not been able to significantly advance the project of many poor African Americans since. Starting in the late 1960s, liberalism came to be associated with the idea that a color-blind, or a gender-blind, or later a sexual orientation–blind law did not guarantee equity and that difference had to be noticed and named in order to make significant progress in overcoming discrimination and inequality of opportunity. Affirmative Action legislation was the first significant movement down this road. However, the gains made through Affirmative Action have been made primarily by middle-class African Americans and women, not by the poor or members of the growing semiskilled work force. Furthermore, Affirmative Action has produced a backlash among conservative whites and even some conservative blacks such as Thomas Sowell (1984), who have argued that as the leaders of the civil rights movement shifted their focus from equal treatment and a color-blind law to equal results regardless of differences or merit, and "preferential treatment," the movement was delegitimated. As Michael Dyson (2000) has observed, it is ironic that even former supporters of the system of segregation in the South now rally around Parks and King in defense of color-blindness and in opposition to the "reverse discrimination" of Affirmative Action.

The limitations of liberal multiculturalism, in its dominant form, first of all have to do with its failure to adequately theorize the public. The public bus, and the conception of citizen rights associated with it, constructs a

public space that, as I have said, is minimalist. Within the public space of
the bus, people may choose to ignore each other completely or have only
superficial conversation, and they have no common ground except the desire
to be left alone and go their own ways and in the meantime to tolerate each
others' presence. Of course, there is more going on in the way of constructing
a public space on a bus than this image implies. People are checking each
other out, some genuine conversations develops, and some of this leads to
bonds of friendship among regular passengers. But the norms of riding a bus,
like the norms of public life more generally, do not require such intimate
bonds and relationships, since the emphasis is upon freedom of association
and a rigid separation between the public and the private (Freeman, 1996).

A more expansive discourse of the public in a democratic society is
suggested by the critical social theorist Jurgen Habermas. In *The Structural
Transformation of the Public Sphere* (1962), Habermas distinguished between
the legal, legislative, and juridical apparatuses of the state, which classical
political theorists defined as the public sphere, and an alternative view of the
public sphere as that arena of citizen discourse, associations, and movements.
In this more radically democratic tradition, as Nancy Fraser (1999) has re-
marked, the public "designates a theatre in modern societies in which political participation is enacted through the medium of talk." It is the space
where people come together across their differences, and in communities of
difference, to "deliberate about their common affairs" (p. 519). The public
thus understood cannot be conflated to the state and public facilities and
institutions, although these are needed to create the conditions for the coming together of diverse and overlapping public conversations and for the
production of diverse cultural narratives through oral histories, film, drama,
art, and other forms of cultural production. In this more expansive discourse
of the public, legal rights would still be needed to make sure all have equal
access to public conversations. But a democratic public cannot be constituted only by the state, through a legalistic discourse of rights and obligations
of citizens. A "strong" democracy requires the continuous construction and
reconstruction of the public through conversation and association. At the
present time, conversation and association are limited in fundamental ways
by power inequalities and the effects of historical systems of domination and
subordination and by the distance established between "public" language and
"private" lives. The democratic agenda thus becomes, from this standpoint,
about making the conversation more equitable, bringing new voices to the
table, developing bonds of affinity and identity, building bonds across differences, and finding some tentative and partial "common grounds" for action.

The other major limitation of liberal multiculturalism is that it is too
individualistic in its conception of the rights of a citizen to adequately account for differences of race, class, gender, and sexual identity. These markers of difference and identity are understood only as they impede the fuller
realization of the American Dream of color-blindness, or gender-blindness,

or sexual identity-blindness. As scholars in Critical Race Theory and Critical Legal Studies have shown, liberalism has recognized group identity only as a problem to be overcome, and only as a basis for discrimination, rather than as a something that is positively valued and is the basis for collective action to overcome injustice. Allan Freeman (1995) has referred to the post-Civil Rights era in America as the "era of contradiction," in which the advancement of African American's historic struggle for empowerment and freedom was framed within a "perpetrator's perspective," that is from the standpoint of those people (whites) who had perpetrated the problem in the first place.

SOCIAL RECONSTRUCTIONIST MULTICULTURALISM: ROSA THE RESISTER

Beyond the problems associated with normalizing multiculturalism, and beyond the current stuck point of liberal multiculturalism, let me suggest a third and more radically democratic form of multiculturalism associated with "social reconstructionism." This term *social reconstructionism* was popularized by progressives in American education and cultural politics in the 1930s to refer to something left of liberalism, entailing the use of public education to help young people demystify the commonsense beliefs and practices that promote and sustain elitism and privilege and engage them in collective activities and projects that challenge privilege and promote the public good. Admittedly, the idea of a unified "public good" is a bit problematic, and the social reconstructionists of the 1930s never had a very expansive or inclusive conception of the public. By and large, they were upper-middle-class males who rarely took into account racial or gender privilege. Nevertheless, they did provide a framework for an approach to education that has continued to influence progressive thinking, including thinking about multicultural education. Let me then close by suggesting some of the ways a socially reconstructive discourse of multiculturalism might reframe Rosa Parks's story in important ways.

First, socially reconstructive multiculturalism would renarrate Parks's bus ride as symbolic of a long historical journey toward freedom, equity, and social justice for Black Americans and for other marginalized and oppressed groups in America, a journey that continues in the face of considerable opposition. Although the terrain of struggle has shifted from the early days of the civil rights era, the struggle continues and takes on new forms. Maxine Greene (1988) has written about Parks that what is often forgotten is that her moment of heroism was made possible by a long history of refusals and demands by African Americans through various associations, through which black people "came together to name the obstacles—the unjust laws, the segregation codes, the fire hoses, the clubs, the power structures themselves" (p. 101). When Parks's story is narrated this way it helps us see how race is itself a historically emergent construct that has no essential or given meaning outside of historic power relations that construct the racial other, power relations that also have been historically resisted and are dynamic rather than static. Through this historic struggle, the identity of "whiteness" as well as "blackness" has changed and evolved (see Omi & Winant, 1994).

To read Parks's story as one scene in a historical drama that is uncompleted is to renarrate it as part of a long journey out—what Nelson Mandela called the *Long Walk to Freedom* (1995), and Myles Horton called *The Long Haul* (1998). Of course, such narratives can be disheartening and demoralizing if they only serve to make people accept "the way things are" today, based on the hope or belief that at some later, promised date, some "end of history," they or those that come after them will get their freedom. Stories of long roads to freedom are only truly progressive when they help people situate their own commitments and actions within a collective memory of struggle and when they encourage people to view themselves keepers of this memory and promise today (Carlson & Gause, 2007). If we are on a long road to freedom, it is a road that is not already there before our feet. It must be built one step at a time, and in the face of efforts by others to open different paths that lead toward new forms of domination and oppression.

A second characteristic of a socially reconstructive multiculturalism I associate with the ideas of solidarity and praxis. Solidarity implies a stronger commitment to change, and change through personal commitment and action, than does either sympathy or tolerance. According to Paulo Freire, "true solidarity with the oppressed means fighting at their side to transform the objective reality" which keeps them oppressed (2000, p. 49). In other words, solidarity is something you do. Solidarity means taking a stand against racism and other forms of oppression in our everyday lives and acting with African Americans and others marginalized by class, race, gender, and sexual identity, to build and support inclusive communities where difference is not marginalized and "othering" is not practiced. Freire argued that when members of dominant groups face up to their own privilege, and the reality of oppression, the result may be merely a feeling of guilt that does not translate or transform itself into solidarity. If left unchecked, the desire to escape from guilt can lead back to an earlier form of racism, which is less threatening to one's self-esteem. Or it can lead, as Freire wrote, to a "paternalistic treatment of the oppressed, all the while holding them fast in a position of dependence" (p. 49). The point is not to deny the feeling of guilt but to get beyond guilt through what Freire called "true solidarity," a form of intervention in the world, or praxis, that "requires that one enter into the situation of those with whom one is in solidarity" (p. 49).

In the civil rights era, a good example of practicing solidarity is provided by the "Freedom Summer" movement in 1964. Freedom Summer brought together approximately seventy thousand college students—including many middle-class, white students from northern campuses—under the leadership of the Student Nonviolent Coordinating Committee (SNCC), led by black students in the South. Together, the students had a significant impact on expanding black voter registration in the South, in establishing "Freedom Schools" to teach reading, math, and African American history to black children, and to open community centers where poor blacks could obtain legal and medical assistance. What might solidarity look like today? How can we enact solidarity in this post–civil rights era? I am sure that Freire would say that as a nation, we did not act in the spirit of true solidarity with the poor black people of New Orleans when Hurricane Katrina hit in 2005, although there were many individual and collectives acts of solidarity that gave cause for hope. The poor black citizens of New Orleans had a right to a seat on a public bus, thanks to Rosa Parks, but all the buses had disappeared. They also had a right to a seat in the public Superdome, no matter that the roof leaked and there was no food, sanitation, or security. Much could be done in public schools and colleges to teach and practice solidarity through, for example, the expansion of "service learning" programs. But if such programs are to be about solidarity, they must offer more than "feel good" experiences for young people who view themselves as engaged in charity work, or worse yet, missionary work.

Finally, a socially reconstructive retelling of Parks's story, I believe, would need to temper the idealistic language of solidarity with a more pragmatic language of "interest convergence." Critical race theory scholars, such as Derrick Bell, have argued that the civil rights era settlement of the 1960s was based on a particular "convergence of interests." It would be foolhardy, he suggests, to believe that U.S. Supreme Court decisions that put an end to Jim Crow laws in the South were based only on the obvious unconstitutionality and injustice of segregation. They reflected the emerging view among some whites in policymaking positions who were "able to see the economic and political advances at home and abroad that would follow abandonment of segregation" (1995, p. 22). First, according to Bell, there was the issue of providing credibility to America's struggle with international communism and its efforts to win the "hearts and minds" of Third World peoples. For example, the first editorial in the *New York Times* to mention Parks's arrest and the subsequent bus boycott, published February 24, 1956, noted: "All over the world the Communists, who hate democracy, will have this tragically true story to add to their existing assortment of lies." When 115 American Americans were arrested for conspiring to incite an illegal bus boycott in Montgomery, a *Times* article noted that the mass arrests "attracted the attention and sympathies of a large part of the world. And this in turn lent an impetus to the protest movement . . . [It became] 'a battle for the oppressed people of the world' " (Phillips, 1956). A growing number of influential whites thus came to believe that civil rights legislation was needed to fix America's "image problem" around the world.

Second, according to Bell, the civil rights legislation and court victories "reassured" black Americans that the principles of equity and freedom heralded during World War II would be given meaning here at home. With the end of Jim Crow segregation in the South, and with a seat on an integrated bus, black Americans were given some reason to invest in the system and move away from militant demands. Third, Bell argues that economically powerful whites "realized that the South could make the transition from a rural plantation society to the sun-belt with all its potential and profit," but only if it ended state-sponsored segregation (p. 23). His point is that the gains of the civil rights era, consistent with the agenda of liberal multiculturalism, were based on some convergence of interests among blacks and whites. The question then becomes, What basis exists for a new convergence of interests, one that significantly extends the gains of the civil rights era and takes on continued racial inequalities in public education and elsewhere in public life? One answer is a convergence of interests among poor blacks, Latinos, and whites. Those on the political right have been quite successful over the past several decades appealing to working-class and poor white Americans, particularly those who are also male and heterosexual. They have played into their fears of being victims of "reverse discrimination" and their resentment of gains made by people of color, women, and gays (McCarthy et al., 1998). But if progressives can appeal to the economic interests of poor whites, then their resentment may be redirected at economic elites rather than at other marginalized groups. There may then be room for a broad "Rainbow Coalition" politics in America to coalesce that takes on discrimination and oppression in its diverse forms but also brings various groups together around a "common ground" of social and economic justice.

CONCLUSION

In a biography of Sojourner Truth, the nineteenth-century abolitionist and women's rights activist, historian Nell Painter concludes that there is no "real" Truth, only a series of representations by various authors who turned Truth into a legendary hero that they could use to support their own set of interests. Unmoored to any verifiable facts or any account of her life by Truth herself, Painter writes that "the idea of Sojourner Truth has been available for several purposes and been put to a multiplicity of uses." Painter finds that the "truth" about Truth is that she lives an "invented" life, a life "consumed as a signifier," transformed into "a symbol without a life" (1996, p. 263). Much the same could be said of Rosa Parks. It is less important to know the "real" truth about Rosa Parks and what she did than it is to know what use she has been put to and by whom. It is more important to ask how her life has been narrated and mythologized, according to whose interests, and based on what set of commonsense beliefs. It is important to deconstruct what Stuart Hall (1999, p. 513) has called the "preferred reading" of popular texts about Parks. This includes readings that "normalize" Parks by setting up neat binaries between "good" and "bad" blacks and whites, or between the "bad South" and the "good North," and it includes liberal readings, where the emphasis is upon winning legalistic rights, narrowly defined. Finally, it is important to ask where we as a nation stand today relative to where we stood a half century ago, when Rosa Parks took that famous bus ride.

REFERENCES

Bell, D. (1995). *Brown v. Board of Education* and the interest convergence dilemma. In K. Crenshaw, N. Gotanda, G. Peller, & K. Thomas, (1996), (Eds.), *Critical race theory: The key writings that formed the movement*. New York: New Press.

Bennett, W. (1993). *The book of virtues: A treasure of great moral stories*. New York: Simon & Schuster.

Bhabha, H. (1984, Spring). Of mimicry and man: The ambivalence of colonial discourse, *October, 28*, pp. 125–133.

Bhabha, H. (Ed.). (1990). *Nation and narration*. New York: Routledge.

Butler, J. (1990). *Gender trouble: Feminism and the subversion of identity*. New York: Routledge.

Carlson, D., & Gause, C. (Eds.). (2007). *Keeping the promise: Leadership, democracy, and education*. New York: Lang.

Collins, P. H. (2000). *Black feminist thought: Knowledge, consciousness, and the politics of empowerment*. New York: Routledge.

Davey, M. (2005, October 26) "Two sets of Parks memories, from before the boycott and after." New York Times, p. A20.

Foucault, M. (1979). *Discipline and punish: The birth of the prison* (A. Sheridan, Trans.). New York: Vintage.

Fraser, N. (1999). Rethinking the public sphere: A contribution to the critique of actually existing democracy. In S. During (Ed.), *The cultural studies reader* (pp. 518–536). New York: Routledge.

Freeman, A. (1996). Legitimizing racial discrimination through anti-discrimination law: A critical review of supreme court doctrine. In K. Crenshaw, N. Gotanda, G. Peller, & K. Thomas (Eds.), *Critical Race Theory: The Key Writings that Formed the Movement* (pp. 29–45). New York: New Press.

Freire P. (2000). *Pedagogy of the oppressed; 30th anniversary edition*. New York: Continuum.

Greene, M. (1988). *The dialectic of freedom*. New York: Teachers College.

Habermas, J. (1991). *The structural transformation of the public sphere: An inquiry into a category of bourgeois society, reprint series*. Cambridge, MA: MIT Press.

Hall, S. (1999). Encoding, decoding. In S. During (Ed.), *The cultural studies reader* (pp. 507–517). New York: Routledge.

Horton, M., with Kohl, J., & Kohl, H. (1998). *The long haul: An autobiography*. New York: Teachers College.

Johnson, W. (1980, December 21). Wheelchair lifts increase bus ridership. *New York Times*, p. A30.

Kohl, H. (1991). The politics of children's literature: The story of Rosa Parks and the Montgomery bus boycott. *Journal of Education,173* (1), pp. 35–50.

Mandela, N. (1995). *Long walk to freedom: The autobiography of Nelson Mandela*. Boston: Back Bay Books.

Margolick, D. (1985, April 25). Court ponders suit on job bias over obesity. *New York Times*, p. B1.

McCarthy, C., Rodriguez, A., David, S., Meecham, S., Godina, H., Supriya, K., & Wilson-Brown, C. (1998). Danger in the safety zone: Notes on race, resentment, and the discourse of crime, violence, and suburban security. In D. Carlson, & M. Apple (Eds.), *Power/knowledge/pedagogy: The meaning of democratic education in unsettling times* (pp. 203–226). Boulder, CO: Westview.

New York Times (1956, February 24). *The Nation:* Segregation fronts, p. E2.

Omi, M., & Winant, H. (1994). Racial formation in the United States: From the 1960s to the 1990s. New York: Routledge.

Painter, N. (1996). *Sojourner Truth: A life, a symbol.* New York: Norton.

Parks, R. (1997). *Dear Mrs. Parks: A Dialogue with Today's Youth.* New York: Puffin.

Parks, R. (2000). *Quiet strength: The faith, the hope and the heart of a woman who changed a nation.* New York: Scholastic Inc.

Peller, K., & Thomas, K. (Eds.). Critical race theory: The key writings that formed the movement. New York: The Press, pp. 29–45.

Phillips, W. (1956, March 4). Montgomery is stage for a tense drama. *New York Times*, p. E6.

Rorty, R. (1998). *Human rights, rationality, and sentimentality, in truth and progress: Philosophical papers.* Cambridge, UK: Cambridge University Press.

Schumach, M. (1968, April 5). Martin Luther King Jr.: Leader of millions in non-violent drive for racial justice. *New York Times*, p. 25.

Sowell, T. (1984). *Civil rights: Rhetoric or reality?* New York: Morrow.

Tarcov, N. (1996). Democracy, nurturance, and community. In R. Soder, (Ed.), *Democracy, Education and the schools* (pp. 1–36). San Francisco: Jossey-Bass.

Transformations of Cinder-Ella, The *New York Times* (July 8, 2000), p. A1.

CHAPTER TWO

A SPACE OF THEIR OWN

WOMEN EDUCATORS IN THE NEW SOUTH

KATHERINE CHADDOCK AND SUSAN SCHRAMM-PATE

INTRODUCTION

During the Progressive Era of the early twentieth century, the United States experienced social and democratic reform endeavors that infiltrated institutions of government, industry, charity, and education. In academic institutions—elementary, secondary, and postsecondary—these reforms tackled a wide range of issues concerning learners, curriculum, and pedagogy. Best known are the curricular theories and experiments heralded by John Dewey, William Heard Kilpatrick, and others under the broad umbrella of "progressive education." Also well known are the efforts of urban social reformers to assure public education for all children and to provide opportunities for immigrants and others to acquire literacy and functional job skills.

Women, and particularly women in the southern United States, have acquired little attention for educational contributions during the Progressive Era. They are generally remembered for spearheading suffrage activism, social service clubs, and community outreach to the poor, all undertaken primarily in northern and midwestern population centers. Yet, valuable educational advances did take place in the South during the Progressive Era with women as dominant initiators. Southern women, black and white, forged important educational improvements by founding new institutions, spreading access to the underserved, creating state-level legislation, and developing heightened levels of community involvement. Their lesser notoriety in narratives about educational advances demonstrates the concept of a 'hybrid' space at work in the history of educational change (Bhabha, 1994). The historical circumstances of southern women educators required them to work in an in-between, hybrid, space that was defined by neither the new and experimental nor the status quo.

The hybrid space that provided a niche for the work of southern women educators of the Progressive Era was largely occasioned by the realities of a region marked by isolation, poverty, racial tensions, and official neglect. Operating outside areas of activity generally viewed as the purview of education reform during the early twentieth century, the accomplishments of these women are not found in the curricular and pedagogical narratives of educational experimentation and progressive advancement. Nor are they found in the professional leadership narratives of the male colleagues who published nationally about educational change and founded the Progressive Education Association. Nor are they found in the endeavors that occurred in the urban centers of New York, Chicago, Baltimore, and others where a small advance could affect many and spread quickly.

Instead, the contributions of southern women are seen in endeavors such as scattered night schools for mill workers, classrooms started in church basements, private schools and colleges based on student work in exchange for tuition and board, and lobbying state governments to fund the education of those in poverty-stricken communities. These and other advances toward an educated southern citizenry could not be categorized as notable mainstream reforms of the Progressive Era. Yet they combined to become the essential and opportunistic first steps toward widespread literacy and learning in a region where poverty, racial tensions, and distance had conspired against educational reform.

In this chapter, we aim to highlight the lesser-known contributions of southern female educators working in a hybrid space where change is situated not only as the new and the exciting but also as the opportunistic and the necessary. We do this by calling attention to three significant contextual markers that emerge from the deconstruction of typical dualistic extremes, such as North-South, rich-poor and black-white. Those markers, which define three key factors of the context in which southern educators worked, comprise realities of time and place that can be perceived as either limiting or enlarging. They are:

1. *Material poverty* or extreme lack of resources;

2. *Cultural inhibition* rooted in the context of southern religious values and conservative traditions; and

3. *Personal isolation* stemming from close and closed communities and families located in relatively isolated, rural settings.

While these markers limited the work of southern progressive reformers by tightly circumscribing gender and cultural expectations, they also sometimes enlarged the opportunities for women to make important strides with limited resources. In this way, they describe the environment in which southern women sought to advance education during the Progressive Era as a context of both restraining and driving forces. These forces required reformers to shape their endeavors in ways that adhered to regional particularities but also accomplished necessary advancement, prompting a great deal of creativity in finding a small niche of acceptable working space for appropriate work. Thus, educational reform efforts of southern women occurred in a space between the extremes of progress and status quo and had implications not only for students and schools but also for the careers and personal lives of the educators themselves.

Recognizing that southern historiography implicates race relations and struggles for equal opportunity, we cannot ignore class and race in a discussion of that region in the Progressive Era. However, our larger purpose is to understand and reconceptualize both black and white southern women as educators whose work and outcomes can redefine and enlarge the meaning of "progressive education."

THE NARRATIVE CANON OF PROGRESSIVE EDUCATION

Typically, the label "progressive education" has been the purview of a group of northern and midwestern classroom reformers—generally, but not always working in urban areas. Upper-middle-class men and women, university educated and affiliated, were most prominent in the discourses swirling enthusiastically about Deweyan thought concerning problems of interest as a starting point for the curriculum and classroom community as a key ingredient for successful pedagogy. Such conditions of operation for "progressive" school reform were central to the widespread and well-accepted narratives of the American Progressive Era school reform discourses.

Nevertheless, the school reforms of the Progressive Era encompass a complex history of power and interests related to American education; and their discourses may be appropriately considered in terms of poststructuralist theorists call "transcendental signifieds" (Cherryholmes, 1988). For example: Where did the stories of Progressive Era school reform come from? How were they produced? Why did they originate? Why are they authoritative? What do they assert? The critical lens of poststructuralist thought requires an examination of dualisms that draw—or continue the already drawn—rigid boundaries between notions of what is central to reality and what is marginal. For example, Progressive Era narratives about educational reform, often initiating with Northern and Midwestern reformers, rarely approach issues such as feminism, racism, rural poverty, and the unequal access to higher education for women and blacks. However, when the same era is examined for indications of educational "progressivism" in the South, we note reforms well beyond the classroom taking multiple directions toward new institutions, newly served populations, policy and systems changes, and other social reforming endeavors (Filene, 1970; Mirel, 1990).

Rural examples—often led by women and African Americans—are key in southern educational efforts of the Progressive Era. For example, in the isolated farming fields of Maysville, South Carolina, we find Mary McLeod Bethune (1875–1955), a child of freed slaves whose sparse and occasional church schooling sparked her struggle for further education at a more formal Bible school. During the early decades of the twentieth century termed the Progressive Era, she gave up her hopes to become a missionary to Africa and instead founded one of the South's first schools for African American girls. Later she emerged on the national policy scene by first founding the National Council of Negro Women and then becoming an advisor on minority and youth affairs to President Franklin D. Roosevelt.

Accomplishments like those of Mary McLeod Bethune generally were dispersed and seemingly unrelated. The southern circumstance, with its scattered rural population, its wide-ranging racial and class mix, and its uncertain economic bases, provided little fertile soil for a clustering of endeavors that could be seen and labeled by later historians as a "movement" or a "cause." Similar to the observations made by Joseph Kett of southern women in humanitarian, "socially progressive" causes, women working in education undertook different routes to reform than their northern counterparts because "advocacy of education in the South was less specialized, less tied to the narrow disciplines being spawned by schools of pedagogy in the North" (Kett, 1985, p. 174). Kett perceived two elements that may have been largely responsible for the impulse of southern women educators toward reform work that developed individually and in relative isolation: (1) their need to reach out in their work to isolated and rural circumstances and (2) their lack of formal training aimed at pedagogical concepts and advanced and/or adequate access to state government agencies concerned with education.

FROM DUALISTIC OPPOSITIONS TO SOUTHERN MARKERS OF REFORM

Most prominent among the binary oppositions that highlight the distinct characteristics of southern education during the American Progressive Era are those that elaborate the differences between communities and schools in the industrialized North and the agrarian South. The elements that distinguished these two geographic areas were nearly opposite in nature and called upon reformers to take very different routes in their work toward local educational advances. Therefore, our understanding of the reform-minded educators of this era is enhanced by an initial construction of North-South binary oppositions. Following is a list of North/South dichotomies that is adapted from Paul Nachtigal's (1982) binary construct illuminating the differences in urban versus rural education:

Progressive Era South	Progressive Era North
Rural/agrarian	Urban/industrial
Smaller/less density	Larger/greater density
Geographically isolated	In close proximity
Tightly linked communities	Loosely coupled communities
Make do	Rational planning
Less spendable income	More spendable income
Less formal education	More formal education
Self-sufficiency	Problem solving left to experts
Protestant hegemony	Diverse religions
Non-bureaucratic	Bureaucratic
Oral communication	Written communication
Conservative	Liberal
Cultivating land/farming	Factory labor force
Time measured by seasons	Time measured by clocks
Who said it?	What's said?

SOUTHERN WOMEN WITHIN SOUTHERN CIRCUMSTANCE: THREE MARKERS

For southern women of the Progressive Era some of the characteristics of the rural South were particularly relevant to their efforts and have remained relevant in the historical narratives about their work. For example, northern reformers acquired notoriety for serving immigrants, serving the homeless, and serving large numbers of children in well-populated classrooms. On the other hand, southern women gained less notice as they worked in the smaller schools of sparsely populated farming areas and in communities where a church basement class held for a few hours after Sunday service was what passed for schooling. However, these southern reformers had similar objectives as their northern counterparts in terms of literacy, social uplift, and public support for education.

Southern women educators also experienced differences in the educational experiences they brought to their work. The coeducational colleges and larger state normal schools were found more prominently in the North and Midwest (Ogren, 2005). Further, the great need to educate African American children in the South often necessitated the employment of African American teachers who had only a year or less of specialized training. Thus, their personal resources often were as limited as the material resources available to develop schools, hire teachers, and supply classrooms.

The markers we have identified as key contextual elements shaping the work of early twentieth-century southern educators combine and collapse a number of Nachtigal's dichotomous categories in order to emphasize realities and necessities of time and place: *material poverty, cultural inhibition,* and *personal isolation.*

These markers indicated extreme need for caring assistance and acted as beacons that attracted women into educational endeavors that took them outside their usual spheres of home and family. But at the same time they acted as barriers that limited women's work and accomplishments in education to what could be done within the confines of the traditional social, economic, and cultural realities of the southern region. Thus, while such situational markers provided a path for women to venture beyond the safe spheres of homes, churches, and women's clubs, they narrowed those paths to an extent that left women with achievements that seemed far less notable than those of Progressive Era educators in other regions of the country.

The "cultural inhibition" marker emphasizes southern traditionalism rooted in conservative and religious values. Such values played out to include political adherence to individual and local determination, with a subsequent suspicion of government intervention. They also played out in traditional notions of family, with its patriarchal dominance and home-bound mothers, and in conservative moral values that required proper places for male and female members of a community. "Personal isolation" takes traditional self-sufficiency to the next step in close-knit, agrarian communities with oral communication and extensive interest in personal lives within— but not outside—the immediate local area. Finally, "material poverty" highlights the pervasive economic struggles of the early twentieth-century South. Individuals who wanted to influence education would have to do so with a great deal of boot strapping—a circumstance that may be at least partially responsible for women's involvement, since they had few other options for professional contribution and were willing to nurture small beginnings into larger endeavors. The extreme poverty urged one analyst of southern education circumstances to note, "Economic retardation is largely responsible for the backwardness of [southern] white as well as Negro schools" (Noble, 1924, p. 406). At first consideration, these elements could be viewed as nearly impenetrable obstacles to women's work educational reform. However, they also can be perceived as assisting in the empowerment of women, since they acted to locate educational work in the same neighborhood as much other social reform work that was already acceptable for women of the Progressive Era.

MATERIAL POVERTY

In 1924, southern journalist Gerald W. Johnson recalled the long shadow of the Reconstruction era when he reminded, "We cannot forget the pit where we digged, nor the crushing toil that went into the digging. What went on in the South between 1870 and 1900 was too completely tragic to furnish the material for theatrical tragedy" (Johnson, 1924, p. 43).

Southern economic and social upheaval following the Civil War occasioned material deprivation throughout the region that resonated into the Progressive Era. Perhaps no sector was more affected by the widespread poverty than education, especially the education of black students. During the first decade of the nineteenth century, the taxable wealth backing each school-age southern white child was one-fifth the amount available in the northern and western regions of the United States. In southern cities, such as New Orleans and Atlanta, per pupil expenditures in public schools were less than half the national average for urban centers with populations over 25,000 (Rabinwitz, 1990). The average southern school term was ninety-three days (fewer still for African Americans), and 25 percent of those working in the South's large mill industry were under sixteen years old. By 1910, the region's public school average annual teacher salaries ranged from $200 in North Carolina to $384 in Texas, while the national average was $485 (Russell Sage Foundation, 1912; Dickerman, 1901).

It is not surprising that a visitor in 1900 to the recently founded Voorhees College, a vocational institution for African American youth in South Carolina, commented of founder Elizabeth Evelyn Wright and her school:

> I found Miss Wright full of zeal and ambition to build an institution. However, I must state frankly that I did not see much to represent the institution she was so enthusiastic about. They had only two meals a day. . . . The teachers got what they had to eat mainly by going around the neighborhood asking the patrons to share their own table provisions with them." (Morris, 1982, p. 54)

In South Carolina at the time, annual state education expenditures for African American school children totaled less than $2 per student, compared to approximately $7.50 per white pupil (Hand, 1902).

Wilbur Cash, a southern scholar who rarely gave up on the region's potential, found himself uncharacteristically admitting that in terms of early twentieth-century southern education, "The standard, to be sure, was still pathetically low. The rural school was ordinarily a one-room shack and ran only three to five months in the year. And the teachers, grotesquely ill paid, were literate only by the most elementary measure" (Cash, 1941, p. 218).

Economic deprivation and its effects on southern education, however, created an opening for women who may not have otherwise sought professions outside their homes and churches. Just as urban blight and unjust labor practices sparked reform impulses in the North, illiteracy and skill deficits ignited the charge in the South. Southern women, who would have been ill prepared to address the government and corporate reform needs more prominently voiced in the North and Midwest, felt ready enough to teach, to found new schools, to push for increased public funding, and to fight for higher educator pay. Their zeal was both missionary and maternal, marked by spiritual leaps of faith and persistent nurturing of tiny ventures (Kett, 1985; Scott, 1970; Sims, 1997). Undoubtedly, most of their male counterparts would not have involved themselves in causes that required long and uncertain startup work that might entail begging for pennies or working without pay. Work in southern rural education typically did not pay in the immediate or pay off in the long run. Combined with the notion that school work was not a huge step from hearth and family, the economic realities of southern schooling made it a perfect venue for southern women taking early steps beyond the domestic sphere.

During this period those who embodied deprivation more often than not remained at the bottom of the social scale. Although Elizabeth Evelyn Wright as an African American woman understood deprivation and embodied its consequences, she was nevertheless persistent in her penny by penny fund raising and religious affiliations. These efforts and connections led her to establish several faltering schools for African Americans in rural South Carolina before she managed to found Voorhees College, which continues today. An African American whose schooling emphasized vocational subjects and just a smattering of teacher training at Hampton Institute, Wright offers an example of the claims by recent scholarship that Northern philanthropists were not completely responsible for the support of southern educational strides for African Americans during the fifty years following the Civil War. In fact, such philanthropy is estimated to account for $57 million to black educational institutions, while African American contributions—often in dimes and quarters—amounted to $25 million (Anderson & Moss, 1999).

Wright's own initial schooling, in Talbotton, Georgia, was confined to lessons a few months each year in the basement of an African Methodist Episcopal church on the wrong side of the tracks. The daughter of a Cherokee mother and African American father, she was the seventh of nineteen children. When she was sixteen, she found a flyer tossed into the trash that described Tuskegee Institute in Alabama, about one hundred miles to the west, where poor black students could work their way through to obtain vocational training. The first letter she ever received was a reply from Booker T. Washington to her inquiry about the place. Determined to attend, Wright began working part time to save train fare for the trip to Tuskegee. She entered in 1888 as a night student whose daytime work paid her expenses (Morris, 1983).

For Wright, material poverty deleted any security of homestead to return to once she left Talbotton. There was no identifiable domestic sphere beckoning from the door of the three-room cabin her father had built on a dirt road to house his many children. As deprivation tightly circumscribed available personal choices for women of nearly no means, it also exposed limitless needs among a large population of rural southerners with substandard opportunities for education, employment, and personal welfare. Wright knew upon seeing

Tuskegee Institute and meeting Booker T. Washington that her own contributions would be in the field of education. She later recalled,

> I made up my mind to try to be the same type of woman as Mr. Washington was of a man. The talks which he gave us on Sunday evenings in the chapel . . . influenced me to try to help my fellow men to help themselves. The teachers were models for me. I had never seen such refined ladies and gentlemen. Their lives influenced me for good, and it was my desire to hurry and get out into the world, connect myself with some school and try to set a living example for those who came under my charge. (as quoted in Coleman, 1922, p. 25)

Wright's path to founding a school in South Carolina on the Tuskegee model included teaching positions at several newly founded rural schools for African Americans in South Carolina. She moved several times to pick up and start new ventures, tirelessly convincing rural blacks and their churches and clubs to donate pocket change and supplies toward creating access to education for their children. Finally, in Hampton County, South Carolina, she received some Board of Education funding to pay her for four months a year to teach young African Americans in an abandoned building she had acquired. She then also opened a night school in the building that, in 1895, became the first adult education opportunity in the region for literacy and math training for African American men. Wright continued to search for land and funding that would move her toward her goal of an industrial and farm school with student labor as student skill practice. She explained to Booker T. Washington that farming should be the "leading industry" for her students because "most of them come from the country and when they return we want them to know more about tilling the soil and to be capable of making better crops" (Source Material on the Life of Elizabeth Evelyn Wright, n.d.).

The emphasis on vocational education for African Americans as promoted by Washington, while arguably slowing progress toward racial equality, did enable white northern benefactors to donate to a cause for which they sensed little threat. Word of mouth and mail campaigns netted donations to Wright from New York, Massachusetts, Pennsylvania, and the Midwest for a farm school on twenty acres in Denmark, South Carolina, that opened in 1897 as Denmark Industrial Institute. A year later, it had two hundred students. After six letters and a visit from Wright, Mr. and Mrs. Ralph Voorhees of Clinton, New Jersey, donated five thousand dollars toward buildings and a 280-acre property for the all-grades vocational institute Wright had long envisioned. The Voorhees Industrial School opened its first building in 1902. By the time it opened, Wright had been instrumental in the founding of eight different schools for African Americans in rural South Carolina, including one in a church, one in an abandoned log cabin, and one above a grocery store. She had begged for money, supplies, and food, and she had gone without salary more often than with salary. The deprivation she experienced and the deprivation she observed undoubtedly spurred her ability to rise above restrictions of gender, race, and class in order to build educational institutions from scratch. Voorhees Industrial School (now Voorhees College) continued past her death in 1906 to become the first accredited junior college for African Americans in the Southeast and eventually a respected four-year college that continues today.

The struggles and slow successes that mark the story of Elizabeth Evelyn Wright and her contributions in education are similar to those experienced by numerous other women educators who worked in the South during the Progressive Era. They were heightened for women who worked with rural African American students, where the needs were most extreme and the resource most lacking. Notable among these women were Mary McLeod Bethune, the founder of the Daytona Beach, Florida, school that became Bethune-Cookman College; Lucy Craft Laney, the founder of Haines Industrial Institute in Augusta, Georgia; Charlotte Hawkins Brown, founder of the Alice Freeman Palmer Memorial Institute in Sedalia, North Carolina; and Nannie Helen Burroughs, founder of the National Training School for Women and Girls in Washington, D.C. (Easter, 1995; McCluskey & Smith, 1999; Wadelington & Knapp, 1999).

White women from the North, typically socially conscious and benevolently motivated, also came to the South to spread educational opportunities to deprived areas in the early decades of the twentieth century. In rural Appalachia, the impulse took the form of schooling for unschooled mountain dwellers. There, Alice Lloyd arrived from New England to start a school with little welcome from locals in a ramshackle cabin. At its founding in 1918, "she and her mother were the only faculty present and the curriculum consisted of whatever they felt called to teach, primarily such fundamental things as the desirability of windows and baths. She was concerned with the health conditions first" (Turner, 1987, p. 109). The school eventually became Alice Lloyd College, which continues to educate leaders for Appalachia today.

Martha Berry, from a wealthy family in Georgia's southern fringe of Appalachia, started a Sunday school, then a boarding school not far from her home "to meet the educational and industrial needs of the poor white country boys of Georgia . . . to make them independent, thrifty, and self-respecting" (Berry, 1904, p. 49). Her school opened in a cabin in 1902 and was serving seventy students, ages twelve to twenty-three, by 1904. By 1930, it became the full four-year institution that is now known as Berry College (Eller, 1932; Searles, 1995).

These and other women began their educational ventures with little or no financing in communities that badly needed educational opportunities but could not possibly mount the resources to support them. Typically, they first partnered with churches for facilities and plate passing, although sometimes for full sponsorship; they then moved on to court local white donors, northern philanthropists, and foundations. They saw themselves as both teachers and missionaries and quickly schooled themselves in skills of negotiation, financial management, and leadership. The very deprivation that made their missions so difficult also gave them a foot in the door to professional accomplishment that would have otherwise been well beyond their reach.

Southern reformers who sought to make a difference in social, political, economic, or educational welfare needed to start from scratch not only in terms of garnering resources and changing attitudes, but also in terms of confronting their own limited professional experiences and training. With healthy doses of intuition and commitment, but limited development of professional expertise, they struggled for the most basic needs in terms of institutions and classrooms.

Additionally, many rural whites and African Americans limited their own access through learned attitudes of inferiority. Referring to them as "degraded masses," W. E. B. DuBois saw the issue among these southerners as failure to credit their practical learning over "book learning" and a tendency to "assume that knowledge is for higher beings and not for the 'likes of us' " (DuBois, 1935, p. 637).

This attitude combined with economic necessity for child labor among rural families whose youngsters contributed essential work on farms and in mills, inspiring widespread reluctance to support compulsory education. Thus, the question about education in the South by the time of the Progressive Era was still to be prefaced by "whether;" while in the North and Midwest, educators were already concerned with "how."

Interestingly, the necessity of confronting resource deprivation and the need to start reform efforts from scratch created some new opportunities for women desiring to work in education. Generally shut out of the hierarchy of policy-making or profit-making ventures, women who went beyond the domestic sphere turned to service realms where their missionary and maternal impulses were valued. Perhaps because they were grateful for a chance to contribute, or perhaps because they had learned to expect a service role, women educators willingly pitched in to the foundational work of searching for start-up resources, seeking out students, and begging favors of county agents and school board policy makers. In this way, many women were able to enter the education profession at the point of initial policy making, program development, and institution building; whereas in other places and times, they would need to start as teachers who might or might not ever advance to decision-making capacities.

Wil Lou Gray, a South Carolina native from an educated and financially secure family, arrived on the educational policy-making scene in South Carolina when local and state governments first began to concern themselves with issues of rural schooling and literacy. After graduating from

Columbia College and attending graduate school at Vanderbilt University, she taught at Martha Washington College in Virginia for a year before serving as supervisor of rural schools in Laurens County, South Carolina, from 1914 to 1916 and supervisor of rural schools in Montgomery County, Maryland, from 1916 to 1918. When the South Carolina Illiteracy Commission formed in 1918, Gray returned to her home state to take over as its field secretary and to create, from scratch, a model statewide effort to promote literacy (Carlton, 1982; Gray, 1915; Neufeldt, 1970).

Gray had an uphill battle in bringing attention to illiteracy as a problem, later recalling, "[W]e couldn't convince the people. But the war came along . . . World War I; and when they examined our veterans, so many of them were illiterate. And the *New York Times* carried the headline, 'South Carolina Leads the Union in Illiteracy'" (Gray, 1975). For the next two years, Gray took on a one-woman lobbying crusade at the state capitol. Eventually, with energy, a forceful personality, but no material resources, she prodded state legislators into funding the nation's first statewide, state-supported adult education program. Its endeavors started immediately, fanning out to mill towns where illiteracy was particularly concentrated and mill facilities were available for night school.

Gray then moved on to institutional building, again from scratch, developing residential adult summer schools on college campuses, largely for female mill workers. Called "opportunity schools," they included classes in arithmetic, civics, health, arts and crafts, and etiquette. For many, this schooling served as a gateway to college education. A year-round opportunity school opened in 1947. It remains active today as the Wil Lou Gray Opportunity School.

Many other southern women who undertook unusual opportunities to start from scratch were those whose work included building new institutions to address the needs of unserved or underserved populations. Charlotte Hawkins Brown, for example, was an African American and native of North Carolina whose family moved to Massachusetts in 1888 when she was six years old. By the time she was nineteen, after only one year of normal schooling, she was teaching back in North Carolina in a small rural school for African Americans founded by the American Missionary Association in a Sedalia, North Carolina, church. When the school closed due to lack of funding the following year, Brown quickly taught herself the fine art of fund raising and negotiation in order to start a new school nearby, the Alice Freeman Palmer Memorial Institute. Within eight years, Palmer Institute had more than one hundred male and female African American students, five faculty members, dormitories and classroom buildings, extensive acreage, and a college preparatory curriculum. By the time Brown retired in 1952, the school included a junior college, a reputation for selectivity, a student body drawn from twenty-four states, and a campus valued at nearly $1 million (Reynolds & Schramm, 2001).

Brown had initiated an academically respected opportunity for thousands of black students in an area where none had previously existed. Mary McLeod Bethune, schooled only as a missionary, similarly began with no evident resources beyond borrowed furniture and a rented room to found the Daytona (FL) Institute in 1904 with five young female pupils and a commitment to "uplift Negro girls spiritually, morally, intellectually and industrially" (Bethune, 1999, p. 77). Her school grew into the well-respected Bethune-Cookman College, and her own prominence extended nationally to a key role in the Franklin D. Roosevelt administration. Bethune and Brown were joined by another well-known African American school founder, Nannie Helen Burroughs, to be dubbed "The Three B's" for their widespread reputations in African American uplift through increased educational opportunities.

The work of these southern reformers was far less scientific and studied than the usual concepts of "progressive education," but more grounded in crucial local and immediate needs. They were not able to seek improvements in program structures, teaching methods, or student learning because they worked in places where to reform education was to start it from scratch rather than to improve it. They worked from personal experiences and intuitive notions of what was needed, whether it was legislation for funding or land for facilities. Context mattered, and the educational landscape of the rural South typically offered a particularly fertile environment for boot strappers willing to make do with little or nothing for as long as it took to establish a stable footing. This may have been the only context that could give so many women a chance to become the key agents of achievement.

CULTURAL INHIBITION

Throughout the post–Civil War era, southern women confronted the paradoxical necessity of dealing with Victorian Era ideals and sanctions while exploring the new educational and vocational opportunities that characterized the dawn of the New South. To illustrate, the traditional doctrine of spheres—the private and the public—posited a clear separation between the domestic and the political worlds. The separation of work roles in modern industrialized American society relegated women to the home, and the "cult of domesticity" emerged as a direct response to modernization (Freidman, 1985). Thus, many women were inhibited in expanding their roles by traditional cultural expectations that urged them to cling to the status quo.

The relationship between home and community and the delicate balance between accepted standards of femininity, sexual purity, and genteel behavior emerge as pivotal to the Progressive Era. Anne Firor Scott (1984), Anastatia Sims (1997), Jean Friedman (1985), and Dewey Grantham (1983) demonstrated that the South had its own unique brand of Progressivism in which southern women were vigorous advocates of such humanitarian causes as education, settlement houses, the abolition of child labor, better schools, and public health. The route that allowed many southern women to adhere to traditional roles and provided them with the comfort of what was familiar and acceptable was what Joseph Kett termed "social Progressivism," emphasizing issues traditionally identified with the domestic sphere—the welfare of children, the family, the poor, and the neighborhood (Kett, 1985, p. 166) According to Kett (1985), "social Progressivism" provided them with a "spacious theater for their reformist activities" (p. 166).

Although Scott's (1984) work in particular emphasizes the importance of the concept of the 'southern lady,' the maintenance of a color line in southern society during this period demonstrates the limits of that notion in application. White southern women progressive reformers, as a group, responded favorably to the ideals of human progress and uplift, often venturing outside the color line. As a result, the causes they eagerly and outwardly championed often made them targets of conservative, antireform politicians (Edgar, 1998). Critics warned that ladies' club work and social agendas interfered with their domestic duties and accused them of neglecting their husbands, homes, and children. Some of the changes of the Progressive Era were a result of the economic developments that were influencing the lives of women. The fruits of the Industrial Revolution, such as electricity and commercial manufacturing, allowed white, middle-class women more leisure hours and a chance to look beyond the roles of wife and mother.

Influenced by these changing times, Cora Wilson Stewart, founder of the Moonlight Schools for adult illiterates in Kentucky, found herself torn between her career ambitions in the field of education and the conventional life of wife and mother (Nelms, 1997). Even so, she became a powerful political figure in national and international anti-illiteracy campaigns. While her founding of the Moonlight Schools brought her national attention, she was also elected the first woman president of the Kentucky Education Association in 1911, and she chaired the illiteracy section of the World Conference of Education Associates five times. After serving on the prestigious Executive Board of the National Education Association, she founded the National Illiteracy Crusade in 1926.

The prevailing Victorian era view of a woman's future called for marriage and home making—nurturing a husband and children. Clearly, that meant that a woman's role in society was to be determined by her husband's prestige and position, while her personal reputation was determined by her success as a wife and mother. This ideology was embraced by Stewart's mother, Anne Halley Wilson, a very religious woman, who doubtless expected her daughter to adhere to society's view of a domestic mold for females. These traditional values and cultural inhibitions are reiterated in her diary:

> A Woman's affections are sacred. They are her life and he who takes upon himself their guardianship assumes a holy and responsible duty. A true woman loves independent of all worldly circumstances . . . A

true woman loves when she loves truly and tenderly and if she unites with the opposite sex in the bond of holy matrimony and feels assured that her love is appreciated she is ready to lay her life at the feet of the man she loves and if the task could be allotted to her of making the path in which he were to walk it would be straight and sweet and soft as a bed of roses . . . Yes, the love of a true woman for her husband is more precious to her than the miser's affection for his hoarded gold. These are my imperfectly expressed ideas of a women's true love. (Quoted in Nelms, 1997, p. 80)

Stewart never reached the matrimonial paradise described by her mother. Cora Wilson and A. T. Stewart married for the first time in 1903, divorced in 1904, and remarried just three months after the divorce. A pattern of domestic abuse elevated by alcoholism led to their second divorce in 1910. According to sworn court depositions, at midnight on March 21, 1910, A. T. Stewart came home in a drunken state and tried to kick in the door of the room where Cora and her two sisters were sleeping. When Cora opened the door to let him in he said, "I've come to blow you up." He violently cursed Cora, told her he detested her, and threatened to kill her (p. 24).

When Stewart's only child died in 1908, gossip erupted about "unfit motherhood" throughout the local community (p. 22). A few people went so far as to claim that if she had taken better care of her baby instead of making so many public appearances, the child would not have died. During a time when domestic problems were stigmatizing and certainly not publicized, in characteristic fashion, this extraordinary woman found the strength to confront her personal tragedies with uncommon courage in her professional life.

Southern women reformers continually struggled to be heard above established male educational, political, and economic agendas in their fight for social justice concerning better schools, better working conditions, and better salaries. For example, heirs to a long tradition of republican independence, the mill operatives were especially insulted by "do-gooders" trying to tell them what they could and could not do regarding child labor (Edgar, 1998). The rise of the textile industry in the South made cotton mills and mill villages a major feature of southern landscape. A class of dependent, propertyless, white mill workers—including women and children—flooded into the mill villages from the rural areas, and Progressive Era reformers sought to use the state systems, especially public schools, to break the "cycle of ignorance" among mill workers (p. 11).

South Carolina's Wil Lou Gray, for example, responded by developing a system of night schools in both rural and mill areas of Laurens County, patterned after the work of Cora Wilson Stewart in Kentucky (Gray, 1915). A large part of Gray's traditional agenda as a public educator was as an acculturating agent of the fast-growing modern industrial society, especially in the realm of citizenship. The learning of the "Three R's" was designed to break down the barriers between the classes and gain mill operatives and other poor whites access to middle-class leadership. Gray's classroom materials and assignments preached not only thrift and good health habits but also more political causes such as civil government, good roads, and, especially, public education. Moreover, her zeal for providing her students with moral inspiration and civic uplift stemmed from her evangelical Protestant and social gospel roots. She enjoyed a privileged middle-class rural South Carolina upbringing, and her affluence both shielded her from the poverty most blacks and many whites experienced and enabled her to benefit from the educational opportunities available to women in the early twentieth century (Neufeldt, 1970). Since teaching was a genteel way for cultivated young women to simultaneously conform within the traditional gender hierarchy and enter the public sphere, Wil Lou Gray—not one to challenge the status quo—intended to teach.

Constructions of gender and race that deemed white women pious, pure, submissive, and domestic and that deemed black women as lethargic, backward, marginalized, and sexually loose produced the ideological glue that held southern traditional culture together for so many years. The "cult of true womanhood" acknowledged white women to be naturally spiritual and motivated only by an unselfish concern for others (Muncy, 1991). What W. E. B. DuBois would later characterize as "plantation mentality" lingered and served to keep blacks in their place (DuBois, 1935).

At this time racism remained in the foreground, even among white reformers. That is to say, southern white women's sense of collective female identity and difference enabled them to slowly venture into the workplace, the market, and the polity, although the needs of families framed and limited the public domain for them. Entreating their maternal duties to protect children and care for the working-class poor, many women, both white and black, organized around local issues: the improvement of working conditions, especially for the poor, blacks, and child wage earners; maternal and child welfare; clean water; pure food and milk; adequate sanitation; improved housing; and most important, schooling. While their careers and records of accomplishments present a valuable reminder that many southern white women worked to expand the values of southern traditionalism, it was their commitment to traditional curriculum that enabled them to venture out of the private sphere while still remaining socially acceptable.

PERSONAL ISOLATION

"Personal isolation" is indicative of the close-knit and isolated community life in small and relatively isolated rural southern communities. To illustrate isolation as a signifier, this section includes a discussion of Alice Geddes Lloyd, born in Athol, Massachusetts in 1876, and Martha McChesney Berry, born ten years earlier in Rome, Georgia. These women founders of schools that eventually became colleges in remote Appalachian communities could be viewed as somewhat typical of women of means, intelligence, and independence whose interests were sparked by the social ideals so vividly demonstrated in Jane Addams' urban settlement work.

Lloyd arrived from New England to start a school in one of Kentucky's most isolated Appalachian regions. It eventually became Alice Lloyd College, which continues today. Berry decided to start a boarding school not far from her home in Georgia's southern fringe of Appalachia to "meet the educational and industrial needs of the poor white country boys of Georgia . . . to make them independent, thrifty, and self-respecting" (Berry, 1904, p. 4986). Both women relied heavily on close and personal communication with locals and on forging relationships by participating in all aspects of community life in the small towns where they started their schools, and they had a particular interest in Appalachian people and their lives. Although in many ways they romanticized the agrarian way of life and were intrigued by Appalachian cultural distinctions, they nevertheless held fast to middle- and upper-class, white value systems. Their earnest beliefs in the necessity of an educated citizenry and their desire to enhance the social welfare of those less fortunate prompted them to create new programs and institutions among southern highlanders. Along with their counterparts working throughout the South, Berry and Lloyd built educational institutions in Appalachia by relying on their communication skills and the force of their personalities to approach wealthy individuals one at a time for support for their causes.

The work that engaged Lloyd and Berry was oriented toward Appalachian uplift through schooling for those who had little or none within reach. Although training to enhance local practices in fields such as agriculture and home economics was readily accepted as part of that education, it was not necessarily central. Religious piety, personal hygiene, morality, citizenship, and basic academic subjects were far more prominent as these women built their one-room schools into fully accredited colleges. For Berry, who started her program as a Sunday school for nearby children, the shift to academic and vocational fare came naturally as numbers increased and lack of adequate schooling became apparent. For Lloyd, whose work in Kentucky began with development of community civic and social betterment activities, the move to concentrate on the development of an educational institution occurred when "it became apparent, at least to Lloyd, that the region's educational needs were more pressing. The local primary school was inadequate; there was no high school within reasonable reach; and a college education was deemed irrelevant for all but a tiny handful" (Searles, 1995, p. 55).

Personal communication of a compelling message was the most essential weapon in the struggle to gather resources for funding their schools. For example, Berry successfully made friends with the Carnegie and Ford families on behalf of the Berry Colleges, which she founded near Rome, Georgia. Lloyd, for her Caney Junior College (later renamed Alice Lloyd College) in eastern Kentucky, received regular financial support from two spinster sisters in Passaic, New Jersey, and got the most out of her fellow classmates from Boston's Chauncy Hall School and Radcliffe College (Reynolds & Schramm, 2001).

Clearly, Lloyd and Berry benefited in their reform efforts by becoming part of the mountain communities where they located their schools. They interacted with local families, purchased local goods, and tied their schools to local activities from fairs to club meetings. They became not just women with reform agendas—which may have made skeptical highlanders suspicious—but neighbors with personal interests who communicated face-to-face, one-on-one. They succeeded where others may have failed because they were able to match their skills in participation and interaction with the needs of the people who responded best to close community.

CONCLUSION

Anne Firor Scott (1970) reminded that before going north to college and leaving her native Georgia for the first time, she believed in the authenticity of the fabled antebellum image of the "southern lady," noting, "like the fish who has to be landed to perceive water, I became seriously aware of southern history only at Harvard, away from the South" (p. 234). Many southern women struggled to free themselves of earlier cultural expectations, and Scott's work described their lives as realities that often defied the "lady" image.

In the South, the social role of women was "unusually confining" and the sanctions used to enforce obedience "peculiarly effective" (p. xi). However, whether white women of educated and/or wealthy families or rural black women of working-class backgrounds, many of these women emerged from domestic circles to work, live, and act in a broader society and leave their mark on the historical and public record. Typically, they also developed strong coping mechanisms to deal with the demands of an insensitive, traditional patriarchal society.

The unprecedented achievements of women in the public sphere during the Progressive Era, especially in the arena of educational enhancement, were gained not by reconceptualizing institutionalized sexist, racist, and classist practices but by thinking and acting within the constructs of those realities in ways that were s socially acceptable for women. As noted, they held fast to existing contexts such as traditionalism and personalization and made their strides by pushing envelopes rather than breaking new trails. Education itself was viewed as a respectable occupation for women, one of the few routes for women in paid employment. Many southern women of the Progressive Era however, managed to use this respectable arena to exercise ideologies that embraced social, political, and religious motives (Seller, 1994). Clearly, their work illustrates a distinctive conception of Progressive Era school reform that deviates substantially from the well-known endeavors concerned with Deweyan notions of pedagogy and curriculum—that is, group activities, socialized learning, child-centered education, the project method, and the educating of social imagination.

While coping with the realities of Jim Crow and bounds of segregated communities, as well as Victorian era norms for women and the limitations of public and private spheres, southern Progressive Era women made a difference though community activity in general and through educational advancement in particular. They did so by employing strategies that respected the boundaries of time and place while enabling them to carve out a new "hybrid" space of activity within those boundaries. That space meant acceptance not only as teachers but also as school administrators and founders. It meant acceptance not only as recipients of policy decisions but also as lobbyists for policy creation. In other words, southern women created new options for their work but did not create entirely new spheres that might have made their work unacceptable within the prevailing contexts. In doing so, they increased their influence in civic and educational affairs and successfully made their cases to the white, upper- and middle-class men in power. While their stories often become marginalized amid the more popular discussions of Deweyan Progressive education, their achievements were real, significant, and enduring.

REFERENCES

Anderson, E., & Moss, Jr., A. A. (1999). *Dangerous donations: Northern philanthropy and southern black education, 1902–1930*. Columbia: University of Missouri Press.

Berry, M. (1904). Uplifting backwoods boys in Georgia. *World's Work* (8), 4986.

Bethune, M. M. (1999). Sixth annual catalogue of the Daytona Educational and Industrial Training School for Negro Girls. In T. McCluskey & E. M. Smith (Eds.), *Mary McCloud Bethune, building a better world: Essays and selected documents*. Bloomington: Indiana University Press.

Bhabha, H. K. (1994). *The location of culture*. New York: Routledge.

Carlton, D. L. (1982). *Mill and town in South Carolina, 1880–1920*. Baton Rouge: Louisiana State University Press.

Cash, W. J. (1941). *Mind of the south*. New York: Knopf.

Cherryholmes, C. (1988). *Power and criticism: Poststructural investigations in education*. New York: Teachers College.

Coleman, J. F. B. (1922). *Tuskegee to Voorhees*. Columbia, SC: Bryan.

Crocco, M. S., Munro, P., & Weiler, K. (1999). *Pedagogies of resistance: Women educator activists, 1880–1960*. New York: Teachers College.

Dickerman, G. S. (1901 April). The south compared to the north in educational requirements. *Proceedings of the Fourth Conference for Education in the South*. Winston-Salem, NC.

DuBois, W. E. B. (1935). *Black reconstruction in America, 1860–1880: An essay toward a history of the part which black folk played in an attempt to reconstruct democracy in America*. New York: Atheneum.

Easter, O. V. (1995). *Nannie Helen Burroughs*. New York: Garland.

Edgar, W. (1998). *South Carolina: A history*. Columbia, SC: University of South Carolina Press.

Eller, R. D. (1932). *Miners, millhands, and mountaineers: Industrialization of the Appalachian South, 1880–1930*. Knoxville: University of Tennessee Press.

Elshtain, J. B. (2001). (Ed.). *The Jane Addams reader*. New York: Basic Books.

Filene, P. G. (1970). An obituary for the progressive movement. *American Quarterly, 22*.

Freidman, J. E. (1985). *Women and community in the evangelical South, 1830–1900*. Chapel Hill, NC: University of North Carolina Press.

Goldfield, D. (2002). *Still fighting the civil war: The American South and southern history*. Baton Rouge: Louisiana State University Press.

Grantham, D. (1983). *Southern progressivism: The reconciliation of progress and tradition*. Knoxville: University of Tennessee Press.

Gray, W. L. (1975). *South Carolina Educational Television Interview with Wil Lou Gray, February 11, 1975*. Columbia, SC: Museum of Education Archives.

Gray, W. L. (1915). *A night school experiment in Laurens County*. Columbia, SC: State Department of Education.

Gray, W. L. (1914). *Our paper*. Columbia, SC: State Department of Education.

Hand, W. H. (1902, July 1). An issue fraught with evil. *The State*, p. 8.

Johnson, G. W. (1924). Critical attitudes North and South. *Journal of Social Forces*, 43–50.

Kett, J. F. (1985). Women and the progressive impulse. In W. J. Fraser, Jr., R. F. Saunders, Jr., & J. L. Wakelyn (Eds.), *The web of southern social relations: Women, family, and education*. Athens: University of Georgia Press.

McCluskey, A. T., & Smith, E. M. (1999). *Mary McLeod Bethune, building a better world: Essays and selected documents*. Bloomington: Indiana University Press.

Mirel, J. E. (1990). Progressive school reform in comparative perspective. In D. N. Plank & R. Ginsberg (Eds.), *Southern cities, southern schools: Public education in the urban South*. New York: Greenwood.

Morris, J. K. (1983). *Elizabeth Evelyn Wright: Founder of Voorhees College*. Sewanee, TN: University of the South Press.

Morris, J. K. (1982). *Source material on the life of Elizabeth Evelyn Wright, Vol. 2*. Typescripts in Wright Collection, South Caroliniana Library, University of South Carolina, Columbia, SC.

Muncy, R. (1991). *Creating a female domination in American reform, 1890–1935*. New York: Oxford Press.

Nachtigal, P. M. (1982). (Ed.). *Rural education: In search of a better way*. Boulder, CO: Westview.

National Training School for Women and Girls. (1926). *Only on north of Richmond*. Nannie Helen Burroughs Papers.

Nelms, W. (1997). *Cora Wilson Stewart: Crusader against illiteracy*. Jefferson, NC: McFarland.

Neufeldt, H. G. (1970). South Carolina's Wil Lou Gray: A study in education and gender. *Vitae Scholasticae, 16*(2) 52–55.

Noble, S. G. (1924). Education of the Negro. In I. L. Kandel (Ed.), *Twenty-five years of American education*. Freeport, NY: Books for Libraries.

Ogren, C. A. (2005). *The American state normal school: An instrument of great good*. New York: Palgrave Macmillan.

Rabinwitz, H. N. (1990). Continuity and change: Southern urban development, 1860–1900. In A. Brownell, & A. Goldfield (Eds.), *The city in southern history*. New York: Lang, 112.

Reynolds, K., & Schramm, S. L. (2001). *A separate sisterhood: Women who shaped southern education in the Progressive Era*. New York: Lang.

Russell Sage Foundation (1912). *A comparative study of public school systems in the forty-eight states*. New York: Russell Sage Foundation.

Scott, A. F. (1970). *The southern lady: From pedestal to politics 1830–1930*. Chicago: University of Chicago Press.

Searles, P. D. (1995). *A college for Appalachia: Alice Lloyd on Caney Creek*. Lexington: University Press of Kentucky.

Seller, M. S. (1994). *Women educators in the United States 1820–1993: A bio-bibliographical sourcebook*. Westport, CT: Greenwood.

Sims, A. (1997). *The power of femininity in the new South: Women's organizations and politics in North Carolina, 1880–1930*. Columbia: University of South Carolina Press.

Source Material on the Life of Elizabeth Evelyn Wright (n.d.). *Elizabeth Evelyn Wright to Booker T. Washington May 1906*. Columbia, SC: South Caroliniana Library, University of South Carolina.

Spring, J. (2001). *The American School, 1642–2000*. Boston: McGraw Hill.

Turner, C. C. (1987). *Patterns of Educational Initiative, Reorganization and Decline in Eastern Kentucky, 1889–1940*. A doctoral dissertation. Lexington: University of Kentucky.

Wadelington, C. W., & Knapp, R. F. (1999). *Charlotte Hawkins Brown and the Palmer Memorial Institute*. Chapel Hill: University of North Carolina Press.

CHAPTER THREE

HORTON HEARS A WHO

═══════════════════════

LESSONS FROM THE HIGHLANDER FOLK SCHOOL IN THE ERA OF GLOBALIZATION

PEPI LEISTYNA

INTRODUCTION

The global economy, a product of the last five hundred years of invention and imperialist expansion, has entered a new phase made possible by innovative technologies, transnational institutions, and the logic of neoliberalism. This new era of global social and economic relations is affecting not only how we think about economics but also politics and culture and the complex interrelationships among these forces.

As capitalism has been undergoing radical change, the new political order of globalization simultaneously emerging differs in many respects from previous forms of imperialism (Bauman, 1998; Castells, 1996; Hardt & Negri, 2000; Harvey, 2001; Lash & Urry, 1987). Obsessed with privatization, deregulation, and restructuring, elite private powers have been successful in using the state to protect corporate interests and dismantle many of the rights and protections achieved internationally by grassroots activists, organized labor, and social democracies.

Needless to say, globalization is by no means a monolithic entity, and there is a radical difference between the top-down economic versions whose proponents are looking to ensure access to cheap labor and raw materials in order to maximize their profits and what is being referred to as "globalization from below"—transnational networking to democratize global technologies, environmental resources, and media, information, and financial systems (Brecher, Costello, & Smith, 2000; Danaher & Mark, 2003). As a response to the injustices produced by the neoliberal and neoconservative models of globalization (Harvey, 2003; Kim, Young, Joyce, Irwin & Gershman, 2000), vast multi-interest coalitions have sprung up that include human rights, antiracist, environmental, faith, indigenous, student, and consumer groups, along with trade unionists, feminists, antisweatshop activists, anarchists, and antiwar protestors. These networks are demonstrating how a critical and inclusive public can effectively wage war against abusive states and international actors and institutions. Confronting oppression from economic, political, technological, and cultural fronts, this transnational collective action is helping people understand and fight to transform how these forces currently organize societies.

Contemporary cultural activists and social movements are compelled to adjust to shifting power relations that are the result of globalization, especially when it comes to their organizational frameworks, collective identities, and actions (Porta & Tarrow, 2005). However, while these activists are crossing into uncharted territory, many of their theoretical orientations and effective organizational styles and strategies are by no means new. In fact, activists have inherited an immense legacy of radical thought, research, and action.

An indispensable part of praxis is to make use of existing theory and research in order to study historically significant events and the actors and organizations therein that have worked toward economic and social justice. A few examples follow: the Abolitionists; the First and Second Internationals; the Cuban, Mexican, and Russian revolutions; anarcho-syndicalism; experiments in social democracy; first- and second-wave feminism; and anticolonial, civil rights, indigenous, and antiwar movements. There is also much to learn from the histories of trade union revivals, labor and environmental coalitions, antinuclear protests, and the global networks that have developed in the fight against AIDS. The intent of exploring the history of activism is not to generate nostalgia in these conservative times, nor does it offer up a recipe book to be followed to the last grain of salt; rather, it is a way to inspire the critical appropriation and reinvention of revolution as these struggles offer theoretical, empirical, and practical springboards for contemporary efforts.

The history, goals, and grassroots achievements of the Highlander Folk School[1] are also an important place to look for insight about the role and power of civil society, that is, "those areas of social life—the domestic world, the economic sphere, cultural activities, and political interaction—which are organized by private or voluntary arrangements between individuals and groups outside the *direct* control of the state" (Held, 1996, p. 57).

The past and continued efforts of Highlander are especially important given that the contemporary global justice movement, when it comes to participation in public life—far beyond simply voting for candidates to represent them (who usually do not come from the same social class and experience), or merely volunteering to join civil society organizations—is striving for active involvement and communicative autonomy. As Simone Chambers (2002) explains, "Communicative autonomy refers to the freedom of actors in a society to shape, criticize, and reproduce essential norms, meanings, values, and identities through communicative [as opposed to coercive] interaction" (p. 93). Voting-centric democratic theory is rapidly being replaced by talk-centric models of participation that move away from the corrupting influences of mainstream media and economic and political party interests and toward a democratized public sphere that creates the conditions within which all people, even those that have historically been excluded from the political process, can express themselves and work to shape the future.

As progressive and radical transnational movements have learned much from the Left's successes and failures, there is a real effort to avoid the dangers of sectarianism as dogma of any type inevitably leads to an extremely limited sense of community, solidarity, and agency. The goal of achieving unity in diversity while also maintaining an activist stance requires that we work through what need not be a contradiction between a Gramscian vision of civil society and war of position intended to use cultural and political practices on multiple fronts to lead to revolutionary change rather than just mere representation (Gramsci, 1975), while creating and protecting a Habermasian public sphere that can burgeon within a liberal democracy to serve as a venue for the free exchange of ideas (Habermas, 1991)—an exchange through which mobilization can germinate. Highlander offers some important historical lessons and inspiration in achieving this radical goal.

THE THEORETICAL ROOTS OF THE HIGHLANDER FOLK SCHOOL

> I think that it's important to understand that the quality of the process you use to get to a place determines the ends, so when you want to build a democratic society, you have to act democratically in every way. (Horton, as cited in Kohl & Kohl, 1998, p. 227)

The Highlander Folk School was founded in 1932 by Myles Horton and Don West in the Appalachian Mountains of Monteagle, Tennessee. The small school blossomed from the hopes of developing a residential adult education center that not only would serve the needs of the people of one of the poorest counties in the country, who were left behind by formal education and corporate greed, but also reinvigorate and celebrate the indigenous cultural heritage of the people of the mountains.

Horton (1905–1991), who dreamed up the idea of the school, was born into a white, working-class family in Savannah, Tennessee—"the grandson of an illiterate mountain man" (Smith, 2003, p. 1). His parents, who were by no means progressives, valued faith, education, and community service. With limited financial means, Horton worked his way through high school and got his feet wet politically by helping to organize a tomato packers' strike for higher wages. In 1942, he attended Cumberland University in Lebanon, Tennessee, and it did not take long before he involved himself in local politics and successfully organized the freshmen class against the abuses of hazing.

Toward the end of his undergraduate career, at the request of the Presbyterian Church, Horton traveled to the nearby town of Ozone, Tennessee, to offer Bible classes. It was during this period in his life that he realized that the pedagogy and curriculum of the church did little to name the problems and address the needs of the mountain communities that had long been oppressed by big business, in particular, by timber and coal mining companies (Bledsoe, 1969). In place of the church's more traditional classroom format, he offered "community meetings" in order to tap the locals and listen to their problems and concerns. It was at this point that Horton realized that everyday folks, regardless of their poverty and level of literacy, could get together and solve their own problems if given the opportunity. The idea of creating a setting that would nurture community interaction, education, organizing, leadership, and activism thus took root.

Looking to develop a deeper theoretical understanding of oppression and empowerment and to fine tune his skills in order to bring his dream of a mountain school to fruition, Horton studied at the Union Theological Seminary in New York City where he witnessed firsthand the horrors of the Great Depression. He was energized by intellectuals who reinforced his growing conviction that people can transform their existential realities through personal initiative and collective action.[2] As such, he immersed himself in the pragmatism of William James and John Dewey, the economic theories and analyses of Thorstein Veblen and Karl Marx, the socialist ideas of George Counts and Richard Tawny, and the work of such scholars as Eduard Lindeman and Joseph Hart, who viewed adult education as a stepping stone to actualizing social justice (Glen, 1996).

While both disgusted with and politically motivated by the realities and politics of poverty, Horton was also appalled by Jim Crow segregation and the racism that saturated the country. Finding great inspiration for social change in the work of African American writers and the efforts of E. Franklin Frasier and W. E. B. Dubois, he struggled to expand his understanding of the intersection of race and class and how these two categories function to "doubly exploit" working-poor blacks while keeping oppressed groups at each others' throats.

Horton was also interested in utopian societies and their vision of human liberation; but upon deeper analysis he turned away from their rebuttal to the harsh realities of modernity, feeling that it was more important to transform, rather than simply escape from, society.

Struggling with how to use education as a force for social justice, Horton developed a profound intellectual relationship with his professor Reinhold Niebuhr—a self-declared Christian Marxist who vigorously confronted the political limitations of liberal Christian ethics, something that Horton himself had grappled with in his work with local communities back in the Cumberland Hills.

Taking a brief hiatus from the seminary, Horton went to the University of Chicago to study with sociologist Robert Park and explore conflict resolution and the transformative power of social movements. While in Chicago, he developed a friendship with Jane Addams, the antiwar activist, feminist, and cofounder of Hull House—the settlement house movement in Chicago that served the needs of the poor. She once told him:

> To arrive at democratic decisions, you need to have a bunch of ordinary people sitting around the stove in a country house or store and contributing their own experiences and beliefs to the discussion of the subject at hand. (as cited in Adams, 1975, p. 18)

Looking for a model school to use as a foundation for his own participatory democratic vision of public education, Horton was encouraged by Danish-born Lutheran minister Reverend Aage Moller and his mentor, Niebuhr, to travel overseas to explore the Danish folk school movement, which began in the late nineteenth century as a result of the efforts of Bishop N. S. F. Grundtvig (1783–1872). These residential adult education programs were designed to combat the stigma imposed on Danish culture— the residue of centuries of conquest and life under harsh feudal regimes.

At a workers' folk school in Esbjerg, Horton experienced for the first time a formal learning environment in which students were conducting analyses of the actual conditions of the working class, which included a local, national, and international focus (Glen, 1996). Engaged in participatory learning about their culture and history, the education taking place embodied the goals of developing pride in students' cultural heritage, having them actively engage knowledge so as to be able to make meaning rather than merely reproduce it, and consequently, in having students make their own decisions about how to approach the future.

Horton returned to the States, deeply committed to the idea of developing community spaces where ordinary citizens could engage in praxis—the on-going process of reflection and action that enables people to understand and transform the conditions within which they live. Before coming home, he wrote:

I can't sleep, but there are dreams. What you must do is go back . . . Get a simple place . . . move in . . . you're there . . . the situation is there . . . you start with this and let it grow . . . it will build its own structure and take its own form. You can go to school all your life and you'll never figure it out because you're trying to get an answer that can only come from the people in the life situation. (1989, p. 221)

LESSONS FROM THE EARLY DAYS AT HIGHLANDER

Highlander's beginnings were humble to say the least. In search of a building to transform into a functional, residential, adult learning center, Horton and West were lucky enough to be offered a house by Lillian Johnson, a wealthy local who was known for her support of women's suffrage and for working to spread the idea of cooperatives after studying them in Italy (Smith, 2003. p. 14).

Buoyantly Horton and West moved in on November 1, 1932. They started immediately to make the house into a residential center. The spacious attic was turned into a dormitory. The living room became a place for classes, meetings, square dancing, and dining. Extra beds were added in the three bedrooms on the second floor. They mailed out requests for books to start a library and took $50 from their meager treasury to publish a collection of West's poems, *Between the Plow Handles.* They sold poetry and mistletoe, which they gathered, in order to buy groceries. (Adams, 1975: 27)[3]

With Horton at the helm, where he would remain as director for the next forty years until he retired, the tiny school worked to nurture curious, creative, critical individuals and diverse coalitions through a simple form of "communicative autonomy"—literally sitting around with folks in big rocking chairs, in "learning circles,"[4] and dialoging about the world and how to go about democratizing and changing it.

"From its inception, Highlander was controversial because education was seen as a way to understand and change one's world rather than as a way to advance within the existing socioeconomic system" (Jacobs, 2003, p. xv). In approaching "education through action and action through education" (p. xv), the themes of the day were generated by the students themselves and by the sociohistorical realities that shaped life in the local mountains.[5]

What was particularly radical about the school was its approach to pedagogy. "Myles frequently asserted that he was not a leader or an organizer but an educator" (Kohl & Kohl, 1998, p. ix). But his idea of an *educator* presupposed that a teacher be first and foremost a learner and that students also be allowed to assume the role of teacher. In this way, educators do not simply impose their convictions on the classroom, rather they learn about students' lives and help them work through their problems by engaging both their own as well as the teacher's experiences and expertise, exposing them to available resources and expanding their knowledge base and moral, critical, and political consciousness.

In the early years, through the 1930s and 1940s, the small staff focused much of its energy on economic injustice and union organizing. Taking up the concerns of local farmers and workers being exploited by the coal-mining and timber industries, the folk school provided workshops, leadership seminars, and a diversity of programs intended to offer support, insight, and the "seeds of fire" to get people rallied for change.

Highlander's first real challenge came in the form of a coal strike in 1932, in the company-owned town of Wilder, Tennessee. As Frank Adams (1975) describes the situation:

> The town's only store was owned by Fentress Coal and Coke Company, as were its few unpainted shacks. Miners were paid in scrip good only at the company store, which charged higher prices than independent stores in the area. The company made weekly deductions for rent on the shacks, for a bathhouse that didn't exist, and for a doctor who was infrequently available. No matter how hard or long the men worked in the mines, they couldn't break even, much less get ahead. As their debts piled up, and food at home dwindled, their indignation and desperation mounted. Finally, they struck. (p. 31)

Enduring the frigid winter temperatures, exacerbated by the coal mine owners' orders to have the doors removed from the residential shacks and their electricity turned off, the strikers quickly found themselves in dire need of help if they were to survive, let alone continue their struggle for more humane work conditions (Smith, 2003). However, instead of meeting the workers' demands, the coal companies were filling their vacated posts with prison labor and scabs from out of state. At one point, the mines were temporarily closed as a strategy to break the strike.

Even when workers tried, early on, to compel the mining companies to abide by the eight-hour workday that President Woodrow Wilson had helped put into place, government protections proved unreliable. After a dilapidated train trestle was mysteriously sabotaged, the National Guard was brought in by the governor, and thus taxpayers' money was being used to support the private interests of the owners of the mines and their hired strikebreakers.[6]

The exploited workers would also get the cold shoulder from the Red Cross, which had responded to the bleak situation in Wilder by coming to the town to hand out food and provisions. But such charity would only make its way into the hands of the strikebreakers because "the county chairman of the Red Cross was the wife of the mine superintendent" (Adams, 1975, p. 31).

The staff and students at Highlander learned as much as they could about the situation in Wilder, and they prepared to give assistance to the strikers (Smith, 2003). Meanwhile, Horton would travel back and forth the one hundred miles that separated Monteagle and the company town, to investigate. Given the gravity of the situation, Highlander made effective use of the media by sending out a barrage of articles and letters statewide, informing people of the harsh conditions and asking for political intervention and charitable contributions in the form of provisions for the protestors whose families were literally starving. The public responded generously, and the school helped coordinate the efforts to relieve the destitute workers and their families.

On one of his trips to Wilder, Horton was arrested and charged by a member of the National Guard with "coming here and getting information and going back and teaching it"; the charges were dropped (Smith, 2003, p. 17).

The power of the mine owners in Wilder proved to be overwhelming. Not only were the miners' demands rejected, but the strikers were evicted from their homes, and their leader, Barney Graham, was murdered by company guards on April 29, 1933, a crime for which they were unjustly acquitted. The mines would eventually reopen and remain nonunion.

But the defeat was not a total loss for Highlanders. Getting their feet wet organizing and using the center as a home base, the event proved to be an important learning experience for the students and staff as it taught them "about the role of newspapers, public outreach, networking, public officials, union officials, and industry in labor conflicts" (Smith, 2003, p. 21). In addition, as Angela Smith (2003) points out, the actions of Highlander residents and staff also drew a great deal of attention to the school, both good and bad. Given its growing popularity and for some its notoriety, the forces that opposed organized labor and the democratization of economic and social relations attacked the Folk school and worked diligently to publicly brand it as a Communist training post.

The constant use of the red-scare tactic would eventually generate a great deal of tension between the center and the AFL-CIO.[7] Since the early 1930s, Highlander had developed a solid working relationship with organized labor, and the center was a popular site for training union members, leaders, and organizers. However, by the late 1940s, as the country was moving into the cold war/McCarthy era, union brass stopped sending representatives to the school (Adams, 1975).

> Reacting to the change in the CIO, unions in general, and their increasingly oppressive racist attitudes Zilphia [Horton] commented in 1952, "[The unions] have become so reactionary and . . . so complacent they've lost their ideals, and I don't care anything about singing for people like that." Sometime earlier in her 1945 CIO school evaluation, Zilphia had somewhat prophetically noted an-

other union issue, that of gender, when she described the bitterness expressed by male students against women in industry. (Carter, 1994, pp. 4–5)

Instead of capitulating to the demands of big labor, and refusing to cut ties with the more radical factions of the labor movement, the residents and staff at Highlander marched onward in support of the Farmer's Union that had developed throughout Tennessee, Alabama, and Virginia. When their attempts to forge a farmer-labor coalition in the South failed, they realized that in order to develop a more effective movement for social change, they would also need to directly confront the oppressive and divisive realities of racism.

THE CIVIL RIGHTS MOVEMENT GETS A BOOST

Realizing that substantive social change would be impossible without a broad coalition of activists, Highlander expanded its attention to include a fight against white supremacy. "A small group consisting of Myles, Zilphia, and three new staff members were responsible for coordinating the emerging integration and civil rights program at Highlander" (Carter, 1994, p. 5). As it progressed developmentally, this program would play a significant role in energizing the civil rights movement in the United States.

In 1953, while already taking heat publicly for having integrated class-rooms, Highlander went ahead and established workshops dealing with integration, focusing in particular on desegregating public schools. The center would also begin to develop literacy programs to serve the disenfranchised, especially poverty-stricken African Americans who were denied voting rights because of their inability to read government documents.[8] The Highlander literacy program evolved into what were referred to as Citizenship Schools and by the 1960s this model had already been adopted by the Southern Christian Leadership Conference (SCLC) and was used to educate over one hundred thousand people and prepare them to vote.[9]

"Through these programs Highlander became the educational center of the Civil Rights Movement during the 1950s and early 60s" (Glen, 1996, p. 3). The folk school was honored by the presence of such influential figures as Septima Clark, Fanny Lou Hammer, Martin Luther King, Jr., Andrew Young, and Stokeley Carmichael, among others. In fact, Rosa Parks participated in one of the school's workshops before her heroic act of civil disobedience. In addition, young leaders of student organizations such as SNCC (Student Non-Violent Coordinating Committee) used the center as a staging ground to strategize and initiate their own activist agendas.

As Highlander was gaining a reputation for itself as an outpost of democratic revival, southern white segregationists heightened their assault on the residential adult education center by recycling the earlier claim that it was a Communist training school, while also arguing that the school had integrated classrooms (a ploy to provoke public outrage among likeminded racists given that the *Brown versus the Board of Education* Supreme Court decision against segregation was handed down in 1954) and that it was promoting antagonistic race relations.[10] On one occasion,

> Georgia's segregationist governor, Marvin Griffin, dispatched infil-trators to the celebration of Highlander's 25th anniversary in 1957, where Martin Luther King, Jr. was the keynote speaker. Pictures were taken of King, Horton and others, turned into billboards, and plastered around the south with the label, "King at a Communist Training School." (Bell, Gaventa, & Peters, 1990, p. xxviii)

This volatile political climate culminated in Highlander being investigated by the state and dragged into court in 1961 on trumped up charges of ille-gally selling beer and profiteering from the schools' operations. When asked by the presiding judge why he looked so amused during the legal proceedings, Horton responded:

> I was just thinking what a waste this trial is. I know what you're going to do just as well as you do. You're going to convict us on what the state calls evidence, confiscate our property, and put High-lander Folk School out of business. Then you'll all settle back and think you've got the job done. But Judge, you won't have done a thing. You'll only have been wasting the taxpayer's time and money, along with a lot of ours. Highlander isn't just a school. It's an idea, and you can't put an idea out of business by confiscating property. We'll go right out regardless of what's happening in this courtroom, and five years from now Highlander will be doing more good, what you folks call bad, than it ever did before. We've been at it 29 years, judge, and they haven't licked us yet. You're not going to stop us now. (as cited in Bledsoe, 1969, p. 4)

As Horton had anticipated, the school was found guilty. As a conse-quence of the conviction on these minor charges, Highlander's charter was revoked by the state, and the property was confiscated by authorities. Not long after, the school burned to the ground under what were, needless to say, peculiar circumstances.

The day after the court's decision, Horton defiantly pursued a new charter, and the school was soon reincorporated as the Highlander Research and Education Center; however, the program was relocated to Knoxville, Tennessee. It would remain there for the next ten years, until in 1971, when it was moved to the town of New Market.[11] In Knoxville, the school was warmly received by local activists. "In a three-year period, from 1961 to

1964, the attendance at Highlander workshops increased by more than 400%"
(Bledsoe, 1969, p. 15).

EXPANDING THE COALITION

Over the next few decades Highlander would continue to expand its horizons.
In the 1970s, it helped start the Southern Appalachian Leadership Training
(SALT) program. It also participated in jumpstarting the environmental justice movement in the area by taking up the hazards of strip mining and industrial toxic waste, as well as the healthcare concerns of local workers.

Joining forces with the Appalachian Alliance, Highlander also helped
prepare local folks to take part in a participatory land survey research project
designed to investigate and expose who owns and controls the local land and
its rich natural resources. Laying bare the raw corporate power that had been
exploiting the region and giving nothing back to the people, the research
project mobilized the public and even "eventually encouraged some state
governments to demand higher taxes from corporations—often foreign
owned—that were not paying their share of the costs of schools and roads
and hospitals" (Kohl & Kohl, 1998, p. x).

The contemporary globalization movement could learn a great deal
from the way that the folks at Highlander have approached the production
of knowledge through participatory research. Much like Kurt Lewin's original
model of action research in 1946 (Reason & Bradbury, 2004), Highlander
has challenged the traditional researcher/subject binarism and as a consequence has embraced the idea of doing research *with* others rather than *on*
them, and thus speaking *with* rather than *to* subjects. As such, the center has
been successful in using theory and the production of knowledge in action
to address systemic social problems. In addition, it has placed great importance on reflexivity (deep self-analysis of all those involved in the project)
and on people's existential realities, lived experiences, emotions, and cultural
sensibilities and how these elements can contribute to community development and on-going community action. Recognizing the existence of multiple
realities and identities, these participatory action-based researchers continue
to work to create spaces within which subaltern voices can emerge under
their own volition—a priority of the contemporary global justice movement.

In recognition of its work and achievements with civil and human
rights, in 1982, Highlander was nominated for a Nobel Peace Prize. Through
the 1980s and 90s, the education and research center continued to grow in
focus, taking on heterosexism and homophobia, youth issues, and the discrimination and exploitation of immigrants. Researchers also recognized that
many of the problems that they were confronting were the byproducts of
neoliberal globalization, and as a consequence, they generated more national
and international projects and worked to gather together activists from far

and wide that engendered the aforementioned goals of "globalization from below"—transnational networking to democratize global technologies, environmental resources, and media, information, and financial systems.

THE ROOTS OF GLOBALIZATION AT HIGHLANDER

While Horton had retired as director of the center in 1971, he remained very active in the organization's operations. In fact, he spearheaded much of the school's efforts to develop cross-border coalitions, long before the current global justice movement got its legs. By the mid-1970s, Horton had already traveled to Brazil and Peru with the hopes of bringing together adult educators from Central and South America.[12] While this particular effort bore no immediate fruit, five years later, upon return from his visit to Nicaragua, where he was invited in 1980 to witness the return to Managua of the thousands of people who had been teaching reading in the countryside during the literacy campaign, he was encouraged by the Nicaraguan Ministry of Adult Education to assemble a meeting at Highlander and make plans for a larger gathering of educators in Nicaragua, an event that would later be called the "International Conference on Popular Education for Peace" (Kohl & Kohl, 1998). Additional support and input for the conference were provided by the International Council for Adult Education and the Latin American Council of Adult Education (an organization directed by Brazilian critical pedagogue Paulo Freire). As Horton recounts:

> One of the main purposes of the conference was to get people from the Americas acquainted with each other so that those of us on the adult education leadership level could recruit people from our various countries—people who worked in unions, cooperatives and social action groups of various kinds—to help facilitate the exchange of working people throughout these countries. As an example, before we left Nicaragua, one of the people who came from the United States, John Zippert of the Federation of Southern Cooperatives (an organization of black farmers in Mississippi), arranged for a counterpart from the Nicaraguan cooperative movement to speak at their next convention. That has been followed up by fifteen to twenty exchange visits between people in the United States, Central, and South America. (As cited in Kohl & Kohl, 1998, p. 205)

Horton would work diligently to keep this international solidarity alive. A couple of years after the conference, he was invited back to Nicaragua to participate as an official witness for the elections.

The literacy campaign in Nicaragua, which took place during the Reagan administration's Contra war, which was dead set on crushing the Sandinista government that had removed the former dictator, Anastasio Somoza, in 1979, was based on the pedagogical ideas of Paulo Freire. This Freirean-based campaign augmented the country's literacy rate from 50 to 90 percent among the general population and dramatically increased people's active political participation in public life.[13]

It seemed only a matter of time before Horton and Friere would cross paths, which they did in 1973. But it was not until 1987 that the two men from very different parts of the world actually sat down together and recorded an extensive dialogue about their influences, philosophies, and democratic vision.[14]

One of the many fascinating things to emerge from this dialogue is the abundance of similarities that exist between the philosophy of Myles Horton and Paulo Friere's work in critical pedagogy.[15] Both models value students' existential realities and expertise, the dialectic of teacher/learner, using generative themes and dialogue, and developing a sense of history and moral and political consciousness. Perhaps this common foundation should come as no surprise given that both individuals came from economically devastated regions. Friere felt that it was really important to have this recorded dialogue with Horton—to "speak a book" as Friere put it—because he strongly felt that his ideas were not just intended for the so-called Third World. "No," he said, "the story of Myles and of Highlander Center show that the ideas apply to the First World, too" (Freire as cited in Bell, Gaventa, & Peters, 1990, p. xvi). They were both also influenced by critical social theory and radical Christian thinkers,[16] and both men had read a bit of each other's work.

However, while activists can surely learn from each other, it is important to note that both educators recognized that an integral part of any political project is a pedagogy that encourages individuals to evaluate, based on their own experiences, expertise, and insight, the strengths and weaknesses of any conceptual and practical movement and *recontextualize* and *reinvent* its possibilities for one's own predicaments. In this way the goal is not to search for fixed solutions to problems, but rather, dialogue and theorizing presents a constant challenge to imagine and materialize new political spaces and flexible identities and more just and equitable economic, social, and cultural relations.

CULTURE AND RADICAL ACTIVISM AT HIGHLANDER

The global justice movement has been pushing the boundaries of protest and borrowing aspects of the carnivalesque approach to politics that have been around since the Middle Ages (Bakhtin, 1984): making effective use of street theater, puppets, block parties, art, music, and dance. Instead of perpetuating the false binaries between artistic expression and social responsibility, radical street activists have learned much from the Brazilian Theater of the Oppressed of Augusto Boal, as well as from the Butoh Dancers of Japan, Bread and Puppet Theater, and the San Francisco Mime Troupe (Starr, 2001).

The folks at Highlander have long understood the power of using culture to reinforce activist efforts; in large part due to the important work of Zilphia Horton, Myles Horton's first wife. From 1935 until 1956, when she was tragically killed in an accident, Zilphia used her artistic talents in music, drama, and dance as an essential part of her organizing strategies, curriculum development, and popular pedagogical style (Adams, 1975; Carter, 1994; Glen, 1988). Heavily influenced by feminism and African American gospel music, Zilphia, who would later be anointed "the singing heart of Highlander," used culture as a means not only to motivate people, raise their spirits, and bring dignified recognition to their rich cultural heritage, but also to prepare them for social action. Rather than falling into the trap of cultural relativism and the romanticization of existing cultural practices, Highlander "maintained both a sensitivity to southern culture and a commitment to transforming it" (Glen, 1996, p. 5). As the music and drama director of the folk school, Zilphia made effective use of role-playing and singing as an integral part of the process of helping activists become literate in government procedures and labor organizing—for example, in setting up a shirt workers' union in 1937. In fact, all of her classes at Highlander began with singing—a strategy that would become one of the school's traditions (Horton, 1989).[17]

Zilphia's energy and voice would soon make its way on to the national stage.[18] In 1938 she attended the first Southern Conference for Human Welfare convention in Birmingham, Alabama, in the company of Eleanor Roosevelt and Supreme Court Justice Hugo Black. This interracial coalition worked to confront and eradicate racial and economic injustice throughout the country. In 1940, at a benefit in Washington DC, which Eleanor Roosevelt helped organize, Zilphia performed alongside blues singer Huddie "Leadbelly" Ledbetter and poet Archibald MacLeish. It was at this event, attended by congressional representatives and other members of government, that Zilphia encouraged Leadbelly to perform, for the first time, his famous diatribe against racism, "Bourgeois Blues" (Carter, 1994; Glen, 1988).

While working at Highlander, Zilphia overheard some guests singing the religious folk song "We Shall Overcome"—a version adopted and reworked from the older tune "I'll Overcome Someday." Joining forces with Pete Seeger, Frank Hamilton, and Guy Carawan, she revamped the song in the 1940s. Through its frequent use at organized labor and civil rights events, and circulation through popular culture with the help of Pete Seeger, the hymn became not only the theme song of Highlander but also the anthem of the civil rights movement both in the United States and abroad. As Carter (1994) notes, crossing geographical and generational obstacles, a prodemocracy student in Tiananmen Square, China, in 1989 was photographed wearing a t-shirt inscribed with "We Shall Overcome."

CONCLUSION: ONWARD AND UPWARD

In order to assist people and organizations in securing human, economic, and political rights in this age of globalization, we need to continue to critically appropriate from the past, actively theorize the present, and forge new frameworks of analysis, new research methods, and creative and courageous actions that, when realized and mobilized with others allow us to work together toward short- and long-term strategies directed at radical but achievable democratic change (Leistyna, 2005).

As part of using the past to inform and inspire us to mobilize against the plethora of injustices that we face in this new millennium, Highlander offers great insight and energy. The center, while it continues to do important work, is home to an inventory of radical documents, transcriptions of speeches, recorded songs and dialogues, and other important resources that should not be forgotten given that they offer a stepping stone for future acts of justice.[19]

NOTES

1. It is important to note that while the continued efforts of Highlander are awesome, this chapter focuses in large part on how the school got started and on its early efforts. Not only are the center's achievements far too extensive to capture in this brief discussion, but the goal here is to show how grassroots mobilization is possible through courage, the power of dialogue, and praxis.

2. Veron Louis Parrington's *Main Currents in American Thought* had an impact on the young scholar/activist.

3. *Highlander* was the popular name for a person living in the Appalachian Mountains.

4. This pedagogical strategy was utilized by women's study groups and clubs of the late 1800s.

5. Highlander also had an unconventional approach to assessment in that students were not formally evaluated, and they received no diploma or academic credits upon completion of their work at the center; instead, progress was based on the actions of students subsequent to their educational experience.

6. Many locals, including Horton, figured that the company destroyed the old trestle so as to justify bringing in government forces to crush the strikers' efforts.

7. Since 1937, Highlander had worked closely with the Committee for Industrial Organization, which soon became the CIO: the Congress of Industrial Organizations.

8. In 1954, "Zilphia represented the school at a Charleston, South Carolina NAACP dinner attended by Justice Thurgood Marshall and J. Waties Waring, the judge who had outlawed the exclusion of Blacks from Democratic primaries" (Carter, 1994, p. 5).

9. The pilot site was the South Carolina Sea Islands Citizenship School on Johns Island. Zilphia oversaw its development.

10. Highlander was getting it from all sides: the media, politicians, etc. In 1957, the Georgia Commission on Education published a pamphlet entitled "Highlander Folk

School: Communist Training School in Monteagle, Tennessee." That same year, James Eastland, a Mississippi senator (D) who was the chairman of the Senate Internal Security subcommittee took charge of the investigation of the school.

11. Highlander financially stays afloat through the generosity of a private foundation, individuals, and fund raisers and drives. With a paid staff of about twenty, the center's current annual budget is about $750,000.

12. Curious about the possibilities of revolution in countries other than the United States, Horton stated: "I've always wanted to see a country during the beginning stages of a revolution, and after an abortive effort to follow up my visit to Cuba three months after their revolution, I was determined to try to see something of the Nicaraguan revolution that overthrew Somoza in 1979" (as cited in Kohl & Kohl, 1998: 202–03).

13. The literacy campaign also had its roots in Marxist class analysis, the theoretical forces of anti-imperialist, revolutionary Augusto Sandino (1895–1934), and Liberation Theology.

14. See Bell, Gaventa, and Peters (1990), *We Make the Road by Walking: Conversations on Education and Social Change, Myles Horton and Paulo Freire.*

15. As the educational arm of critical social theory, critical pedagogy, which emerged in the early stages of decolonization, has been used to help understand and respond to oppressive social practices, especially those that manifest in educational institutions. Arguing that education is an inherently political act where values and beliefs are transmitted, or at best struggled over, critical pedagogy encourages, as a fundamental part of the learning process, examination of the exploitation of labor and the concomitant class divisions and conflicts that reveal different economic, political, and cultural interests in society.

In its more mature form it also addresses how oppression affects people of all walks of life who fall outside of mainstream norms of identity and "acceptable" behavior. In order to be active "subjects" of history rather than passive "objects" to be acted upon, manipulated, and controlled, critical pedagogues argue that literacy needs to work in a way that helps people read the economic, social, and political realities that shape their lives in order to develop the necessary critical consciousness to name, understand, and transform them.

16. Friere was impressed and motivated by progressive Christian intellectuals, in particular: Jacques Maritain (1882–1973) and his view of knowledge analysis and "critical realism," liberal Christian humanism, and the defense of natural rights; the critical voice of Geroges Bernanos (1888–1948); Emmanuel Mounier (1905–1950), who called for people to take and active role in history; and like Horton, the religious socialism of Reinhold Niebuhr (1892–1971). Spiritually grounded, Freire also maintained a symbiotic relationship with liberation theology. Liberation theologists emerged in the 1960s out of the economic, political, and military turmoil in Latin America. Among its many important voices, Gustavo Guiterrez (1970) has worked to reveal the compassion rather than anger of God and answer the call to learn from and help the poor and oppressed. Influenced by critical theory, ecological ethics, and feminist, black, and minjung theology, religious practice in this sense includes taking a political stance and opposing the exploitation and tyranny of market forces, thus making a profound link between Christianity and socialism.

17. The daughter of a coal mine owner in the town of Spadra, Arkansas, Zilphia Mae Johnson was born on April 14, 1910. She took serious interest in the

labor movement when she met a radical Presbyterian minister who was working to establish the Progressive Miners' Union in order to collectively bargain with her father. As Vicki Carter notes, rejecting her father's insistence that she cease working with the minister and his church, "she was disowned and forced from her home because of her 'revolutionary Christian attitudes' " (1994, 2). In 1935, Zilphia visited Highlander with the hopes of learning more about the labor movement, as a stepping stone to furthering her formal education.

18. She was also a member of the YWCA national subcommittee on music.

19. The collection can be found online at www.lib.unc.edu/mss/inv/htm/20361.html.

REFERENCES

Adams, F. (1975). *Unearthing seeds of fire: The idea of Highlander.* Winston-Salem, NC: Bair.

Bakhtin, M. (1984). *Rabelais and his world.* Bloomington: Indiana University Press.

Bauman, Z. (1998). Globalization: The human consequences. New York: Columbia University Press.

Bell, B., Gaventa, J., & Peters, J. (Eds.). (1990). *We make the road by walking: Conversations on education and social change; Myles Horton and Paulo Freire.* Philadelphia: Temple University Press.

Bledsoe, T. (1969). *Or we'll all hang separately: The Highlander idea.* Boston: Beacon.

Brecher, J., Costello, T., & Smith, B. (2000). *Globalization from below: The power of solidarity.* Cambridge, MA: South End.

Carter, V. K. (1994). The singing heart of Highlander Folk School. *New Horizons in Adult Education,* 8 (2). Retrieved May 5, 2006, from http://web.bilkent.edu.tr/nova/education/horizons/v8n2/3.html.

Castells, M. (1996). The rise of the network society. Oxford: Blackwell.

Chambers, S. (2002). A critical theory of civil society. In S. Chambers & W. Kymlicka (Eds.), *Alternative conceptions of civil society.* Princeton, NJ: Princeton University Press.

Danaher, K., & Mark, J. (2003) *Insurrection: Citizen challenges to corporate power.* New York: Routledge.

Glen, J. N. (1996). *Highlander: No ordinary school.* Knoxville: University of Tennessee Press.

Gramsci, A. (1975). *Prison notebooks.* New York: Columbia University Press.

Habermas, J. (1991). *The structural transformation of the public sphere: An inquiry into a category of bourgeois society.* Cambridge, MA: MIT Press.

Hardt, M., & Negri, A. (2000). *Empire.* Cambridge, MA: Harvard University Press.

Harvey, D. (2003). *The new imperialism.* Oxford: Oxford University Press.

Harvey, D. (2001). *Spaces of capital: Towards a critical geography.* New York: Routledge.

Held, D. (1996). The development of the modern state. In S. Hall, D. Held, D. Hubert, & K. Thompson (Eds), *Modernity: An Introduction to Modern Societies.* Cambridge, MA: Blackwell.

Horton, A. (1989). *The Highlander Folk School: A history of the major programs, 1932–1961.* New York: Carlson.

Jacobs, D. (Ed.) (2003). *The Myles Horton reader: Education for social change.* Knoxville: University of Tennessee Press.

Kim, J., Young, M., Joyce V., Irwin, A., & Gershman, J. (Eds.). (2000). *Dying for growth: Global inequality and the health of the poor*. Monroe, ME: Common Courage.

Kohl, J., & Kohl, H. (1998). *The long haul: An autobiography*. New York: Teachers College.

Lash, S., & Urry, J. (1987). *The end of organized capitalism*. Madison: University of Wisconsin Press.

Leistyna, P. (Ed.). (2005). *Cultural studies: From theory to action*. Oxford: Blackwell.

Porta, D., & Tarrow, S. (Eds.). (2005). *Transnational protest & global activism: People, passions, and power*. Boulder, CO: Rowman & Littlefield.

Reason, P., & Bradbury, H. (2004). *Handbook of action research: Participative inquiry and practice*. London: Sage.

Smith, A. (2003). Myles Horton, Highlander Folk School, and the Wilder coal strike of 1932. Retrieved May 3, 2006 from http://www.highlandercenter.org/pdffiles/wilder_horton.pdf.

Starr, A. (2001). Art and revolution: Revitalizing political protest. In N. Welton & L. Wolf (Eds.), *Global uprising: Confronting the tyrannies of the 21st century*. British Columbia: New Society.

CHAPTER FOUR

WILLIE LEE BUFFINGTON AND FAITH CABIN LIBRARIES

DOING PRACTICAL GOOD IN A DISORDERED WORLD

Tamara Powell

The American South during the 1930s can be defined through its predominantly rural lifestyle, through its caste society, and through its resistance to provision of adequate educational facilities for its children, but most significantly, it can be defined through its racial problem. The issues surrounding the emancipation of slaves and how they would be assimilated into society or kept at arms' length were at the root of the socioeconomic and educational life at all levels of southern society. The South's economic, social, and financial structures were based on cash crops, extractive industries, and a large unskilled labor force (King, 1980). The South of the early twentieth century defined by historian Vance (1932) was a region of farmers and farm workers who were barely supported by agriculture. Per capita annual income was less than half that of the rest of the United States. Cotton, the major cash crop, controlled the routine of the early twentieth-century southern rural lifestyle with a cycle of tenancy at the heart of farmers' lives (Tindall, 1967).

The tenant farmers of both races were the victims as well as the supporters of the economy that gave large landowners control over large parcels of land and the power to exploit laborers. The tenant farmers were near the bottom of the southern social hierarchy and were also the poorest residents. They were reliant on the landowners to furnish their planting needs, but the costs for their dependence were frequently inflated by double digit interest

75

rates (Poe, 1935). Nine of ten black Americans lived in the South in 1917; about three-fourths of them in rural areas (Litmack, 1998). Rural life for them was more difficult than for tenant whites. It was philosophically accepted by whites of all classes in the South that blacks were an inferior race. That philosophy was made into practice through the laws and customs of Jim Crow.

Jim Crow laws dictated the normative social and legal standards in the South. Reactionary white citizens also used the Jim Crow traditions to support their vigilante activities, that is, house burnings and lynchings. Whites were determined to keep blacks from enjoying the privileges of American citizenship (Packard, 2002). Jim Crow pervaded all social strata of whites, influenced business, religious, and educational, and public policy formation and impacted private, individual, and family decision making.

School reforms made in the first decades of the twentieth century in the United States' burgeoning population centers initiated by noteworthy educators such as John Dewey looked different than those seen in the American South. While women in the Progressive Era South were dominant initiators of educational change, little is recorded about white men who worked in an in-between niche, a "hybrid" space, which was neither defined nor supported by contemporary practice or experimentation (Bhabha, 1994). The niche for one such white man, Willie Lee Buffington, was comparable to that of the women celebrated in this book: he worked in an area of South Carolina that was characterized by poverty, racial tension, isolation, and neglect by the authorities.

At a time when Jim Crow ruled and when libraries in South Carolina existed only in the population centers of Columbia and Charleston primarily used by whites (Wilson & Wright, 1935), Buffington founded libraries that provided a means of knowledge production to the marginalized rural blacks over a span of twenty-one years in South Carolina and longer in Georgia but received limited recognition. Buffington established his first community library in an African American church and then moved it to a community-raised log cabin, which was the first to be known as a "Faith Cabin Library," before later integrating the library movement into school sites. These libraries were completely organized and operated through volunteer effort; they were stocked with used books, old newspapers, and periodicals and provided to rural black citizens an opportunity for literacy that was previously inaccessible to them. One of the few contemporary articles in South Carolina publications about Buffington's work appeared on May 1, 1933, in The State newspaper praising a "young white man" for extending "goodwill towards his Negro neighbors." The editorial further affirmed his work with the first library in saying that "inter-racial relations would improve far faster in South Carolina if there were more Willie Lee Buffingtons."

The gaps in the paper trail that document the life of Willie Lee Buffington are wide, but it is clear from the existent paper that from any analytical perspective, his accomplishments are amazing. The man followed his childhood dream of serving those in need, and through the sacrificial giving of his resources he contributed to improving the quality of others' lives. From 1932 to 1943 Buffington facilitated the establishment of twenty-eight libraries in South Carolina for use by African Americans, many in connection with Rosenwald schools. Two South Carolina libraries were affiliated with Christian schools established for blacks earlier than the Rosenwald initiative in rural South Carolina. Buffington saw his missionary endeavor as a method to build attitudes and habits that would change behavior with results that would be found in the uplift of the community but would not be found in quantitative reports made to project sponsors (Carter & Geil, 1943).

Buffington dedicated his life to the Faith Cabin Library movement because he understood extreme poverty and the difficult situations his African American neighbors balanced; he grew up in the community where he established the first of the libraries. He believed that individual and community uplift could be achieved through education. Perhaps most important to Buffington, he was putting into practice the teachings of the scripture through the ministry he felt led by God to complete.

Buffington's awareness of the lack of interracial understanding emerged from the Jim Crow tradition. According to his autobiographical information (1942), while walking in Edgefield, South Carolina, Buffington met a black woman with a preschool-aged child. The child screamed and ran into the street when he encountered the white man coming toward him. The incident engendered in Buffington a desire to bridge the racial misunderstandings in his town (Kuyper, 1933).

In an autobiographical article, Buffington (1942) wrote of the impact of others on his own life. After his mother's death, when he was two years old, he was sent to live with his grandmother. Even though she could not write and struggled to read, she had read the Bible through several times and based her own life on the teachings of the scripture. She told young Buffington bedtime stories from the Old Testament. His grandmother said the acts of the boy David exemplified her belief that "one on God's side is a majority" (Buffington, p. 45). It is likely that his observation of his grandmother's struggle with literacy inspired Buffington's own yearning to read and learn.

Four years later, according to Carr's (1958) report on her interview, Buffington went back to live with his father and new stepmother. The elder Buffington had stepped up from farm tenancy to farm ownership when he remarried, but every member of the family was needed to work the crops. Seven months of the year, Buffington walked three miles to the white school. Both the white and the black schools were old, dilapidated, recycled shacks made of slabs with strips of batten covering the cracks. The blackboards were boards painted black that were nailed across part of a wall. The white school had a ceiling that held the heat from the fireplace better than the black school with its unlined roof. His father was a member of the school board who appointed teachers for both schools (Buffington, 1942).

Euriah W. Simpkins, a teacher at the Red Hill School, a black school in Saluda County, had thirty years' teaching experience. Euriah, one of Clark Simpkins' eleven children, was self-taught and widely respected in Saluda County (E. B. Brown, personal communication, 2005). Buffington tells of meeting Simpkins when he was about nine years old, crying at the top of his lungs over a squabble with his black playmates. Simpkins told Buffington to "be a man, my son" which, Buffington (1942) recounted in his autobiographical writing, reminded the child of his grandmother's stories of the boy David. Simpkins walked across the Buffington farm daily to school and stopped frequently to chat with young Buffington (Curtis, n.d.). In his role as a Saluda County school trustee, Buffington's father had to sign Simpkins' monthly salary claim. Simpkins' monthly visits to the Buffington home presented further opportunity for the black man and the white boy to nurture a deep and lasting friendship over the next three years (Brown, 1937). Simpkins died in 1944.

During these years the elder Buffington supervised a community Sunday school organized in the white school building where training focused on sharing what you had. Buffington recollected with amazement that the children in the school gave their coins to help pay a Bible teacher's salary in Africa when they did not have a regular pastor themselves (Buffington, 1942).

It was through his study and teaching in this school that the younger Buffington decided to become a minister. According to his interview with Sprinkle (1948), when Buffington confided his career aspiration to others, they were doubtful that he would accomplish his goal because he did not have the skills thought to be necessary for preachers. He was shy, awkward in both speaking and on social occasions, and he had no money to pay for college and seminary (Sprinkle, 1948). According to the information Buffington shared with Neal (1959) the need for his labor on the farm prevented him from attending high school after completing the seventh grade. However, his family and his friend Simpkins encouraged Buffington to pursue his dream (Sprinkle, 1948).

In his autobiographical article, Buffington (1942) recounted how the members of his family worked hard on the farm until the boll weevil reduced the cotton production from a bale an acre to two bales from an entire twenty acres planted. When he was twelve years old, at his completion of the seventh grade, Buffington's family lost their farm; he and his father went to work in a sawmill making a total of $1.25 for their day's labor. Money was scarce in the rural South during the 1920s, and for the Buffingtons, with six children younger than Willie Lee, the sawmill work must have barely kept them from starvation. Throughout the community, impressionable young Buffington saw people helping each other get by (Maynard, 1950). While the life of a sawyer was harsh, it would provide Buffington with knowledge he would need to carry out his dream. In November 1925, Willie Lee Buffington left Saluda County for the first time in his life to go to the Martha Berry School in Georgia where he could work his way through high school (Buffington, 1942). Buffington related to Styler in 1947 that it was his father who heard of this school, and knowing of his son's intense desire to learn, the elder Buffington put $3.85 together and sent Willie Lee off. The seventeen-year-old student worked digging sewer lines at Martha Berry School at first and then he was assigned to driving the school trash wagon. This second job was fortuitous as it gave Buffington opportunity to read the newspaper clippings and old magazines he found in the trash. He even made scrapbooks of the clippings. After the school principal saw the young man reading from the trash, he arranged for him to work as a library assistant. Reading opened the world to Buffington, who had little experience aside from the daily struggles of survival. Books granted him access to the wisdom of the ages. In his mind, he contrasted his access to books with that of the people in his home community. A small number of families subscribed to a newspaper (Buffington, 1942). Some families there owned a Bible, and some had a copy of *Pilgrim's Progress*, and while there were very few books in the white community, Buffington knew there were fewer still in the black community (Styler). Not only did access to books drastically expand Buffington's world as well as remind him of the lack of opportunity to read afforded his friends and family, but it also was important to his future to know that the library at Martha Berry School was stocked with many used books that had been donated from people around the nation (Neal, 1959).

During his tenure at Martha Berry School, Buffington received a letter from his father every other week (Buffington, 1942) and monthly letters and a dollar for spending money from his mentor, E. W. Simpkins, who was still teaching in Saluda County where he earned forty dollars per month. This dollar sent out of Simpkins' monthly paycheck was essentially all the pocket money Buffington had during the time he was at Berry (Neal, 1959). Simpkins encouraged Buffington to live a Christian life, to complete his education, and to remember his desire to be a pastor (Brown, 1937). Buffington admitted that the gift of this mailing from a poor black man to a poor white man changed his life. One of his Berry teachers, Ernest Hall Buell, later wrote that Buffington was hardworking and earnest in pursuing his studies (1937). And after two years of constant studying and working at Berry, Buffington became so ill that he was forced to go back home to his family, now living in Ninety-Six, South Carolina. After eight months of recuperation, he went to work in a textile mill (Buffington, 1942).

Buffington eventually moved with his family to Edgefield County and at twenty-three years old, married his childhood sweetheart, Clara Rushton. He worked as a cotton mill doffer, (Department of Commerce—Bureau of the Census, 1930) earning twelve dollars a week and lived with his wife in part of a company house (Buffington, 1942). As a doffer, Buffington's job was to "change the bobbins on the spinning frames when they were filled" (Carlton, 1982, p. 177). A year or two after moving to Edgefield, Buffington's long-time friend Simpkins invited him to tour the new Rosenwald-funded school in the Plum Branch community. While touring the new three-room schoolhouse, Buffington was struck by the fact that there were no books for the three teachers to use. He was pained because he was aware of the differences between the new school facility and the two-room, two-teacher school for white children in the community. He wrote:

> In the Centennial School for white children there were shelves for books and a glass case with a key and lock for books or displays; but in the school of which Mr. Simpkins was so proud, there were no books and no place where books could be placed. It was unbelievable and unthinkable to me that a school should not have any books. I had just read Booker T. Washington's "Up from Slavery," and I was ashamed of the unequal opportunities and struggles Negroes encountered. When I asked Mr. Simpkins about his books, he replied that the books will come. "I have faith the books will come. The Lord will provide." (Carr, 1958, pp. 9–10)

Buffington prayed for a way to help Simpkins and his students. The answer came to him in a dream of a cabin full of books on a familiar spot of ground. Late in 1931, as he continued to wrestle with how to help the black school, Buffington was reminded of his grandmother's adage, "A little bit, blessed by the Lord, goes a long way, Willie Lee. God makes the miracle" (Buffington, 1942).

In 1932, although Buffington was working eleven-hour shifts in the mill, he, his wife, and infant son were striving to make ends meet on his twelve-dollar-per-week-salary (Buffington, 1942). In his interview with Beard (1933), Buffington described the strong call he felt to prepare for the ministry, and he knew he had to finish his own education.

Buffington told his children, William, Jr., and Ethel, the way he got his own education "was almost magical" (E. B. Brown, personal communication, 2005). A labor negotiation shortened his work shift from eleven to eight hours per day, and Buffington, twenty-four years old and a new father, took advantage of the extra time to return to public high school. He described his educational experiences to Carr in 1958. He attended school in the morning, walked back to his house, ate, and then went to work from 2:00 p.m. until 10:00 p.m. He graduated Saluda High School in 1935 and entered Wofford College because there he could work in a mill while attending classes, although he was dissuaded by an administrator at the college who thought Buffington had no business in college while trying to provide for a family (Brown, personal communication, September 16, 2005). The mill work proved to be too much for Buffington to do while attending to the responsibilities of being a student, so he arranged to leave Wofford to attend Furman College in Greenville, South Carolina, where he had less demanding work and a scholarship. He earned a baccalaureate degree in 1938.

Buffington then moved his family to Chester, Pennsylvania, where he attended Crozer Theological Seminary, served on a church staff, and worked in the shipyard during summers. At the time, Crozer was interested in students who were on the cutting edge of social reform. One of Buffington's classmates was Martin Luther King, Jr., whom he described as being charismatic, always followed by a crowd of other students wanting to hear what King had to say (E. B. Brown, personal communication, 2005).

His work with the Faith Cabin Libraries satisfied Crozer's interest in educating students who were involved in social reform. While at the institution, Buffington's tuition was free, his family lived in campus housing for $10 per month, he had a $150 annual scholarship, and he received an annual $200 grant from the Phelps-Stokes Fund. He was also paid by the black church where he served as director of Christian education (Beard, 1933). In 1942, Buffington was awarded a Bachelor of Divinity from Crozer and a master's degree in sociology from the University of Pennsylvania. From 1932 through 1942, while he worked and attended school, Buffington continued to conduct the Faith Cabin Library project (Carter & Geil, 1943). He asked that books during this time be shipped to his father, M. W. Buffington, in Edgefield (Beard, 1933).

Buffington achieved his goal of becoming a minister; he preached his first sermon at Pendleton Street Baptist Church in Greenville, South Carolina, during his second year at Furman. After completion of his formal education, he accepted a position as professor of sociology and church history at Benedict College in Columbia, South Carolina, where he was employed when he was interviewed by Carter and Geil in 1943. He taught at this historically black college from 1942 until 1945. The professor and pastor collected books for the Starks School of Theology at Benedict and arranged for the establishment of two other libraries during this time (Carr, 1958).

By his own admission to Carr in 1958, Buffington was so haunted by the need for books in the new Plum Branch schoolhouse that in late 1931 he acted on impulse in spending the last money in his pocket on five two-cent postage stamps. He wrote to five ministers in various parts of the country whose names he gathered from old Sunday School literature. He chose these persons because they had contributed to the writing of the lessons, and Buffington reasoned that they might show interest in his appeal. His simple writing style clearly conveyed the need:

> The Negroes here have no books. Good books will help them more than anything else and I want to start a library for them. Could you send me a book for it? If you have none to send, would you send me a postage stamp so that I might write to someone else? (Neal, 1959, p. 3)

Buffington did not hear from any of the five for a while and never received a response from four of the addressees. An air mail letter arrived two months later from Dr. L. H. King, pastor of St. Mark's Methodist Episcopal Church, a black congregation in New York City. The letter read:

I have your letter and I know from experience something of the conditions of which you speak. I have presented your appeal to my people and they are responding splendidly. Over 800 books are on hand, and more are coming in every day. Will make shipment soon. (Buffington 1942, p. 47)

More than one thousand books—fiction, biography, religion, and textbooks— were shipped in barrels to Buffington from this church congregation in Harlem (Buffington, 1942). The number of books proved to be problematic because after selecting books to house in Simpkins' school, the men had no pragmatic plan to make the rest accessible to the community, nor could they locate a suitable place to store them (Carr, 1958). They called a community meeting in the Lockhart Baptist Church, where Simpkins taught a Bible class for men (Buffington, n. d.).

In an interview, Buffington told Maynard (1950) that the books were said to have been stacked all over the sanctuary, up the aisles, on the altar, and on the pews. Buffington described the overwhelming effect of that scene to Carr (1958):

You should see a pile of a thousand books some time to realize how impressive books can be; perhaps you can imagine the effect on these people who, "backwoods" though one might call them and lacking in formal education as most of them were, they still know the value of books. They were bread and meat to the starving. The lives of people changed that day.

At that meeting, it was determined that this African American community would do as they had done in the past—work together for the common good. The black community formulated plans to build a log cabin to serve as library. The question of what to name the library came up in one of the community meetings that were on-going through the building process. A woman who could neither read nor write suggested "Faith Cabin Library" based on the fact that at the outset of the project, the community had faith but no physical resources to use in building the library (Carr, 1958). The term was also descriptive of the faith that Buffington had that the books would be donated as a result of his five letters. Further, the name reflected the faith that Simpkins had that the community's Rosenwald school would be fitted with books (Buffington, 1942). Faith Cabin Library named the movement that resulted in thirty such facilities in South Carolina between 1932 and 1943 (Buffington, 1954).

The building at Plum Branch was eighteen feet by twenty-two feet with a rock chimney and an open fireplace (Kuyper, 1933). Farm prices had been low since the early 1920s, and the project was being planned in the midst of the nation's Great Depression (Buffington, n.d.). The South Carolina tenant farmers had no money to invest in the venture. Some in the community had logs to donate, others worked with Buffington to solicit trees from white landowners in the county, and they cut the trees on the school property. The men in the black community felled the trees, and those who had mules and wagons hauled them to the planning mill in the town of Saluda (Buffington's knowledge of sawmills must have been valuable at this time!) The trees were cut into lumber for floors, walls, and ceilings, and extra trees were traded to pay for the sawing or sold for cash to buy hardware and windows (Buffington, 1942). A stonemason came from a neighboring community because there was not one in the Plum Creek area, and Buffington told Carr (1958) that the community had to pay him for building the fireplace and chimney. There were hundreds of labor hours logged into building the cabin, and everyone helped as they could.

The work had to be done around the crop cycle, so the work "bees" were community events. An old piano was converted to serve as a table (Sprinkle, 1948). The black women made chairs for the library out of barrels with cushions covered with a cotton upholstery fabric, cretonnes. It is not a leap to imagine that St. Mark's Church furnished not only the books for this library but also the barrels for the chairs. The women also sold barbecue hash at the gatherings and put the money in the library fund (Buffington, 1942).

The library was located five miles from a power supply line, so the people of the community found kerosene lamps to light the building. Buffington went through the donated books and magazines to cull those he considered "undesirable" (Carr, 1958, p. 15). The criteria used for culling books are not evident, but Buffington's background and life goals as well as the fact that the books were donated through a church would suggest that books were shelved or culled based on Christian values. Books were sorted and placed on the shelves according to reader age brackets, with sections for children's books, for young people, and for adults. The religious materials were organized conveniently for use by black pastors in the area (Carr). There was a sign in the library and in the successive ones that read "Others" as a reminder to all patrons how the library had come about (Neal, 1959).

On December 31, 1932, Buffington led the community in dedicating the library to "the glory of God and the uplift of mankind" (Carr, 1958, p. 15). What a celebration this pivotal event must have been as members of the community reviewed their long hours of labor and looked forward to the promises to come from access to more than a thousand books. J. B. Felton, the state's supervisor of Negro schools, attended the dedication and made a fifty-dollar donation to the library. He described the library as "the rarest spiritual and intellectual institution in America" (p. 15). This quote was then used, according to Buffington, as the library movement's motto and was printed on the official Faith Cabin Library stationery (Carr).

A battery-operated radio was given by a Pennsylvania woman, and school recesses were timed with news broadcasts so that children could learn of current events (Buffington, 1942). There was storytelling. There were weekly reading clubs for adults and children. Children's clubs began on Sunday afternoons with prayer and singing before each child talked about the book she or he was reading (Buffington, 1942). A nickel per week was collected from children who could pay, and the money was used to buy books written by African Americans. Buffington described Sunday afternoons as being particularly busy at the library (Jones, 1937).

Books were loaned for three weeks, and in Buffington's assessment (Beard, 1933) about one-third of the books were in use all the time. During the winter, when fieldwork was not demanding, the library was open each evening and every Saturday and Sunday afternoon. Buffington said the school and community used the library facility virtually every day. They had subscriptions to two magazines, and other papers and magazines, although out of date, were still widely read (Carr, 1958). One can envision Buffington enjoying access to the materials as much as did the black members of the community.

Buffington was not the only white person who enjoyed access to the library. Buffington family members have recounted their library experiences as school children. Every Friday, the children from the white school in the community would walk to the Plum Creek branch of the Faith Cabin Library for browsing and check-out (Brown, personal communication, September 16, 2005). The Wilson and Wright (1934) study of libraries in the American South indicates that the closest public library to Plum Creek was the Rosenwald Demonstration Library in Columbia. Circulation data from 1934 indicate that persons from rural areas hardly used the Columbia library. The fact that Buffington family school children used the Plum Creek library makes it plausible to suggest that white children in other communities used the Faith Cabin Libraries as well as the blacks.

Although Buffington remained active in the life of the library, he lived sixteen miles away from the building, so it was practical that Simpkins be named superintendent of the library (Beard, 1933). Members of the school staff and the community were appointed to committees to look after all the phases of the library work. During the second year of operation, the Lizzie Koon Unit family focused on beautification of the library grounds with the aim of making them the loveliest school campus in the South. More important, during the second year of establishment of the original unit, Buffington, Simpkins, and other leaders began developing plans for expanding the Faith Cabin Library movement to other rural South Carolina communities (Kuyper,

1933). It is said that success breeds success, and this is highlighted through the phenomenon of the Faith Cabin Libraries. By the end of the first year of its existence, the Plum Branch library had a two thousand volume collection and Buffington's appeals during the year for books to enlarge the unit had yielded fifteen hundred books for a second library (Buffington, 1942).

On August 20, 1933, Simpkins and Buffington met with T. F. Hammond, the Saluda County Jeanes Supervisor, to discuss the establishment of a second library on the Ridge Hill Rosenwald School campus. This was the beginning of Buffington working through county school leaders to ascertain needs for libraries and to identify communities that could pull together to raise the facility (Maynard, 1950). Buffington told Carr that it was not as complicated to build a library at the Ridge Hill School as it had been to build the Plum Branch cabin because the community donated the lumber, rather than logs, and laborers were paid a dollar per day by the Works Progressive Administration (WPA) (Carr, 1958). This was probably done through the Civil Works Administration, which was funded from late 1933 through 1934. The money provided through this arm of the WPA was used to construct, repair, and renovate libraries throughout the southeastern United States (Anders, 1958).

To distinguish between two libraries located in the same county, each unit was named. The Lizzie Koon Unit was named for Buffington's mother, who had died in 1910, and the second unit, at Ridge Spring, was known as the Annie Bodie Unit (Carr, 1958), named for Buffington's stepmother, with whom he had enjoyed a rich relationship. A third library was opened in Newberry at the Drayton Street School. The 2,200 volumes housed in a specially planned room in this new high school building were surplus from the Bodie Unit. This unit was named after L. H. King, pastor of St. Mark's Baptist Church in Harlem, who had responded to Buffington's initial request for books (Plumb, 1938).

Lessons learned from organization, acquisition, and operation of the original Faith Cabin Library provided the foundation for establishing twenty-nine more in South Carolina over the next decade. Buffington continued his campaign to secure used books by writing letters to friends of friends and to strangers. He explained to Jones that he told his story wherever he had an audience, asking for no monetary contribution aside from shipping donations by prepaid freight or postage stamps to support his letter writing appeals (Jones, 1937). He asked for donations of used but not outdated books and magazines of general interest to both children and adults (Maynard, 1950). The letters of solicitation indicated a strong pay-as-you-go philosophy that was integral to keeping the library development healthy. In his letters, Buffington asked for a stamped, self-addressed envelope to be included in shipments of books for the acknowledgment of the gift (Carter & Geil, 1943).

As members of other black communities heard about the Faith Cabin Library movement, they contacted Buffington and asked for help in developing their own community libraries (Sprinkle, 1948). Log cabins were built to house the acquisitions for the first six libraries, and the next half dozen were housed in independent structures made of other materials. Most of the later libraries were located in specially designated rooms in the school buildings (Neal, 1959).

The libraries were stocked with books donated by specific groups and organizations outside the state of South Carolina. These donations came about through articles in magazines and church-related materials as well as through the personal appeals from Buffington made through letters and public appearances. Some of the Faith Cabin Libraries had interesting characteristics other than their association with supporting groups. The library at Pendleton, on the campus of the Anderson County Training School (Buffington, 1954), was built on land formerly owned by John C. Calhoun (Buffington, n.d.). The Abraham Lincoln Unit on the Fountain Inn Negro School in Fountain Inn opened in 1937. The 2,800 books in this library were given due to the collection work of Isaac Diller of Springfield, Illinois. The unit was named for the sixteenth president of the United States, according to Buffington, because Diller was the only man known to be living at the time who had been photographed with President Lincoln (Carr, 1958). The citizens of Hanover, New Hampshire, and students from Dartmouth College joined forces to gather books for the shingled library that matched the teachers' quarters and other buildings on the campus of Simpson Junior High School in Easley (Plumb, 1938). Merchants in Hanover posted signs in their windows and allowed books to be dropped off in their businesses; local Scouts gathered the books daily and delivered them to a central location. The 3,000-volume collection was described as "attractive and well balanced, with a wide variety of books, most of them in excellent condition. It is quite apparent that they were chosen with care and thought for their purpose and not merely discarded because one no longer wanted them" (Carr, 1958, p. 27). Included in this collection were 400 textbooks and encyclopedias that were earmarked by the Simpson school principal for adult education courses he planned to conduct for blacks in Easley (Plumb, 1938). The people in Hanover and at Dartmouth were assured that the books would be cared for "since they belong uniquely to the people who use them" (Carr, p. 27). Both an annual supplement and additional books were donated by the Hanover and Dartmouth communities to the library in Easley (Buffington, 1942).

The community members in Chapman Grove, Greenville County, planned a log building for their Faith Cabin Library. They brought logs for planing into lumber, but the desks and blackboards were falling apart in the schoolhouse, so Buffington negotiated with the library leaders to use the newly acquired lumber to build new furnishings for the schoolroom and to remodel the old classroom to serve as the library. This pragmatic use of materials and resources yielded the Bessie L. Drew Unit, which was dedicated in 1936 (Plumb, 1938). The teacher-librarian at the library in Chapman

Grove was able to attend a summer session of library science training at Paine College (Buffington, n.d.).

Seneca Institute in Oconee County was founded in 1899. Black male and female students were offered nondenominational Christian education at the institute until 1926 when it began to offer two additional years of educational opportunity. The institute was renamed Seneca Junior College in May of that year (Seneca Junior College, 1929–1930). This institution was not a recipient of Rosenwald funds, but a Faith Cabin Library was established on the campus in 1937. The 4,000 books for this unit were donated by students at Oberlin College in Oberlin, Ohio, following a personal appeal made on the Oberlin campus by Buffington. Buffington accompanied his lecture with lantern slides (Carr, 1958). The library was out of service by 1950 (Buffington, 1954) and may have closed when Seneca Junior College closed in 1939 (Brown, n.d.).

Reverend Caspar C. Garrigues, pastor of First Christian Church and president of the Ministerial Association of Iowa City, Iowa (Carr, 1958), organized the Faith Cabin Library Club. The club united members of ten different faith groups and denominations with the Kiwanis, Elks, and Lions and the public library, the University of Iowa library, and the School of Religion in a drive that yielded 6,000 books and 1,500 magazines for the Iowa City Unit at the Bettis Academy in Trenton, located in Edgefield County, South Carolina, as recounted by Buffington to Plumb in 1938. This library building was a forty-foot square building made of concrete blocks. Located in a sandy region of the state, it was practical for Bettis students to use the sand in the area to make the blocks on site (Buffington, n. d.).

The Bettis Academy was not a Rosenwald School. It was founded in 1881 by the Reverend Alexander Bettis for the purpose of educating black youths from grammar school through junior college. In addition to intellectual training, spiritual and industrial training were emphasized (Bettis Academy, 1939). Bettis Academy had an expansive influence on the education of rural South Carolina African Americans in the years following the Civil War. Hortense Woodson reported in 1943 that the institution had five hundred students enrolled; three hundred of these were boarders, and there were thirty faculty members. The Academy's Independence Day celebration that year drew approximately ten thousand blacks from the area (Woodson, 1943). Following the dedication of the Faith Cabin Library at the institution in 1938, many black students benefited from their accessibility to the large collection of books contributed by the Iowa City coalition.

The citizens of the Elyria, Ohio, community sent a truckload of books, enough to supply the Elyria Unit at Edgefield Academy with 1,600 books and the George A. Brown Unit at the Edgefield County Training School in Johnston with an 1,800-volume collection. W. E. Parker, (1939) principal of Edgefield Academy, wrote a letter published in the Elyria newspaper that expressed the community's appreciation for the donation and indicated that four young men were using the new acquisitions to prepare for studying for the ministry. Both of these libraries were dedicated in 1938 (Carr, 1958).

The Albert Stamm Unit at the Inman Negro School was also dedicated in 1938. The acquisitions comprised the largest single donation to the Faith Cabin Library effort. Four tons of books were collected by Albert H. Stamm of Stryker, Ohio. Stamm, a disabled World War I veteran, gathered the books from people in four neighboring counties according to Buffington (Styler, 1947).

A Faith Cabin Library was established in 1939 at the Batesburg Negro School with two thousand acquisitions sent from Decatur, Indiana. Mrs. S. D. Beavers, wife of a physician, responded to an article in a religious publication by soliciting books in her community. This library burned in 1950 and was not rebuilt (Carr, 1958).

Miss Margaret Hanesfield was in charge of the Mount Gretna Players, a theater troupe who did outdoor summer performances in a Pennsylvania community. The players appealed to their audiences through the summer of 1937 and collected 2,400 volumes to send to the Mount Gretna Players, Pennsylvania Unit, on the campus of the Saluda Rosenwald School (Carr, 1958).

Buffington was a guest on Dave Elman's *Hobby Lobby* radio program in 1939, (Carter & Geil, 1943) which featured unusual hobbies. Buffington's description of his hobby of collecting things for others and his appeal for book donations was heard by people all over the nation (Carter & Geil, 1943). Buffington acknowledged that this appearance in combination with an article published in the *Christian Herald* at about the same time yielded almost 7,500 books, which were dispersed to four Faith Cabin Libraries. The Hobby Lobby Unit on the Lexington Rosenwald School campus was not built of logs but of shingles as the pine trees in this part of the state do not grow tall enough to use in a log cabin. This library was also used as a classroom part of the time because the school was overcrowded, but Buffington insisted that one corner of the room was always designated as a reading space (Buffington, n.d.). The other libraries that were established through donations made from the radio appeal and the *Christian Herald* article were the Lucy Harris Unit at Howard High School in Georgetown, the Jamestown Unit at Jamestown Negro School, and the E. W. Simpkins Unit at the Baugknight Negro School in Edgefield County (Carr, 1958).

Reverend J. Earle Edwards invited Buffington to speak to representatives of churches, clubs, and fraternal organizations at his church in Queens Village, New York. This group developed a community campaign to collect books, entitled "Ten Thousand Books in Ten Weeks" (Buffington, n.d.). The books collected were placed on the shelves of the Queens Village Unit at the Marlboro County Training School in Bennettsville (Buffington, 1942).

Buffington reported to Carr (1958) that the Philadelphia Matinee Musical Club donated the volumes to stock the shelves of the Harry A. Mackey Unit in Greenville County. The club was stimulated to become involved in this project from hearing Mrs. Mary Rose Collins, a professor of speech at Crozer and member of the club, talk about Buffington's work.

Mrs. Oscar, a member of the Lutheran Church, took an interest in the Faith Cabin Library phenomenon in South Carolina. Her efforts to collect books led to the building of the Rockford (Illinois) Unit in Aiken on the campus of the Aiken Negro School (Buffington, 1954).

Faith Cabin Libraries were a step toward the realization of an ideal. Contemporary French theorist Pierre Bourdieu argues that cultural capital is increased through individual learning and that this self-improvement increases an individual's power (Swartz, 1997). If reading good books has been the foundation of the development of whites, Kuyper (1933) argued, it is likely even more important to the development of the African American people at this particular time. Establishing libraries in rural southern communities made learning accessible to individuals, thereby increasing what Pierre Bourdieu calls "cultural capital" for blacks. For example, the original unit, the Lizzie Koon Unit, served two thousand blacks (Kuyper, 1933).

These thirty libraries were modestly built but were very well stocked with books that Buffington considered to have "lasting value" (Sprinkle, 1948, p. 1). He said, "Boys and girls are rejoicing in the opportunity given them for reading" (Beard, 1933, p. 1). Annie, a Faith Cabin patron, wrote, "Our library has made me a better citizen. Teaching me more about the country in which I live. I wish others, all over, could have a library like ours" (Plumb, 1938, p. 53). The woman who initiated the name *Faith Cabin Library* for the first unit built in Plum Branch learned to read in that library (Carr, 1958).

No one can measure the impact on an ambitious young person reading a book about someone of their own race who achieved success (Kuyper, 1933). Children read books about black leaders who had to overcome great obstacles, such as Booker T. Washington and George W. Carver. At one children's book club meeting not long after the Lizzie Koon Unit was opened, a young boy began his report on Russell Conwell's *Acres of Diamonds* with this introduction, "I've never been out of Saluda County, but this week, I took a trip way up to Philadelphia!" (Buffington, 1942, p. 49). Some of the units were given radios, which opened the world of current events where newspapers were unknown (Styler, 1947). According to Jones (1937) 80 percent of the 8 million blacks in the south still had no access to libraries. The schools were without reference materials and textbooks. It was not uncommon for one student to read from the only textbook aloud while the other students listened. Teachers had no pedagogical materials or guidance for their professional development. The publication of articles about the Faith Cabin Libraries focused some attention to the paucity of books and other materials accessible to rural southern blacks of the day. A school trustee was impressed with the orderliness and widespread use of a library. "I've taken the Negro schools for granted until now. I've just appointed the teachers and let them shift for themselves. From now on I'll take an active interest" (Buffington, 1942, p. 49).

Whites and blacks worked together to build the libraries. In many of the communities, a civic organization or church sponsored the building project. This experience of interracial cooperation to battle the inadequate opportunity for literacy for black citizens was enriching for the entire community (Sprinkle, 1948). The voluntary collaborative projects ushered in a new venue for interracial understanding (Beard, 1933). Many of the groups outside of South Carolina who collected and donated books were comprised of white people who had an inaccurate perception of blacks. Participation in the Faith Cabin Library project improved access to education for blacks, but it also afforded opportunity to the white donors to gain a deeper understanding of the status of disenfranchised blacks and whites (Jones, 1937).

The addition of Faith Cabin Libraries completed the requirements for two schools to meet accreditation standards (Jones, 1937). According to Buffington and reported by Brown (1937), the religious books gathered through church collections were used widely by preachers and church teachers. The contributions from public and college libraries widened the range of books made available through the libraries (Jones, 1937). Buffington recounted that a pastor in Seneca wrote that one of his teachers sent him to the Oberlin Unit to "dig for gold among the books. I found poetry, history, current events . . . thanks be to God for this gold mine! I can preach better sermons because of it" (Plumb, 1938, p. 18).

Unforeseen and unplanned side effects of the Faith Cabin Library movement were varied. Buffington's inspiration to make the libraries community projects helped the citizens realize what they could do when working toward a common cause; the citizens felt the libraries were "peculiarly theirs" (Curtis, n.d, p. 12). Local blacks managed the operation and activities of the library. The libraries served as community centers where black children, teens, and adults could satisfy intellectual needs and participate in social activities (Curtis, n.d.). A school principal described how his community's library became a community center: "We are attempting to make it the first unit of a little community center. At present we are working on a tennis court" (Plumb, 1938, p. 53). One library devised a way of sharing its books with communities who did not have access: "Ours is known as a *traveling library*. It has served thousands of boys and girls, men and women, in the county" (p. 53).

The library movement grew to be so popular that there were two communities who had arranged facilities before Buffington could collect books to fill their shelves. He told Plumb (1938) that he received requests for more libraries than he could honor. At one time in 1937, he had appeals from over a hundred communities who wanted libraries. Donors were eager to help. A librarian in a large library wrote Buffington that she had several hundred children's books to send but had no money to pay to ship the donation.

Buffington did not have the freight money either, so he had to refuse the books. The librarian responded that she would arrange to ship the books; this was the first of several shipments from that organization (Buffington, 1942).

There is evidence of white opposition to Buffington's work. His daughter recalls her years growing up as being very hard; there were threats from local chapters of the Ku Klux Klan. She said that throughout her childhood, she could always feel an undercurrent even though she did not understand it. While it never actually happened, she was concerned throughout her adolescence that she would eventually be involved in a confrontation focused on her father's work. Buffington was aware of potential problems for his children, and for that reason, he enrolled them in school districts where economic levels were higher, making it unlikely that their classmates would be aware of his work on behalf of poor African Americans. Her brother had more problems from Buffington's work than she did. He was enrolled in private schools for a time when he was a teen and finished his high school education at Martha Berry School. Resistance also came from other members of Buffington's family. The elder Buffington worked with his son's ministry, but other family members were opposed to offering assistance to blacks. Much of the family was "not on the same wavelength" (E. B. Brown, personal communication, 2005).

The story of the man behind the Faith Cabin Library movement in South Carolina is proof that individuals, no matter what their resources, can work to alleviate unjust situations for other people. Buffington overcame the obstacles of having a low socioeconomic status, of growing up in rural South Carolina where Jim Crow was a demanding autocrat, and of beginning his life's work during the bleak days of the Great Depression, to impact the lives of thousands of people, black and white. The factors that drove this white man's passion to grow literacy in black communities were instilled in him by his father and grandmother, beginning in his childhood and nurtured by his friendship with Simpkins as well as his passionate Christian beliefs. The determination which pushed Buffington to take practical steps to alleviate the difficulty of others was deeply embedded as indicated during his early adult years when he was a husband, father, and student; held a part time public job; and yet continued the Faith Cabin Library work.

Buffington revealed his empathy for blacks and the passion with which he embraced his advocacy on their behalf in an interview with Kuyper in 1933:

All of my life I have battled with poverty, want, and need, and I am still of the opinion that the poor are not dishonorable. I know that it is possible to live a noble, sweet, and rich life, and be free of prejudice toward any race of God's creation—even in a textile center, where the greater percent of ignorance can be found and where racial prejudice probably reaches its highest peak. Therefore, I shall not be satisfied until I am able to render a service to my community that I feel led to render. I have been the favored one upon a thousand occasions when I have received kindness and courtesy from large host of Negro friends. It has always puzzled me how any Christian could claim the name of Christ and have ill will or hatred for any part of humanity. I am not a preacher, but I study God's word and seek to know His will. As a child of God, my duty is to serve Him by helping others.

Buffington preached in his later years about Jesus' entire life being one of continuous service to God and to men. In that sermon, he spoke of men who live their faith with conviction and named Father Damien, Martin Luther King, and Albert Schweitzer as exemplifying Jesus' demand that Christians dedicate themselves to caring for others. He said that the test of commitment to Christ is to determine if faith is passive or active (Buffington, 1942). Buffington acted out his faith through establishing libraries for the people that he knew and understood. He said that his work was based on a dime, a bank of faith, and a life of sacrifice and prayer. He had faith in the generosity of humanity, and he believed that other people would be stirred to action when they were made aware of the intense need for books.

Buffington realized the great human potential that was lost to society in its denial of educational opportunity to blacks. "For too long we have thought of the Negro as a Negro, not as an American who, contributing boundless energy, talents, and religious enthusiasm, is helping shape our [nation's] destiny" (Buffington, 1942, p. 49). He was zealous in providing books to be a springboard for individual blacks to contribute to America's life. Buffington accepted his responsibility in the building of this library phenomenon, believing his grandmother's teaching, "God makes the miracle, Willie" (Buffington, 1942, p. 49). He had a deep and abiding faith in God and his love for all people. He felt that God had called him to do the library work that was his avocation at first but evolved into his vocation.

Books pass on what is legitimate to know; they set a cultural standard of what should be passed on (Apple, 1988). According to Bourdieu, the cultural capital of the dominant culture is considered the most elite knowledge (Swartz, 1997). Buffington had direct control of the libraries and the acquisitions of each. Additionally, most of the donated volumes probably were written by whites embracing white traditions. In this way, Buffington's weeding of the libraries' collections was an avenue of ensuring that the religious and cultural values that were meaningful to him were reproduced in the African Americans who used the books.

Buffington was a practical man. Poverty had taught him how to do a lot with a little and how to appreciate what he had. His experiences as a farmer, library assistant, student, sawyer, and mill worker prepared him to work with what was obtainable and to have reasonable expectations. Growing up in poverty made Buffington an earnest worker willing to take on tasks and to embrace the value of work. It also taught him to make the most of every available resource.

Living in the country as a sharecropper's child had shown him that he was not different from his black sharecropping neighbors and in fact he shared with them the experiences that came from striving for survival. His life on the farm gave him a contrasting perspective to the life he had as a mill worker where his time was spent with white people. The contrast focused on the fact that despite their poverty in common with blacks, the white mill workers thought they were members of a higher social order than blacks. Diane McWhorten (2001) in *Carry Me Home: Birmingham, Alabama* calls this social attitude "narcissism of small differences"; the closer one is in socioeconomic status, the more one homes in on small differences. Buffington was able to use the white privilege with which he had been born to further the nurture of literacy for disfranchised blacks.

The rural South was insulating through its isolation. Buffington had little access to books and newspapers through his early years; his knowledge of the world's events was limited due to the inaccessibility of the outside world. His involvement in a black community when he was a boy and his immersion as a young adult in the mill society that was rife with prejudice toward poor and black people formed a dichotomy with his expectation that his original five requests for books would actually generate contributions. His naïveté in sending these requests to people who had written for church literature indicates the depth of his childlike faith in God and in his fellow Christians.

There was interracial cooperation in the formation of these libraries. It existed primarily between blacks in the recipient community and the book donors. The donors did not challenge segregation per se, nor does it appear that Buffington confronted South Carolina's political system, which supported the system of dual institutions. It appears that those involved with providing Faith Cabin Libraries to rural communities were primarily concerned that isolated African Americans should have access to books that would in turn enable them to achieve their own religious, moral, and educational uplift.

Buffington and his work with the Faith Cabin Libraries was a paver in the road to full physical access to libraries and lifelong education for rural southern blacks. The work pushed ahead the development of African Americans as a people. While Progressive Era educators in the nation's larger population centers in the Northeast and the Midwest were bringing about change through improved school buildings, better educated teachers, and healthier environments, Buffington was working within the world he knew and using a pipeline of others interested in social reform to quietly offer an opportunity to learn to the marginalized population he knew. The hybrid space that Buffington carved added to the strides accomplished by Progressive Era women in the American South on behalf of the marginalized and was effective in the uplift of southern rural blacks who were stranded with little educational opportunity in the early decades of the twentieth century because of the Jim Crow enforced segregation.

REFERENCES

Anders, M. E. (1958). *The development of public library service in the southeastern states, 1895–1950*. Unpublished manuscript. Columbia University.

Apple, M. W. (1988). *Teachers & texts: A political economy of class & gender relations in education*. London: Routledge.

Beard, F. (1933, August 26). A mill worker and his dreams. *Religious Telescope*. W. L. Buffington Papers. South Caroliniana library. University of South Carolina.

Bettis Academy (Trenton, SC) Records. (1939). *Bettis Academy*. Retrieved September 25, 2004, from University of South Carolina Caroliniana Library Web Site, http://www.sc.edu/library/socar/uscs/1999/bettis.html.

Bhabha, H. K. (1994). *The location of culture*. New York: Routledge.

Brown, G. A. (1937, December 30). By faith Willie Lee Buffington. *The United Presbyterian*, pp. 12–13. W. L. Buffington Papers. South Caroliniana Library. University of South Carolina.

Buell, E. H. (1937). *Establishing libraries as community centers in the colored school sections of the South*. Unpublished manuscript, Connecticut State College. W. L. Buffington Papers. South Caroliniana Library. University of South Carolina.

Buffington, W. L. (1954). *Location of the Faith Cabin Library units*. Unpublished manuscript. W. L. Buffington Papers. South Caroliniana Library. University of South Carolina.

Buffington, W. L. (1942). I had ten cents—and a dream. *Who*, 1(4), 45–49. W. L. Buffington Papers. South Caroliniana Library. University of South Carolina.

Buffington, W. L. (n.d.) *Script describing the Kodachrome slides of the Faith Cabin Library*. Unpublished manuscript. W. L. Buffington Papers. South Caroliniana Library. University of South Carolina.

Carlton, D. L. (1982). *Mill and town in South Carolina*. Baton Rouge: Louisiana State University Press.

Carr, L. D. (1958). *The Reverend Willie Lee Buffington's life and contributions to the development of rural libraries in the south*. Unpublished manuscript. Atlanta University. W. L. Buffington Papers. South Caroliniana Library. University of South Carolina.

Carter, P. C., & Geil, R. H. (1943, November). *Baptist Leader*. W. L. Buffington Papers. South Caroliniana Library. University of South Carolina.

Curtis, A. L. (n. d.). *Libraries by faith*. W. L. Buffington Papers. South Caroliniana Library. University of South Carolina.

Department of Commerce—Bureau of the Census (1930). *Fifteenth Census of the United States: 1930 Population Schedule*. Washington, D.C.: U. S. Government Printing Office.

Jones, K. M. (1937, May). The proper setting for a miracle. *Advance*. W. L. Buffington Papers. South Caroliniana Library. University of South Carolina.

King, R. H. (1980). *A Southern Renaissance: The cultural awakening of the American South*. New York: Oxford University Press.

Kiwanis Magazine, The. W. L. Buffington Papers. South Caroliniana Library. University of South Carolina.

Kuyper, G. A. (1933, May). An adventure in faith. *The Southern Workman.* W. L. Buffington Papers. South Caroliniana Library. University of South Carolina.

Litmack, L. F. (1998). *Trouble on my mind: Black southerners in the age of Jim Crow.* NY: Knopf.

Maynard, E. H. (1950, February). *New hope from old books. Kiwanis Magazine.* W. L. Buffington Papers South Carolina Library. University of South Carolina.

McWhorten, D. (2001). *Carry me home: Birmingham, Alabama, the climactic battle of the civil rights movement.* NY: Simon & Schuster.

Neal, H. E. (1959, April 12). The bookshelves filled by faith. *Sunday Digest,* pp. 1–4. W. L. Buffington Papers. South Caroliniana Library. University of South Carolina.

Packard, J. M. (2002). *American nightmare.* New York: St. Martin's.

Plumb, B. (1938, July). The brotherhood of books. *Christian Herald,* 16–18; 53. W. L. Buffington Papers. South Caroliniana Library. University of South Carolina.

Poe, C. (1935). The farmer and his future. In W. T. Couch (Ed.), *Culture in the South.* Chapel Hill: University of North Carolina Press.

Seneca Junior College. (1929–1930). Catalogue. Seneca, SC: College.

Sprinkle, H. C. (1948). The miracle of the books. *World Outlook.* W. L. Buffington Papers. South Caroliniana Library. University of South Carolina.

Styler, H. (1947, June). He worked wonders—with faith and a dime! *Coronet.* W. L. Buffington Papers. South Caroliniana Library. University of South Carolina.

Swartz, D. (1997). *Culture and Power: The sociology of Pierre Bourdieu.* Chicago University of Chicago Press.

Tindall, G. B. (1967). *The emergence of the new South, 1913–1945.* Baton Rouge: Louisiana State University Press.

Vance, R. B. (1932). *Human geography: A study of the South.* Chapel Hill: University of North Carolina.

Wilson, L. R., & Wight, E. A. (1935). *County library service in the South: A study of the Rosenwald County Library Demonstration.* Chicago: University of Chicago Press.

Woodson, H. (1943). Bettis Academy celebrates the Fourth. South Caroliniana Library, University of South Carolina.

CHAPTER FIVE

DANGEROUS MINDS

CONSTRUCTING URBAN EDUCATION
BETWEEN HOPE AND DESPAIR

Suellyn Henke

INTRODUCTION

The contemporary production of *Dangerous Minds* (1995) serves as a useful point of reference when thinking about the ideological and utopian possibilities of representations of urban education. As Fredric Jameson (1992) and others have argued,

> To explain the public's attraction to a text or medium one must look not only for the "ideological effect" that manipulates people into complicity with existing social relations, but also the kernel of utopian fantasy reaching beyond these relations, whereby the medium constitutes itself as a projected fulfillment of what is desired and absent within the status quo. (Shohat & Stam, 1994, p. 352)

Dangerous Minds marks an endpoint in the mainstream genre[1] of popularized modernistic investment in the tender hope of urban public education. This genre began with the film *Blackboard Jungle* (1955), which opened with the following lines:

We in the U.S. are all fortunate to have a school system that is a tribute to our communities and our faith in American youth. Today we are concerned with juvenile delinquency—its causes—and its effects. We are especially concerned when it boils over into our schools. The scenes and incidents depicted here are fictional. However, we believe that public awareness is a first step for the remedy of any problem. It is in this spirit and in this faith that *Blackboard Jungle* was produced. (Berman, 1955)

The urban education film genre has, since its inception, marked itself as a contested space between fiction and reality. This is the drama that says, This story is not real, but gee whiz, is it true. *Blackboard Jungle* portrayed the juvenile delinquency spilling over into the schools. However, in all the future portrayals "juvenile delinquency" and the "urban high school" became merged as one. Although urban education has always been portrayed as a place of despair (*Blackboard Jungle, 1955; Lean on Me, 1987; Stand and Deliver, 1988*)[2] within the genre was a sense of hope. This hope is not unproblematic but contains severe limitations (which are taken up in the text analysis that follows). However, in the spoof of the genre, *High School High* (1996) all the clichéd narrative elements of the drama are laid bare in hyperbolic fashion, for the gaze of the ironic viewer. Mr. Clark (John Lovitz) caring and naïve, drives to his first day of teaching at Marion Barry High School. As he enters a dirty, depressed, graffiti-ridden neighborhood, loud rap music blares. A metal road sign simply reads "Inner City." Every scene, every character, every element craftily evinces prior films. Lovitz overthrows the evil drug lord, bat-wielding principal, and transforms the school's appearance. The film ends on graduation day when Clark hands out diplomas to all six of the graduating class, and proudly announces the valedictorian, who has a 2.35 G.P.A. The hope that plays here is ironic, distanced, bemused. As parody, it is not meant to be taken seriously or inspire. It is merely a trope for viewers to hang their hats on—an artifact of the past and any sincere powers of investment would certainly be smirked upon. As the cover of the video relates, "With wicked aim, HIGH SCHOOL HIGH skewers feel-good movies like *Dangerous Minds* and *Stand and Deliver* to create a new brand of urban comedy that's laced with slapstick and hilarious spoof of *True Lies* and *The Deer Hunter*" (Dave Kehr, *New York Daily News*). *High School High* is the doorway to a new genre of urban education films, where drama has given away to action/adventure and tragedy. *High School High* illustrates that all the clichés have been combined, and the audience is immune to their effects. The dominant metaphor now is crossover with the war film. This metaphor always existed within the genre itself. Even beginning with *The Blackboard Jungle* there was a sense that urban high schools required a certain militaristic initiative. In this film, Glenn Ford was a returning World War II veteran, and a character in the film states that "the most important war is now to be fought at home." Although there will no doubt still be narratives about urban schools with messages of hope and redemption, in the current context of cynicism and questioning about what is public, it is unlikely that such a narrative will ever explode as wildly again as *Dangerous Minds*; it eulogizes the last hope of public education.

This chapter focuses on *Dangerous Minds*' trajectory as a "hope-filled" popular commodity. Besides its standing as a film about urban schooling, the story of *Dangerous Minds* can be viewed as a fairly typical cultural phenomenon of postindustrial capitalism and the dispersal of meaning. First published as a nonfiction book, *Dangerous Minds* grew much larger and in the process spread and contextualized certain "commonsense" understandings of urban education.

Based on the autobiographical teaching stories of exmarine (which publicity would have viewers believe is an extension of her first name) Lou Anne Johnson, an English teacher who quits after four years of teaching at "Parkmont High School," *Dangerous Minds* is the site of multiple productions. In the film Johnson becomes Michelle Pfeiffer, and in the TV show she becomes Annie Potts. Johnson tells the tale, but it is not her tale after the telling; she is but a ghost haunting the main persona of the teacher. Hence forward "Lou Anne Johnson" refers not to Lou Anne Johnson, a human being, but the representation of Lou Anne Johnson, the teacher, the shimmer of white, middle-class conscience that is the mobile immanence of all the *Dangerous Minds*' teachers. The film *Dangerous Minds* first arrived for the public as a written text: *My Posse Don't Do Homework*; however, the emergence of *Dangerous Minds* simultaneously eclipsed and reinvented its own originary text. Through a mythic process *Dangerous Minds* (1995) ingested *My Posse Don't Do Homework* and regurgitated *Dangerous Minds*, a multitentacle creature capable of creating its text and context at the same time. Perhaps in an effort to save some posited essence, both Johnson and Pfeiffer fought a losing battle to keep the original title, but "Disney boss, Joe Roth . . . decreed . . . [it] is to reach the screen as *Dangerous Minds*" (Nathan, 1995, p. 22). As we now know, *Dangerous Minds* did not just reach the screen but burst forth as a (not so) new nonfiction paperback, a soundtrack, a music video, and a television show; within a year, the film even spawned its own genre spoof: *High School High* (Hamilton, 1996). *Dangerous Minds*, as the object of cultural criticism, is an elusive and effusive spectacle, pointing the same instance to a synchronic and diachronic understanding of culture. The film *Dangerous Minds* invented the phenomena *Dangerous Minds*. The image, the aesthetic constant of postmodernity, injected itself as the code for the fearful allure of the "inner city" so effectively that choice to watch, to consume was never a complete option. Two illustrative examples of the tentacle unfurling are the banding across several radio listening audiences of Coolio's rap "Gangsta's Paradise" and the image of Michelle Pfeiffer, standing in jeans and a leather jacket in front of representations of African American and Hispanic teenagers. Both were burnished in many minds that never had to set foot near a bookstore or a movie theater. In an era where meanings and symbols are put forth instantaneously, then flashed into our minds through a blitzkrieg of publicity, the battle over a title definitely has incalculable stakes. The *Dangerous Minds* narratives are enveloped within the image of the title itself. In these times, the picture, the fragmented phrase, the song played at a high school dance that everyone sways knowingly to, the oversized jeans and "gangsta clothes" fashions, the multitudinous strains of the endless repetitions of the representation in many ways becomes the story itself.

ANALYSIS

Dangerous Minds invented itself under the presupposition of the city as a tourist proposition. It is the bad, the sin-laden detour constructing a gaze of attraction and repulsion. The city is the simultaneous signifier of death of the signified and birth of new signifiers.[3] Inner cities, most concretely symbolized by the concept that is 'Los Angeles' are coded as hotbeds of gangs, violence, and racial and ethnic otherness. Nationally, racial tensions are played out around Los Angeles media events such as the beatings of Rodney King and Reginald Denney, the uprising subsequent to the trial (Fiske, 1993), and the murder trials of O. J. Simpson. In the now, the utterance "inner city" and even to a large extent its muted code, "urban," must be understood as pronouncements and negotiations presupposing the inner city as otherness (Popkewitz, 1998), representing danger to body, to order, to established codes of power. "Inner city" is the allure and the credibility of the concept '*Dangerous Minds*' even as *Dangerous Minds* works to create the allure and credibility of the concept 'inner city.' A notion of transcendent, objective reality wholly outside a text is never a complete proposition in the age of mass cultural productions.

Using *Dangerous Minds* as a starting point it is not difficult to illustrate that inner city is not a social fact as much as a socially constructed representation of a social fact.[4] All the productions of *Dangerous Minds* capitalize upon being tales of inner city experience. On the back cover of the paperback (released after the production of the film) Johnson's class is described: "They were called the class from Hell—thirty four inner city sophomores she inherited from a teacher who'd been 'pushed over the edge.' She was told, 'those kids' have tasted blood. They're dangerous." This epithet is used to describe the class that Johnson started out with as an intern. Her second year teaching she worked in a school-within-a-school called the "Academy." The TV show *Dangerous Minds* centered around this program, whereas *Dangerous Minds* the movie centered on the initial "class from Hell." All the productions blur through faux repetitions of characters with strangely reminiscent attributes and names.

Nearly half-way through the book, (p. 130, chapter 11), Johnson chooses to describe the specific context of the school for the first time (which is not really important since *Dangerous Minds* has been born, and the context has already been created from the image.

> The fifty sophomores who volunteered for the first year of the Academy program were evenly split into three groups—Black, White, and Hispanic. I was surprised, and a little embarrassed, to realize that I had not expected to see as many pale faces in a dropout prevention program, although Parkmont High is located in an all-white high-income community. I was even more surprised to find that only half of the Academy class rode buses from the poverty-stricken East Side; the other half came from Buffy and Jody land where a quarter of a million dollars is considered a reasonable price for a three bedroom house and a Mercedes convertible is the standard birthday gift for the sweet sixteen. The common denominator in our program wasn't money or ethnic origin—it was failure . . . Their scores on standardized reading and math tests ranged from average to excellent. (p. 130)

This description, inserted nearly in the middle of the book, is wasted because a gloss of stereotypic inner cityness is already embedded in the readers' perceptions. Johnson's students have passed standardized reading and math tests and come from a complex range of backgrounds, but the productions of *Dangerous Minds* are careful not to use any "pale faces," except for the character of Johnson, in its advertisements. Inner-city schooling is not simply there; it is deliberately constructed. The opening scene of the film ensnares viewers in this deliberate framework, also. "Gangsta's Paradise" plays as the camera flashes images of graffiti, a homeless person, housing projects, and so on. A typography of the inner city as white, middle-class audiences want to see it, as it is "already known" it exists, is presented before viewers much in the manner of a well-set table; all the senses are attracted to come and dine, simply because that is what is done at such a table. Suddenly, on the screen, a yellow school bus appears, a symbol of education and "normalcy," but it is decayed and decrepit. Viewers are driven through a contemporary "hell," outside one's self and yet within a comfortable viewing distance; of course, the viewer will stay and dine.

And viewers will come to this same table again when Coolio sings "Gangsta's Paradise" reenacting as story of ethnic, adult-looking teens while Michelle Pfeiffer looks on, and again when reading in an article that Coolio, a former gang banger was excited to meet Michelle Pfeiffer because she was in *Scarface* (William, 1995, p. 53). And the audience is back at the table for still more when the TV shows a slow, grainy camera shot of an anonymous arm spray painting graffiti on a locker, and just when viewers think it is time to untuck the napkins and be excused, along will come a young woman who in real life was inspired to teach by "Lou Anne Johnson," and we will realize that consumption has nothing to do with being full.

When discussing or writing about *Dangerous Minds* (and many other "realist" tales) there is a strong compulsion inducing us to talk on the plane of "reality." Critics find the story either very true or not true enough. In either case the truth hangs floating above, an absent signifier, waiting, but never fully able to descend. *Dangerous Minds* the nonfiction narrative resonates as a realist tale. Lou Anne Johnson lands her first gig as a teacher stemming from her internship with the "class from Hell." She is the master inquisitor, a colonial agent exemplar, imploring students *tell me your culture*; and the audience comes along for the ride as students falteringly answer, or glare back at her.[5]

"Why?" I probed. He shrugged and his face closed back up.

"Do you feel mad a lot of time?" He nodded, but didn't speak.

"Why do you feel mad?"

"I don't know," he said. "Things." (p. 226)

After her fourth year, she quits the field and publishes her account of hope: inner-city students can learn, because it functions as a study of culture as experienced by the researcher (Johnson), someone who is *here* and has been *there* (Van Maanen, 1995). *Dangerous Minds* is representative of what could be termed "popular ethnography," the travel writing of our time. Travel writing is steeped in power relationships but through a sense of subjectivity escapes the baggage of "realism" of a documentary, while managing to profit from the feeling that it is evoking something real. In "An End to Innocence: The Ethnography of Ethnography," Van Maanen (1995, p. 2) discusses many of the epistemological debates within the idea of ethnography and explains how the "cultural representation business has become quite tricky." He defines ethnography broadly as "a storytelling institution" (p. 3). In the simplistic version, "an ethnographer is something of a Supertourist who visits a group of natives in their natural habitat and brings back the news of their way of life" (p. 3). MacCannell (1992) outlines tourism as a modernistic invention, a manifestation of middle-class desire. The tourist consumes countries, following a prescribed path, and returns to the comforts of home. Although there is a desire to see the "back room," behind the scenes story, the symbols of the journey are defined before hand.

Realist tales, such as the Mafia film *Donnie Brasco* (1996), news programs,[6] movies of the week, and television talk shows increasingly point audiences toward observing culture as tourists. Examples are everywhere from

Music Television's (MTV) artificial culture lab, *The Real World* series about seven strangers picked to live together in a house, to the Travel Channel as the ultimate getaway in voyeuristic tourism. The viewer knows what will be seen (much in the same way a movie trailer or television commercial for a movie encapsulates the essence of the entire story) and are rewarded by seeing it with an added sense that something extra was revealed. In essence, through filmic images, the viewer feels privy to the "back room," that the real story is being known. Examples such as MTV, the Travel Channel, and broadcast news are segmented moments of cultural study where "real" people become characters in a much larger story of voyeuristic fix. Within this scope it would seem naïve to focus on *Dangerous Minds* only because of its voyeuristic invitation to the inner city, of course it invites a voyeuristic journey.[7] What is pertinent about *Dangerous Minds* is the intensity with which the voyeur is directed toward a moral imperative, which suggests caring about "others" in the same moment it works to construct a reified image of unbridgeable otherness: this points to the double bind, that in many ways is cultural representation.

Each narrative strand of *Dangerous Minds* operates in a semiautonomous fashion, stemming from and yet wholly recreating the original concept. Each strand appears to be a repetition of the story, and it is, but it is never exactly the same story; even *My Posse Don't Do Homework*, which essentially only had cosmetic surgery on its covers, was never the same as the *Dangerous Minds* paperback that usurped its place on the bookshelf. Interestingly, all the narrative productions called "*Dangerous Minds*" were commercially successful, except the television show (Fall 1996), which lasted a mere thirteen episodes; in TV time it was quickly buried, a forgotten prodigal banished from her chance to deeply enhance the collective memory because she did not sell enough product. *Dangerous Minds*, however, will continue to live on in the school saga trophy case—joined by other populars in the same line: *Goodbye Mr. Chips* (1939), *Blackboard Jungle* (1955), *Up the Down Staircase* (1967), *Our Miss Brooks* (1955), *Teachers* (1984), *Dead Poet's Society* (1989) *Lean on Me* (1987), *Stand and Deliver* (1988).

As this list implies, the drama of the teacher as lone individual,[8] fighting the good fight against evil has been well documented in history. In his essay, "A Teacher Ain't Nothin but a Hero: Teachers Teaching in Film," William Ayers (1994) states:

> To begin with, the movies tell us that schools and teachers are in the business of saving children—saving them from families, saving them from the purveyors of drugs and violence who are taking over our cities, saving them from themselves, their own pursuits and purposes. The problem is that most teachers are simply not up to the challenge. They are slugs: cynical, inept, backward, naïve, hopeless. (p. 147)

Despite stating in her introduction that the "bonding" between students and faculty who remain together throughout the three-year period is the "key to the success of the Academy model " (p. 2), the rest of Johnson's book and the film present her accomplishments as connected to her status as a strong, autonomous individual, intent on saving her students. Her story taps into a long-understood notion of the hero. And the story of teaching tends to position the hero as the savior. Popkewitz discusses the "redemptive discourse" of schooling as part of the "deployment of psychological categories" in which psychology replaced moral philosophy as the secular "approach to saving the soul" (p. 24). White student teachers who view themselves as "white knights" (McIntyre, 1997, p. 80) and Teach for America volunteers whose desire to enter into "urban" and rural schools, to "rescue" (Popkewitz, 1998, p. 9), are concrete examples of how practice is discursively produced. The concept of 'teacher as savior' has been around since Jesus and Mohammed, and in spite of its many secular transformations, the idea that within the good teacher is a light shining brighter than anywhere else is still retained.

"Gangsta's Paradise" opens with a biblical allusion: "As I walk through the valley of the shadow of death" and haunts the listener with the drawn out "aaahhhh" of a church choir (which incidentally was the commercial break tag of the short-lived TV series), framing the vision of the transcendent good available in the notion of teacher. Part of this vision entails a vow of poverty, of turning against capitalistic gain. (Vividly illustrated in *Stand and Deliver* when "Escalante" is positioned in contrast to the shiny white flank of his businessman neighbor's new boat). Also, an element of sacrifice is a large component of the image of the good teacher. Fictionally, it is accepted that a truly good teacher must be sacrificed for his or her students, as if implicitly it is known that anyone truly good cannot exist in school: she or he must be sent away. However, as in *Dead Poet's Society* (1991) we know that even when the teacher must leave, disciples will live on to carry the teacher's fire. And indeed, we the audience are instilled with it as well; in fact up until a recent apocalyptic turn (*187, The Substitute*) this transfer of fire, or as Ms. Johnson's students called it, 'light" was the heart of the teaching film.

The highly romanticist conception of teacher definitely hovers around in popular culture. A good teacher kindles human essences, bringing individualism to light. Sexuality is coded through a transcendent "charisma," which renders the teacher capable of igniting our own passions, making us "be all we can be," despite a cruel and oppressive outside world. Poetry, the true art, is the device for reaching souls. Charisma allows the teacher to inject students with an orgasmic rapture of the world, without transgressing any laws or "natural" boundaries. (Though Blanche Dubois and Miss Jean Brodie[9] always remind us this it could be otherwise). In *Dangerous Minds* this "charisma" is negotiated in various ways by the different mediums. In the book Ms. Johnson draws upon a masculinist sense of power from her father:

"Go ahead and hit me," I snarled, "but make it good, because you're only going to get one hit. Then I'm going to kill you." The merciless cold of my voice made the back of my own neck prickle. It was my father's voice and my father's words spoken so often to my teenage brothers as they strutted their stuff and challenged their old man's authority. I glared at Hakim with my father's eyes, which turned black with anger and flashed with fire. (p. 88)

The Michelle Pfeiffer Ms. Johnson pretends to draw upon this masculinist power as well, hence the highlighting of the karate scene near the beginning of the film, but this is a decoy, an illusion, never to be fully believed. Her real draw is the sexuality sedimented within her by so many other roles positioning her exclusively as the focus of heterosexual desire; her sex appeal promotes her charisma with students. The Annie Potts Ms. Johnson from the television series earns her charisma with the love of a mother, speaking sharply because she cares, and looking soulfully at the camera—her signature look as yet another angry young person walks away or commits a futile but nonetheless touching gesture.[10] The role of Ms. Johnson demands "the compassion and cunning of a social worker and a nun, plus the survival skills of a navy Seal and a Zapatista" (Leonard, 1998, 212).

What is ironic about the charisma of Ms. Johnsons is that it instills anything in audiences at all since what is seen in each and every episode is a resolution of failure. Rarely does she seem to understand her students' motives or find herself able to convert them into "disciplined" middle-classish bodies. When she begins to actually connect with her students and lose her status as outside inquisitor, she reminds them that she is not like them. She can quit. She can walk out of the room. Not only can she walk out of the room unproblematically, but she can also represent the room by telling the story. And even though Ms. Johnson leaves, threatens to leave, or is merely canceled, the audience manages to pool affective investment in her story. My Posse Don't Do Homework was excerpted in Reader's Digest (Johnson, 1992) suggesting that the story says something that conservative middle-class audiences want to hear at the same time Coolio's "Gangsta's Paradise" and the clothing of hip hop is making its mark on youthful bodies. In the film, the culmination of the Michelle Pfeiffer Ms. Johnson's Dylan Dylan contest, in which students find the Bob Dylan song most like a Dylan Thomas poem is used to illustrate "success." Success is a montage of "urban" student bodies looking docile and disciplined as they pour through library books, grooving on learning. Poetry by white males is shown to symbolize universal values, which in themselves are transformative. However, the winning students' reward ends in a failed night out in a fancy restaurant, which only serves to heighten the economic and social class disparity between the students' lives and the "reward." Also, the poetry lesson turns into the catalyst forcing a student to drop out of school. The student's mother tells Pfeiffer Ms. Johnson that she is a "White bread bitch" and that "poetry is a waste of time. We ain't raisin' no doctors and lawyers here—find some other poor boys to save." Only after realizing that all her white, middle-class beneficence could not save Emilio, leader of the film "class from Hell," from being shot, does Pfeiffer Ms. Johnson quit. In the film, the "usual suspect" is lined up as the receptacle for audience judgment: an uncaring black administrator. There are no caring adults of color shown in the film. In *Dangerous Minds* the television show, where a caring, growing-through-time Annie Potts Ms. Johnson is on the cusp of a biracial relationship with the school counselor, and has effectively ended a gang war by inviting rival gang members' mothers to come into the negotiating room and make their pleas; this Ms. Johnson, the diachronic Annie Potts Ms. Johnson, gets canceled after only thirteen episodes,[12] canceled before she ever has a chance to quit. *Dangerous Minds* is nothing but a story about failure, failure of the middle-class ideology to seep into every pore, failure of a white woman to go in and change the world with her paternalistic love of the "other," failure of education, failure of liberal ideology, and yet interestingly it continues to operate as a tale of hope and inspiration.

All this failure points toward the more utopian possibilities available within *Dangerous Minds*. The utopian elements of *Dangerous Minds* exist, not in its overt ideological reading, summed up nicely by Giroux (1997) in this passage:

> *Dangerous Minds* functions mythically to rewrite the decline of public schooling and the attack on poor Black and Hispanic students as part of a broader project for rearticulating "whiteness" as a model of authority, rationality and civilized *behavior . . . In this context,* Dangerous Minds *reinforces the highly racialized,* though reassuring, mainstream assumption that chaos reigns in inner-city public school and that White teachers alone are capable of bringing order, decency, and hope to those on the margins of society. (p. 49)

I believe *Dangerous Minds* works in the way described by Giroux and also works to dismantle these very notions at the same time. The representative Ms. Johnsons negotiate a relationship with their students, but this relationship is dimmed in comparison to the economically bleak picture surrounding them.[12] The Academy program Ms. Johnson worked within is aimed at helping students find jobs in a postindustrialist business economy that is really more interested in them as consumers.

Historically "the city" has always been a place peopled with bodies. In ancient Greece Socrates is lead by Phaedrus away from the polis, the rational, public sphere of men and into the realm of irrational nature. The concept of the 'polis' has undergone many transformations before becoming the intersubjective understanding "inner city," which is an often taken for granted raw material in contemporary aesthetic productions such as *Dangerous Minds*.

The construction of inner city, which is discussed for its dystopic function as uncongealing otherness is also not all that far from its older moment as the idea of public sphere and community. "For the Athenian, the polis was the state *and* the community. Members found virtues of personhood and citizenship . . . inherent in the community's own conception of the good life" (Knight-Abowitz, 2000, p. 35).

In the contemporary United States of America, community is considered local ("close knit"), and "the state is a somewhat anonymous official governing body of the public realm" (p. 35). And it should not be ignored that "community" literally meant privileged men. In the invocation that is inner city the concept of 'public sphere' is invoked through its impending absence. Tracing the history of "cities" Mumford (1961) writes:

> The final mission of the city is to further man's conscious participation in the cosmic and the historic process. Through its own complex and enduring structure, the city vastly augments man's ability to interpret these processes and take an active, formative part in them, so that every phase of the drama it stages shall have, to the highest degree possible, the illumination of consciousness, the stamp of purpose, the color of love. That magnification of all the dimensions of life, through emotional communion, rational communication, technological mastery, and above all, dramatic representation, has been the supreme office of the city in history. And it remains the chief reason for the city's continued existence. (p. 576)

This is perhaps the same invocation that draws viewers/readers to the story of teacher, transmitter of the culture, perpetuator of the elusive "common good." Despite their much publicized downfalls, schools are still one of the only remaining public places where people gather to make meaning (Wexler, 1992). The proliferation of charter schools, private schools, and home schooling is a signal that the public sphere, which we never know until we are mourning it, is in jeopardy. In an article (*New York Times*, 1996) about the onslaught of television shows on schools and schooling (during the premiere of *Dangerous Minds*, fall 1996, there were five), Richard Kramer, who produced and wrote the TV series *Thirtysomething*, observed, "When you have a glut of shows that are all about the same thing . . . it's possible that it addresses a fear that Americans have, which is the collapse of the education system. There's some unspoken cabal, to make people feel better about something they are uneasy about" (p. 25).

Perhaps this statement is true enough, except it could be argued that education in popular culture is always a symbolic representation tied to higher stakes. Teacher stories often represent a desire for a common good within a framework of tension that acknowledges that the desires fulfillment, a holistic common good, might not ever be possible. In film, at their best, teachers can only save a handful of individual (even Glenn Ford, with the full discourse of modernistic progress behind his actions, still had to get rid of two students and admit that not everyone could be saved). There is anxiety, but the notion of education is only symptomatic of perhaps never completely knowable concerns.

American audiences consume *Dangerous Minds* in the midst of it consuming us. As aesthetic cultural object it injects a sense of hopefulness, while its depictions reify a sense of dread that what is needed most is hope. The story of teacher as saint is less about promoting individual freedom than it is an acknowledgment of deeply held class antagonisms. Therefore, what is it we look to when we turn our gaze toward "inner city schooling?" What is represented?

In a discussion of the film *Jaws* Fredric Jameson (1992) suggests that what is interesting about the shark is not what it represents—since there are a variety of readings that position the shark as fear of the other and then delve into what the other is from communism to the unreality of daily life— but that the shark represents anything at all. He writes:

> Now none of these readings can be said to be wrong or aberrant, but their very multiplicity suggest that the vocation of the symbol— killer shark—lies less in any single message or meaning than in its very capacity to absorb and organize all of these quite distinct anxieties together. As a symbolic vehicle, then, the shark must be understood in terms of its essentially polysemous function rather than any particular content attributable to it by this or that spectator. Yet it is precisely this polysemousness which is profoundly ideological, insofar as it allows essentially social and historical anxieties to be folded back into apparently "natural ones." (pp. 26–27)

In the United States the construct "inner-city schooling" and even its muted code "urban education" are becoming, have become, natural. In art, in education, in our minds. Mainstream audiences are learning to observe the swirl of youth, low income, and color as disruptive forces, reminding us of the brutality of economic inequity, at the same moment telling viewers that "others" (mainly poor youths with ethnic identities) might be "saved" and thus contained. Foucault (1978) reminds us that "power is . . . a complex strategical situation in a particular society" (p. 93). The representation of inner city is a strategic moment in American society. The image is codifiable, an arbitration of power relations, which mobilizes us even as we marshal ourselves to construct it.

CONCLUSION

As stated earlier, *Dangerous Minds* is the cusp of a genre. It feeds into a sense of hope about the possibilities of urban education at the same time it also

mobilizes a sense of cynicism that the project of public schools actually can
work. (Why else would a strong teacher like Johnson have to quit?) Two
films that illustrate this new dystopic turn toward lack of possibilities for
public education are *The Substitute* and *187*.

In *The Substitute*, Shale, a mercenary (played by Tom Berenger), mas-
querades as a substitute teacher in a Miami public high school, after his
girlfriend (a teacher in the school) has been knee-capped by a Native
American gang member. It turns out that the principal of the school, played
by Ernie Hudson, is not the positive black male role model he appears to be;
instead he is a drug lord operating gangs within the school to market product. The film ends in an all-out battle between Shale's mercenary pals and
the principal's gang members and hired mercenaries. The good, caring teacher
(the shimmer of Lou Anne Johnson) is portrayed by both the knee-capped
girlfriend and a young, African American, male teacher. There is no time for
him to quit the job, because in his attempt to save one of his female students,
he is murdered under the gaze of the principal before the all-out battle
begins—the ultimate sacrifice. The result is that the school is completely
torn apart by grenades, gunfire, and shellfire. Only one of Shale's compatriot's
walks out alive with him. They are seen walking down the street discussing
the possibility of going to Los Angeles. Obviously, still intending to fight the
most important war at home.[13]

The movie *187* follows a narrative of good teacher pushed over the edge.
Trevor Garfield (played by Samuel L. Jackson) represents the glow of "Lou
Anne Johnson" being extinguished. In the hallway, a student stabs him repeatedly with a nail because Garfield does not give him a passing grade. Eleven
months later, Garfield moves to Los Angeles and begins a career as a substitute
in a run down bungalow. In slow-grained shots around the school, primarily
low-income Hispanic high school students are portrayed as violent animals.
Gang members kill Garfield's girlfriend's dog, trash his classroom, and stab his
lab rat with scissors. Garfield does not have any legal rights, so he turns into
a murdering vigilante. Stealthily in the night, he kills one of the gang members
and chops off the finger of another, his in-class nemesis, Cesar.

There is no motivation, no structural understanding, no humanity to
the students. As youth without meaning, they become objects of public fear.
The audience is focalized to deeply understand and feel pathos toward
Garfield's actions. After the murder his class runs smoothly and students
begin to learn. But this success is short-lived. Reminiscent of the *Deerhunter*,
Garfield finally meets his death in a game of Russian Roulette that he is
forced to play with Cesar. Before fatally shooting himself, he tells Cesar that
he has been robbed of something worse than his life a year ago, he has been
robbed of his "passion" his "spark" his "unguarded self." The last scene of the
film is the pretty, blond, LouAnn Johnsonish teacher, who almost started a
relationship with Garfield, throwing her framed license in the waste basket
as she packs up to leave. Her actions are interspersed with the graduation

speech of a young woman who Garfield tried to save. She introduces her essay "My Way Out" by talking about Garfield: "Teachers don't get no respect." She explains the meaning of Pyrrhic victory in which a battle is won at too great a cost. The vision advanced of public education is dystopic. In this film urban high schools are portrayed as a nightmarish reality of a Freddy Kreuger dream. They are beyond understanding and outside of structures of logic. The film lays claim to truth by somberly portraying these lines before the final credits role: "One in 9 teachers has been attacked in school. Ninety-five percent of those attacks were committed by students" (Metropolitan Life Survey). A teacher wrote this movie.

These words illustrate the tension between schools as imagined and real places. Representations of schools are never just entertainment. They are always defining knowledge about urban youth.

The "teaching film" genre is now undergoing a new transformation; the feminized do-gooder missionary is being kicked out for ineffectiveness and instead the masculinized commando is taking "her" place to regain control (or at least punish the guilty). In the scene before he shoots the fatal bullet, Garfield yells at Cesar, "I was a teacher. I wanted to help you. You can't kill me," It is perhaps the futile cry of the modernist project of public schools as progress and public good attempting to live on through dire circumstances.

NOTES

1. This genre is marked by the following films: Blackboard Jungle (1955), Lean on Me (1987), Stand and Deliver (1988), The Principal (1989), and Dangerous Minds 1995).

2. Richard Quantz brought up the film Fame (1980) as a counterexample to this tendency (Fieldnote, May 22, 2000). I have not thought through the ramifications of his suggestion sufficiently. However, based upon my memory, the fact that the school was based upon performing arts and required students to have talent, separates it from the traditional comprehensive high school setting of the genre to which I am referring. Still, the narratives of Fame (both the film and the ensuing series) and their relationship to the general urban education genre would be an interesting area of study.

3. The relationship of "the city" as a site of production for new signifiers and meaning is well articulated by Henry Giroux (1996) in the following passage: "[Y]outh in urban centers produce a bricolage of style fashioned from a combination of sneakers, baseball caps, and oversized clothing that integrates forms of resistance and style later to be appropriated by suburban kids whose desires and identities resonate with the energy and vibrancy of the new urban funk" (228). The Dangerous Minds productions are important aspects of this process. They collate, crystallize, legitimize, and disseminate a notion of "urban chic," which layers itself self-consciously throughout diverse socioeconomic strata.

4. By negating the word fact I am pointing to the discursive production of inner city as part of the construction of a "cognitive perceptual grid" (Shohat & Stam, 1994, 205) or in Popkewitz's terminology part of a "scaffolding" or "amalgam-

ation of discourses" (9). Popkewitz argues that "urban . . . does not signify a geographical place but it gives reference to certain unspoken qualities of the child and the community who belongs in that space" (10). Whereas, much like Popkewitz I want to recognize this discursive production of "urbaness" as an "effect of power," I do not want to ignore that this power operates on actual bodies who are framed as the referent for "urbaness." Poverty, racism, and sexism are material conditions, not merely perceptions.

5. Shohat and Stam (1994) write about this at length: "Many liberal Hollywood films about the 3rd World or about minoritarian cultures in the 1st World deploy a European or Euro-American character as a mediating 'bridge' to other cultures portrayed more or less sympathetically . . . [This character] inherit[s] the 'in-between' role traditionally assigned to the colonial traveler and later to the anthropologist; the role of the one who 'reports back.' The mediating character initiates the spectator into otherized communities; Third World and minoritarian people, it is implied, are incapable of speaking for themselves. Unworthy of stardom either in the movies or in political life, they need a go-between in the struggle for emancipation" (p. 205). The figure of "Lou Anne Johnson" in all the *Dangerous Minds* productions is definitely the "one who reports back."

6. According to Maeroff (1998) since the investigative coverage of incidents surrounding Watergate "[c]omity and decorum have fallen victim to a take-no-victims sort of journalism that illuminates the recesses that had remained unobserved when the media was less zealous about its mission . . . For education, the new style of journalism has meant the piercing of institutional armor. The words of superintendents and school board members, once virtually unchallenged by the press, have become fair game for skeptics, if not outright cynicism. The sanctity of public education has been stripped away by journalists who report on alternatives to traditional approaches and raise questions about how well consumers are served by the status quo" (p. 3). In other words there is an imperative for the "wall" of the back room to collapse and for the audience to see what had been consensually unreported about in the past.

7. This trend continues as illustrated by an excerpt from the *New York Times* article, "On Television, New Voyeurism Shows Real Intimacies" (Carter, January 30, 2000, 1, 17): "[A] new wave of television formats . . . all based on real-life experience voyeuristically captured on camera, is posed to invade prime-time network schedules . . . The shows range from on-camera examinations of people trying to survive on a desert island off Borneo to people trying to get along while locked together in various settings of forced intimacy (p. 1) . . . The shows, many of which will have ambitious Internet components, have been described as various combinations of MTV's cinema verite show *The Real World*, the syndicated talk show *Jerry Springer* and the influential game show from England *Who Wants to Be a Millionaire*." Mr. Moonves, president of CBS, referred to these shows as "reality shows." "Robert Thompson, founder of the Center for the Study of Popular Television at Syracuse University, called the trend toward voyeurism shows an inevitable confluence of advances in technology and basic human interest. 'Popular culture is beginning to catch up with our real behavior,' Mr. Thompson said. "We all talk about family values, but that's not how most of us operate as human beings. In some ways, this is the programmers discovering what TV was always so great at in the first place. This is Peeping Tom to the max' " (p. 17).

8. As Rousmaniere (1999) points out, "[I]n educational media there are few written or visual images of teachers working collaboratively in meetings, sharing duties in the play yard or lunchroom, talking in the teachers' lounge, or exchanging resources . . . In popular culture the teacher appears as a friendless, isolated being, alone in a crowd of children, lacking any need for interaction with other adults" (p. 38).

9. In Tennessee Williams' play and film A Streecar Named Desire, Blanche Dubois is a high school teacher who has had an affair with a student. Miss Jean Brodie is the central character in the novel by Muriel Spark also adapted as a film The Prime of Miss Jean Brodie (Fryer, 1969). Miss Brodie has an affair with a married teacher. Eventually both must leave their positions. Blanche Dubois and Jean Brodie represent the societal sanctions and discomfort associated with thinking about female teachers and sexuality.

10. Leonard (1998) describes the television Ms. Johnson thus, "Annie Potts was in fact far more persuasive in the TV version of Dangerous Minds than Pfeiffer had been as a black-belt biker chick in the movie. Dressed as if in a hurry at night in a burning building, oddly vagrant like a rock-band roadie, fiercely inward, with memories of guns in Texas, Potts had some cool and edgy street in her. From previous duty in sitcoms such as Designing Women and Love and War, she brought not only her usual smart mouth but also a "been-there" credibility to this inner-city "academy" program for grown-up-too-quickly problem children, with their high IQs and low self-esteem and gaudy self-sabotaging behaviors, their gang colors and their babies. She was her own subtext, teaching Of Mice and Men as if with a rodent in her pocket, teaching Look Homeward, Angel as though she'd run away with a circus. She was lots more hands-on than is strictly permissible in today's supersensitive public school system, where an incautious hug can get you suspended for child molestation, and not above bribing kids to perform, and one began to wonder if all her students would wind up living in her house, like in an R.D. Laing therapeutic commune. But good educators always break the rules to save a child. Dangerous Minds was at least nostalgic [sic] for the bygone era when all of us had cherished teachers—instead of border guards—who sought to engage us in classrooms that weren't impossibly overcrowded, in buildings that weren't falling down, in neighborhoods that didn't resemble Belfast or Beirut; back when public schools were trampolines from which we bounced into our futures, instead of warehouses with metal detectors or detention camps for refugees" (p. 212).

11. According to Maeroff (1998, 8) "[F]ictional images of education on the big or little screen tend to be more powerful and enduring than what appears in print. But what appears tends to be stereotypical and in short supply. Education as subject matter for prime-time series has all the appeal of mumps to producers. They seldom give shows that are built around student or school themes the time to build an audience, yanking them off the air so fast that hardly anyone can remember having seen an episode. The visual media shy away from education, whether the issue is news or entertainment." For a more complete discussion of this phenomenon read John Leonard's (1998) "Educating Television."

12. This is illustrated in the film High School High by weekly career days, which include options such as airport security, military militia, Burger Hut, and a banner suggesting, "Have you considered begging?"

13. Two other films were made in the series. Treat Williams stars in The Substitute 2 and The Substitute 3.

REFERENCES

Ayers, W. (1994). A teacher ain't nothin' but a hero: Teachers and teaching in film. In P. Joseph & G. Burnaford (Eds.), *Images of schoolteachers in twentieth century America: Paragons, polarities, complexities* (pp. 147–156). New York: St. Martin's.

Bakalar, S. (Producer), & Mandel, R. (Director). (1996). *The Substitute* [Film]. (Available from Live Entertainment).

Berman, P. (Producer), & Brooks, R. (Director). (1955). *Blackboard Jungle* [Film]. Los Angeles: Metro Goldwyn Mayer.

Carter B. (2000, January 30). On TV, new voyeurism shows real intimacies. The *New York Times*, pp. 1, 17.

Fiske, J. (1993). Los Angeles: A tale of three videos. *Media matters: Everyday culture and political change*. Minneapolis: University of Minnesota Press.

Foucault, M. (1978). *The history of sexuality* (1st American ed.). New York: Pantheon Books.

Fryer, R. (Producer & Director). (1969). *The prime of Miss Jean Brodie*. London: TCF.

Giroux, H. A. (1997). Race, pedagogy and whiteness in dangerous minds. *Cineaste, 22*(4).

Giroux, H. A. (1996). *Fugitive cultures: Race, violence, and youth*. New York: Routledge.

Giroux, H. A. (1995). Is there a place for cultural studies in colleges of education? In H. A. Giroux, C. Lankshear, P. McLaren, & M. Peters (Eds.), *Counter-narratives: Cultural studies and critical pedagogies in postmodern spaces* (pp. 41–58). New York: Routledge.

Giroux, H. A. (1988). *Schooling and the struggle for public life: Critical pedagogy in the modern age*. Minneapolis: University of Minnesota Press.

Giroux, H. A. (1981). Hegemony, resistance and the paradox of educational reform. In H. A. Giroux, A. Penna, & W. Pinar (Eds.), *Curriculum & instruction: Alternatives in education*. Berkeley: McCutchan.

Greenstein, J. (1999, March). Just add color. *Brills content*, pp. 82–85.

Haft, S., Junger Witt, P., & Thomas T. (Producers) & Weir, P. (Director). (1989). *Dead poet's society* [Film]. Warner/Touchstone/Silver Screen Partners IV.

Hamilton, D. (1996, October 25). Review of high school high * dangerous minds spoof. *Atlanta Constitution*, p. 18.

Haran, S., Johnson, B., Locash, R., Nether, G., Whichter, D., Wright, J., & Zucker, D. (Producers), & Bochner, H. (Director). (1996). *High school high*.

Jameson, F. (1992). *Signatures of the visible*. London: Routledge, Chapman, & Hall.

Jameson, F. (1981). *The political unconscious: Narrative as a socially symbolic act*. Ithaca, NY: Cornell University Press.

Jenks, C. (Ed.). (1995). *Visual culture*. London and New York: Routledge.

Johnson, L. (1993). *Dangerous minds*. New York: St. Martin's.

Johnson, L. (1992). *My posse don't do homework*. New York: St. Martin's.

Kaniss, P. (1991). *Making local news*. Chicago: University of Chicago Press.

Knight-Abowitz, K. (2000). *Making meaning of community in an American high school: A feminist-pragmatist critique of the liberal-communitarian debates*. Cresskill, NJ: Hampton.

Labunka, J., Law, L., & Musca, T. (Producers), & Menendez, R. (Director). (1987). *Stand and deliver* [Film]. Warner Brothers.

Lasalle, M. (1995, August 15). New kids on block fare well at weekend box office. *San Francisco Chronicle*, p. E3.

LeCompte, M. D., & Preissle, J. (1993). *Ethnography and qualitative design in educational research*. New York: Academic.

Leonard, J. (1998). Educating television. In G. Maeroff (Ed.), *Imaging education: The media and schools in America* (pp. 209–219). New York: Teachers College.

MacCabe, C. (1974). Realism and the cinema: Notes on some Brechtian theses. *Screen 15*, 2.

MacCannell, D. (1992). *Empty meeting grounds: The tourist papers*. London: Routledge.

Maeroff, G. (Ed). (1998). *Imaging education: The media and schools in America*. New York: Teachers College.

Mayne, J. (1993). *Cinema and spectatorship*. London: Routledge.

McCarthy, C., & Crichlow, W. (1993). *Race, identity, and representation in education*. New York: Routledge.

McIntyre, A. (1997). *Making meaning of whiteness: Exploring racial identity with white teachers*. Albany: State University of New York Press.

McKenna, J. (1995, September 9). Hot 100 singles spotlight. *Billboard*.

Metro Goldwyn Mayer (Producer), & Hiller, A. (Director). (1984). *Teachers* [Film]. MGM/United Artists.

Mitchard, J. (1996, September 28). The family pages. *The TV guide*, pp. 54–55.

Mumford, L. (1961). *The city in history: Its origins, its transformations, and its prospects*. San Diego: Harcourt Brace.

Musca, T. (Producer), & Menendez, R. (Director). (1988). *Stand and deliver* [Film]. Warner/American Playhouse.

Nathan, P. (1995). Short subjects. *Publisher's weekly 242*(6), 22.

Nicolaides, S. (Producer), Singleton, J. (Director). (1991). *Boyz 'n the hood* [Film]. Columbia Pictures.

Nicholson, L. J. (1990). *Feminism/postmodernism*. New York: Routledge.

Pakula-Mulligan, R. (Producer), Mulligan, R. (Director). (1967). *Up the down staircase* [Film]. Warner Brothers.

Pedelty, M. (1995). *War stories: The culture of foreign correspondents*. New York: Routledge.

Peters M., & Lankshear, C. (1996). Postmodern counternarratives. In H. A. Giroux (Ed.), *Counternarratives: Cultural studies and critical pedagogies in postmodern spaces* (pp. 1–41). New York: Routledge.

Pistone, J. (with Woodly, R.). (1987). *Donnie Brasco: My undercover life in the mafia, a true story*. New York: New American Library.

Popkewitz, T. S. (1998). *Struggling for the soul: The politics of schooling and the construction of the teacher*. New York: Teachers College.

Production Information (1995). *Dangerous minds homepage* [On-line]. Available at www.movieweb.com/movie/dangminds/indexhtml.

Profile of Lou Anne Johnson. (1996, March 3). *Chicago tribune*. Section 13, p. 6.

Russo, D. (Producer), & Hiller, A. (Director). (1984). *Teachers* [Film]. Metro Goldwyn Mayer-United Artists.

Saiull, V. (Producer), & Wood, S. (Director). (1939). *Goodbye Mr. Chips* [Film]. Metro Goldwyn Mayer.

Shohat, E., & Stam, R. (1994). *Unthinking Eurocentrism: Multiculturalism and the media*. London: Routledge.

Simpson, D., & Bruckheimer, J. (Producers). (1996). *Dangerous minds* [TV Series]. California: American Broadcasting Company.

Simpson, D., & Bruckheimer, J. (Producers), & Schmeichen, R. (Director). (1995). *Dangerous minds* [Film]. Burbank, CA: Touchstone.

Tucker, R. (Ed.). (1978). *The Marx-Engels reader: Second edition*. New York: Norton.

Turow, J. (1997). *Breaking up America: Advertisers and the new media world*. Chicago: University of Chicago Press.

Van Maanen, J. (1995). An end to innocence: The ethnography of ethnography. In J. Van Maanen (Ed.), *Representation in Ethnography*. Thousand Oaks: Sage.

Wadsworth, D. (1998). *Do media shape public perceptions of America's schools?* In G. Maeroff (Ed.), *Imaging education: The media and schools in America* (pp. 59–68). New York: Teachers College.

Weisbart, D. (Producer), & Lewis, A. (Director). (1956). *Our Miss Brooks* [Film]. Warner Brothers.

Wells, A. S., & Serman, T. W. (1998). Education against all odds: What films teach us about schools. In G. Maeroff, (Ed.), *Imaging education: The media and schools in America* (pp.181–194). New York: Teachers College.

Wexler, P. (with Crichlow, W., Kern, J., & Martusewicz, R.). (1992). *Becoming somebody: Toward a social psychology of school*. London: Falmer.

William, C. (1995, August 18). Dangerous lisaisons: Coolio gives Michell Pfeiffer a piece of his mind. *Entertainment Weekly*, p 53.

Wonder, S. (1995). Gangsta's paradise. [Recorded by Coolio] On *Dangerous minds*. [CD]. Universal City, CA: MCA Records.

CHAPTER SIX

QUEERING THE BODY

THE POLITICS OF "GAYDAR"

JENNIFER ESPOSITO AND BENJAMIN BAEZ

INTRODUCTION

In an episode from the popular National Broadcasting Company (NBC) sitcom *Will & Grace*, Will, a gay man, and Grace, a straight woman, compete for the attentions of a new neighbor, a man whom they cannot identify as "gay" or "straight." They decide to invite him over to determine which of them will get to date the man. They are unsuccessful in determining his orientation, so eventually they call on their gay friend Jack to utilize his finely-tuned "gaydar" to determine the sexual orientation of the man. Jack, whose expert gaydar is based on the fact he has slept with many men, is not quite certain, and by the end of the episode we are (as are Will and Grace) left in doubt. This story provides for us an illustration of what we mean by "gaydar" and its fault lines. *Gaydar* is a term used often by gays and lesbians to explain how they "pick each other out," that is, how they determine that another person is gay or lesbian in a world that presumes heterosexuality. This story illustrates as well that even gays and lesbians with "finely tuned" gaydar may get the "wrong message" or, worse, get no message at all.

Gaydar, from this perspective, focuses on the subject who gazes, that is, the gay or lesbian who uses it to identify other gays or lesbians. But from another perspective, it also implies that the gazee is sending out signals of "gayness"—without saying a word—to another person or to a general group of gazers. The "without saying a word" is important, since gaydar is an implicit form of communication. Indeed, *silence* is absolutely crucial to the existence of gaydar for at least a couple of reasons. First, and perhaps most important, gaydar is necessary because the underlying sexuality must remain silent. Heterosexuality can be explicitly confirmed, but the explicit confirmation of homosexuality, for obvious reasons, is altogether a different matter. Second, given that homosexuality requires, more or less, silence, the explicit announcements that one is gay or lesbian makes gaydar meaningless. Gaydar, as mode of knowledge, is premised on the underlying sexuality being kept silent. Gaydar is then, paradoxically, a way of speaking without speaking. This speaking without speaking—this silence that speaks—gives Michel Foucault's (1978) argument about silences a certain kind of sense. Foucault argues that "there is no binary division to be made between what one says and what one does not say; we must try to determine the different ways of not saying such things" (p. 27).

The notion of gaydar, as a silence that speaks, allows us to think of the body as a site of struggle. In *Discipline and Punish*, Foucault (1977) argues that power works on and through bodies. Bodies also "speak" social codes, Elizabeth Grosz (1995) suggests. Thus, gaydar is "speaking," but also a struggle over speech. All forms of speech are continually contested and changed. For gays and lesbians, given the extent of homophobia in this country, speaking explicitly about their gayness carries particular dangers. In some situations, such explicit statements are by definition grounds for punishment, such as in the military. Gaydar, therefore, represents a kind of speech with words that arises out of necessity. And yet, the idea of gaydar assumes that: (1) "gayness" can be represented in a definitive set of ways; and (2) only those who "qualify" have the ability to use it.

We interrogate this idea of gaydar, which leads us to ask questions about how we communicate, not simply, and perhaps not even primarily, with our words, but with our bodies. If gays and lesbians communicate with each other through gaydar, that is, through bodily representations, then a further question we explore is whether or not such gaydar is inherently something that only gays and lesbians perform. In other words, who gets to use gaydar, and what are the emancipatory possibilities or consequences of extending such performance to heterosexuals? Using narratives from poststructural and queer studies of sexuality, we address these questions: (1) How do we speak sexuality? (2) Who gets to speak sexuality and under what conditions? (3) How might such understanding help educators deal with gay and lesbian students?

SPEAKING SEXUALITY

After a number of years of interpretive analyses, particularly those from feminist, poststructural, and queer theorist perspectives, we can say that "the body" is a significant theme of the canon. And yet, paradoxically, this close attention to the body has made it more, rather than less, elusive, fluid, and uncontrollable. The more sophisticated and eclectic we have become at theorizing the body, the more we must concede that the "problem" of the body cannot be settled (Lock, 1993). Thus, while we now have considerably more diverse analytical tools for thinking the body, those tools shed doubt on our ability to think of the body in any one given way. Thinking about "gaydar," therefore, is beset with a constitutive difficulty; we can think it now as a bodily act, but the more we think it as such the less certain we can be of what it actually is. We do not, because we cannot, offer here, therefore, a definitive take on gaydar, but only a way of bringing the idea into educational discourse.

The body has been theorized from many disciplinary perspectives, but we cannot address most of them within the confines of this chapter. We provide here only a brief account of the certain poststructuralist and "queer" theories of the body since these allow us to think of gaydar as a construct for thinking of "gayness." Judith Butler (1990) questions the idea of the "natural" body and calls it, instead, a "discursive" construction. Here the body is recognized as invested with textual meanings, meanings that are fluid and unstable. But this is a trickier claim than at first meets the eye. Butler (1989) is not simply arguing that the body is inscribed with cultural meanings, for that assumes an order of operation (i.e., the presence of a body that is prior to its attributed meanings); she is asking us to think about rather than to take as given; that is, she is asking us to question the idea that the body exists a priori to the meanings that it acquires. In other words, she is asking us to question the idea of the materiality of the body, the body as a prediscursive domain. If the body cannot be understood simply as a material entity, but as intelligible only through particular regulatory norms (such as those associated with gender), then to give the body a definition, even a materialist one, means that it has been given a linguistic existence; it means that the body has already become an object of and by language.

To say that the body is a linguistic construct means for us that the body cannot be thought outside of the discursive constructions we place on it, those we use not only to name but also to value. The meanings of bodies are historical and cultural, we are told, since bodies are produced and interpreted in specific cultural and historical moments (Grosz, 1994). Therefore, our understandings of bodies are "necessarily mediated by the contexts in which we speak" (Shildrick, 1999, p. 7). We think it is to these contexts, meanings, and constructions that we might attend when we think of "gaydar," "gayness," and "sexuality." What are these meanings, contexts, and so on that "speak" the "gay" body and through which such body speaks?

The body is both signifying and signified. Elizabeth Grosz (1994) reminds us, however, that even though the body is involuntarily marked (by inscriptions such as race, gender, and sexuality), our "voluntary" practices make our bodies "amendable to the prevailing exigencies of power," to the sense that we may collude in our own oppression (p. X). Kathy Davis (1997) furthers this argument by adding that we cannot even make sense of these types of inscriptions without taking into account the ways power works on and through bodies:

> Bodies are not generic but bear the markers of culturally-constructed difference. Understanding what embodiment means to individuals depends upon being able to sort out how sexual, "racial," and other differences intersect and give meaning to their interactions with their bodies and through their bodies with the world around them. Conditions of embodiment are organized by systemic patterns of domination and subordination, making it impossible to grasp individual body practices, body regimes and discourses about the body without taking power into account. (p. 14)

All bodies are marked by race, class, gender, and sexuality, as well as a host of other markings. Some markings are more easily manipulated than others. Some appear also to bear other overriding marks: That of universality and essentiality. We think Davis is referring to the latter kinds of marks, the ones that appear universal and essential, but, as we indicate below, no construct ever "hits its mark" entirely, so to speak, and thus all marks are never as fixed as we tend to think. But marks we bear, so when we say we use our gaydar, what markings are we reading, which are we inscribing, and how manipulable are they? These marks, more or less manipulable, however, are not simply a matter of choice; they are the effects of power relations, and this should imply struggle. Gaydar should be understood as a condition of embodiment that is implicated in power relations. The question is not whether such relations exist, but which.

The idea of the body as a site of discursive practices can be most easily attributable to the work of Foucault. In *Discipline and Punish*, Foucault (1977), examining the history of the penal system in France, traces the forms of power from its concern with "punishment" and "repression" to its current form as a subtle, invisible power that takes as its object the "soul" of the individual. Foucault uncovered how power attaches itself to certain kinds of practices which he calls the "disciplinary mechanisms" or "technologies" of power. The "body," and its "soul," became the new site for, and investment of, power relations, which did not seek to repress the individual but to *produce* him, to make him the subject of knowledge, a knowledge intended to direct its actions and desires, to effectively administer him in relation to others, to make him more useful. These disciplinary mechanisms are everywhere—in civic, scientific, and political institutions— but they become very powerful when the sciences gives "scientific status" to such political technologies.

In other words, disciplinary mechanisms were born when the body, or more accurately, its soul, became the site of a concerted, but not necessarily systemic or organized, calculated manipulation of its elements, its gestures, its behaviors:

> The human body was entering a machinery of power that explores it, breaks it down and rearranges it. A 'political anatomy,' which was also a 'mechanics of power,' was being born; it defined how one may have a hold over others' bodies, not only so that they may do what one wishes, but so that they may operate as one wishes, with the techniques, the speed and the efficiency that one determines. Thus discipline produces subjected and practised bodies, 'docile' bodies. Discipline increases the forces of the body (in economic terms of utility) and diminishes these same forces (in political terms of obedience). In short, it dissociates power from the body; on the other hand, it turns it into an 'aptitude,' a 'capacity,' which it seeks to increase; on the other hand, it reverses the course of the energy, the power that might result from it, and turns it into a relation of strict subjection. (Foucault, 1977, p. 138)

Disciplinary mechanisms are the most significant forms of power of the modern era because, especially if they attain scientific status, they "make up" individuals.

Discipline takes on particular significance, and particular trajectories, when it comes to sexuality. Sexuality is something over which much discourse attends. Indeed, if Foucault (1978) is correct, sexuality has, more than any other construct, attached itself to identity, constitutes it to such an extent that it is presumed to hold an undeniable truth of the self: we direct what we are to sex. With regard to gays and lesbians, what kinds of bodies and souls are produced? What does the gay and lesbian body speak? It was Freud who first spoke sexuality into psychological discourse, or, at the very least, it was Freud (1975) who made sexuality a scientific subject. Freud's intent was to liberate sexuality from the repressive status it had. Although Freud attempted to make sexuality of all kinds a central aspect of identity, it was only homosexuality that soon became a "condition" that was immediately pathologized. By the 1950s, homosexuality was viewed as a psychological disorder that needed treatment. This discourse about the gay and lesbian body created a body that was deviant and sick, a body in need of treatment. It was not until 1973 that the American Psychiatric Association (APA) removed homosexuality from its list of mental illnesses. This move by the APA, however, did not remove the stigma from homosexuality. Indeed, the removal of homosexuality from the list of pathologies, one which arguably one can hardly help having, may have had the negative consequence of deeming it a "choice," and thus it is more easily punishable.

Yet even today the gay body is perceived as a body of sickness (for some, a mental illness, and now because of Auto Immune Deficiency Syndrome [AIDS], to many others, a physical illness) as well as a deviant body, a morally corrupt body. The most common construction of the gay body appears to be the self-hating, closeted homosexual. This is the "straight" by day, "gay" by night individual, who often is depicted as on the verge of suicide. Other images of moral corruption and illness exist as well. The promiscuous gay man, in particular, has been an image that has lingered for many years, and AIDS has made alterations to this image. While the promiscuous gay male has histori- cally been deemed a deviant predator, perhaps also a child molester, the AIDS crisis has made him a pathetic object that has paid for his deviancy, a payment that some conservatives will readily admit to feeling is just. A self-hating Christian gay and lesbian body also exists as well, and this is the object of attempts to cure her homosexuality. In addition, these constructions of gayness have been furthered redefined by gender, race, and class. For example, the white, upper-class lesbian in the first part of the nineteenth century was con- structed as somewhat "normal" if she was in a "Boston marriage," although this had to remain an open secret. The African American male gay body, subject to other constructions about his masculinity, as well as religious restrictions, has attained a specific status that allows it to maintain its heterosexuality *even while engaging in homosexual behavior* (often almost exclusively): These men are deemed on the "down low."

Recent gay-rights movements have sought to create new constructions of gayness, positing the gay body in different, positive ways. We think, how- ever, that such constructions work to the extent they "heterosexualize" the gay body. In these constructions of gayness, gay men and women are posi- tioned as "normal," living in committed, monogamous "marriages" and some- times raising children together. The gay-marriage movements have now sought legal status for such an image. Although this is by no means an exhaustive representation of the constructions of gayness that exist, it is an example of the multiple ways the gay and lesbian body has been spoken, and these form the speech, we think, that gaydar reads.

"Queer" theorists have questioned the fixity of such speech. They have called into question what it is we mean by the term *sexuality*. Sexual identity is, like other identities, deemed "arbitrary, unstable, and exclusionary" (Seidman, 1996, p. 11). Sexuality is inextricably intertwined with, even sometimes constitutive of, power relations (Gamson & Moon, 2004). Rather than defining sexuality as a subject position rooted in biology, queer theorists ask us to see it as always resisting definition. This means that what we can know through gaydar may be nothing at all, or, rather, we "know" only that which certain highly regulatory social norms allow us to "know."

But if gaydar can tell us nothing essential about a person, only about particular social norms, then does this mean that accounting for it with queer theories is, in essence, useless? No, because these theories provide us with a way of thinking of sexuality as not *in* the person but as constituted by social norms. And in this way the queer project is—or should be— everyone's project. This also implies, in a very real sense, that anything can be "queer." But the idea that queer is anything raises concerns for some academics who wonder if it that idea might not be an attempt to coopt a marginalized space in the name of whiteness.

In other words, queerness has been deemed undeniably white and for all its emancipatory intent has left out queers of color (Dhairyam, 1994). Anzaldua (1991) explains, for example, that the term *queer* is used by white academics as "a false unifying umbrella which all 'queers' of all races, ethnicities and classes are shoved under" (p. 250). The idea of queerness, as elaborated in many academic theories, may have ignored the specificities of race in an attempt to mobilize around a sexuality, which such theories then postulate as undefinable. For example, Berlant and Warner (1998) argue that queer social theory is committed to sexuality—which cannot be defined in advance—as an "inescapable category of analysis, agitation, and refunctioning . . . Any social theory that miscomprehends this participates in [the] reproduction [of heteronormativity]" (p. 564). "Heteronormativity" refers to the "institutions, structures of understanding, and practical orientations that make heterosexuality seem not only coherent—that is, organized as a sexuality— but also privileged" (Berlant & Warner, 1998, p. 548). Attention to heteronormativity has the potential of giving a totalizing account of society which ignores, or perhaps even rejects, other vectors of power, such as class, race, ability, and even gender itself.

Although the idea of "queerness" may be problematic to the extent it gives a totalizing account of all identity and power, we find it useful to our discussion because it recognizes sexuality as discursively produced. There is nothing biological or inherent about one's sexuality. Similar to the poststructural understanding of gender, queer theory posits sexuality as performative. Butler (1990) argues that gender must depend upon our repeated acts and bodily presentations that, over time, come to make gender appear natural even as the very notion of gender becomes constructed through our repeated acts. Butler (1990) continues:

> In other words, acts, gestures, and desire produce the effect of an internal core or substance, but produce this *on the surface of* the body, through the play of signifying absences that suggest, but never reveal, the organizing principle of identity as a cause. Such acts, gestures, enactments, generally construed, are *performative* in the sense that the essence or identity that they otherwise purport to express are *fabrications* manufactured and sustained through corporeal signs and other discursive means. That the gendered body is performative suggests that it has no ontological status apart from the various acts which constitute its reality. (p. 173)

Understanding the idea that gender and sexuality are performative requires understanding that we create through our acts or practices that which we call "gender" and "sexuality." In other words, we enact gender and sexuality with our words and actions. The question still remains: What kind of enactment is read by gaydar? Previously, we gave examples of multiple constructions—which we can now call "enactments"—of the gay and lesbian body. Our point here is that such enactments of gayness are complicated and multilayered. There are no definitive ways to be gay or lesbian, and any given definition is simply *a* performance of the cultural and historical ideas and ideals that constitute the gay or lesbian body.

This idea of gender and sexuality as performative opens up the possibilities for individuals to perform gender and sexuality in a variety of ways. Some of these performances, like those of female impersonators, are more challenging to dominant conceptions of gender and sexuality. In fact, the performances of drag queens "articulate political ideas that challenge conventional understandings of male and female, gay and straight, to create new collective identities, and to disrupt existing collective identity boundaries" (Rupp & Taylor, 2003, pp. 212–13). Here we may see drag queens as utilizing embodiment as a political tool to resist heteronormativity and traditional gender norms.

We can note as well how race norms are destabilized by such performances, as when white drag queens "perform" black women, such as Diana Ross, or when black drag queens "perform" white women, such as Cher and Barbra Streisand. One does not accuse these men of racism when they don and parody a racial identity, something that is impermissible in other settings.

Similarly, Sullivan (2001) explains this ability of bodies to rework identities as a "transactional" embodiment:

> Thinking of bodies as transactional means thinking of bodies and their environments in a permeable, dynamic relationship in which culture does not just effect bodies, but bodies also effect culture. This relationship is one in which bodies and culture are formed from the beginning, as it were, by means of mutual constitution. (p. 3)

If culture is affected through bodies, as bodies are affected through culture, then we can infer that gaydar is part of this transactional process. In other words, gaydar is part of how we make culture. Gaydar permits us to read a particular culture's notions of gayness, but then these enactments reconstitute what culture means by gayness.

Thinking of our bodies as transactional, Sullivan (2001) argues, "enables thinking of meaning—creation as socially constituted through an appreciation of the differences of others. It also provides a conception of communication as a transactional circle in which all parties involved in a situation jointly constitute its meaning" (p. 9). Gail Weiss (2002) takes issue with this idea and argues that not everyone is consciously aware of these transactions and their significance. This raises the question of the effectiveness of gaydar in particular but bodily communication in general.

We have argued that enactment of gayness may vary by gender, race, and class. This means that the meanings of gayness may not be as clear as we like to think. If race, class, and gender also shape how gayness is spoken, then our understanding of such speech must attend to the multiple, conflicting constructions of raced, classed, and gendered bodies. How are we to read, for example, a black lesbian body? We may need to be familiar with what performance our culture expects of, say, a black, middle-class lesbian versus a poor, black lesbian. Gaydar, which reflects a struggle over multiple definition of gayness, may miss its mark, since it seeks a "sexual" body that cannot be extricated from its raced, classed, and gendered inscriptions. This "misreading" can happen even among gays and lesbians, but we may also add another layer of misreadings by heterosexuals. Sexuality is coconstructed, so straight people do use gaydar, more or less effectively, and indeed much of gay bashing or harassment of gays and lesbians could not occur without it. Can gaydar by straights, however, also be used to create democratic possibilities? We will explore these questions later in this chapter. But first we examine how gaydar has entered discourse.

Gaydar has become necessary because our society has created a need for it to the extent that its heteronormativity has marginalized gays and created the closet. Gaydar, therefore, is *necessary* in two senses: (1) it is necessary for the same reasons our society has created the need for the closet—"gayness" in many instances can only be spoken implicitly; and (2) it is necessary for gays and lesbians because it allows them to seek each other out for companionship and, perhaps as often, safety.

The first reason needs little explanation. Heteronormativity requires silence about homosexuality, not only because, as we have argued, it is, for all our progress, still a stigmatizing mark but also because homosexuals still face physical violence and other forms of discrimination, sometimes with legal impunity. Nevertheless, what it means to be a homosexual is very much an open question. With regard to the second reason for gaydar that gays and lesbians use it for companionship and safety, Creed (1999) argues:

> The need to construct a sense of community, through dress and appearance, suggests quite clearly that there is no such thing as an essential lesbian body—lesbians themselves have to create this body in order to feel they belong to the larger lesbian community, recognizable to its members not through essentialized bodily forms, but through representations, gesture and play. (p. 123)

Creed explains why lesbians (and gay men) want to be recognizable to one another. Yet, such recognition, to the extent it relies upon particular social definitions of what it means to be gay or lesbian, fixes identities and may reinscribe cultural, and hegemonic, regulatory norms. For instance, gaydar may help a "feminine" lesbian, or "femme" identify a particular kind of "masculine" lesbian, or "stud," but to the extent she relies upon culturally determined views of a "masculine" appearance, albeit, in a woman, she reifies these norms rather than contests them. This fixing of identity, however, will remain elusive, since it can only really read definitively what it means for a woman to perform a "stud" identity? And perhaps there is some contestation of norm after all, if not by the gazer, then by the gazee, since the "stud," as a woman, is performing masculine characteristics and is thus requiring us to acknowledge that what it means to be man or woman is never really as rigid or as "natural" as we are led to think.

The moment one says "gay," "lesbian," or "queer," at any rate, one is necessarily calling into question exactly what one means (Harper, White, & Cerullo, 1993). If this is so, what are we to understand by the term *gaydar*? What exactly is, or can be, the "gay" in *gaydar*? We argue that gayness is irreducible to any particular set of representations, and to argue otherwise should be considered more of an obstacle than an aim of progay politics. If one argues that gayness could be represented and that these representations would ultimately define gayness, one would have to inquire into the social processes and institutions that define gayness and continue to maintain its coherence. Assuming the authority of gaydar without such inquiry would amount to a form of surveillance that, according to Foucault (1977), creates docile bodies. We are not denying that there is such a thing a gaydar, but we ask that rather than assume the stableness of the identities read by it that such identities be made the objects of inquiry into their origins, their institutional bases, and the social constructions that ensure that individuals are deemed "this or that." It is the idea that one is this or that—that one is a gay or a lesbian—and that such an identity is permanent, fixed, stable, *recognizable* and that is also what allows the gay basher to use his gaydar to commit violence.

WHO SPEAKS SEXUALITY?

This last point about the gay basher's use of gaydar requires that we attend to the question of who gets to use gaydar. Who can or should read it? In the *Will and Grace* episode mentioned earlier, Jack, who was positioned as a gay man with particular expertise, an expertise premised on having slept with many men and whose promiscuity is exalted for comedic effect, is called upon to make the definitive decision about the man's sexuality. This makes explicit the sexual component inherent in gaydar. Homosexuality is still defined as "sex," and this may be why homosexuality is so problematic for so many people: It cannot be dissociated from the sex act. For all the talk of gaydar as a political act, to the extent it reads "sex," as in this *Will and Grace* episode, it reinforces a predominant notion of homosexuality as sex and thus as inherently punishable. It is this notion of homosexuality as sex that permits the gay basher to transfer his hate for the sex act to a hate for individual. Or perhaps because homosexual is sex for many, the gay basher feels sexually threatened solely by another person's sexuality, even when no sexual proposition took place.

But perhaps this notion of homosexual as sex is breaking down under pressure from the gay rights movement, which has sought different, more positive, representations of homosexuality. At any rate, we argue that "gayness" is a socially constructed concept, so its predominant images, particularly its negative ones, such as the promiscuous gay man that the Jack character represents, are open to be read by heterosexuals as much as homosexuals. "Gayness," whatever that might mean, is constructed by heterosexuals as much as, if not more than, by homosexuals, who must construct an identity that challenges the negative images presented of them. It is impossible for any group of individuals to claim ownership over how bodies speak. And this is as much the case of the sexual body as it is of any linguistic construct. As Sedgwick (1990) argues, "no one person can take control over all the multiple, often contradictory codes by which information about sexual identity and activity can seem to be conveyed" (p. 79). That neither Will (nor Jack) nor Grace could define the sexual body of the man whose sexual attraction they sought is part of the problem of claiming gaydar for only, and just only, gays and lesbians. There is a danger to reducing the multiple identities and feelings that belong to individuals so totally to their sexuality, and, conversely, to attempt to do so makes it harder for one to protect it from being expropriated by others who seek to use it to do harm.

This claim is not made without some hesitation, however, because it raises questions about "experience," which at least one of us wants to keep open as a possibility for questioning the hegemony of normativity in all its forms. The notion of "experience" is problematic (if essentialist) to the extent that it is not historicized to determine the conditions of its possibility (Scott, 1991). But the notion of experience also undoes the massive project of establishing, in our present case, a heteronormativity in all we see and think. In this regard, attending to the experiences of "the other" may constitute the kind of strategic essentialism that Gayatri Spivak (1988) explains is useful for social action, or put differently, asserting a uniquely gay or lesbian experience may constitute, in the political arena, a "*strategic* use of positivist essentialism in a scrupulously visible political interest" (p. 205).

Nevertheless, the idea that gaydar provides a speech for homosexuals as well as heterosexuals does present us with a particular dilemma. Walters (1996) articulates this dilemma speaking on the subject of straights teaching queer theory:

This is a very touchy issue and one, I must admit, I am very torn over. For, on the one hand, an essentialist position (one must be something to teach it, and that "being" represents the truth of experience) is unacceptable on any number of levels. On the other hand, if we believe that knowledge is always situated—that we always speak and think from somewhere—then to say it does not matter at all is equally unacceptable. (p. 840)

So we have to ask, if problematically, do nongays have the right to read or even speak gayness? The closet is a fundamental feature of the lives of gay people, as Sedgwick (1990) explains, even for out gays and lesbians. Thus, gaydar plays an important part in the lives of gay people, for it allows them to transcend the "open secret" that shapes their lives. But if the closet is such a constitutive aspect of gay identity, then gaydar also destroys the ability of one to keep one's sexuality secret. It may amount to a kind of forced outing, not with the same implications as outing someone publicly, of course, but nevertheless one's agency is stripped by another. So even if the gazer seeks to make a political connection with another person, she is engaging, with an unwilling subject, as in the case of the man Will and Grace desire, in the kind of dangerous play of silence and speech that gay people must play with heterosexuals, always to the benefit of the latter.

But this still begs the question of whether heterosexuals can perform gaydar. If "gayness" is defined in essentialist terms—which is not the same as "strategic essentialism"—if "gayness" is understood solely in terms of particular, authentic experiences, then the answer would have to be no. Heterosexuals cannot use gaydar, because they cannot experience homosexuality—homosexuality, that is, as something more fundamental than sex. And yet they do, as the example of the gay basher illustrates, if only violently, or when a straight woman suspects her lover is gay. And if heteronormativity is what must be challenged, then it makes a certain kind of sense to take the risk of extending gaydar to others, for such is the kind of "strategic use of positivist essentialism [with] a scrupulously visible political interest." This might spark the initiation of new gay bashers, as well as forced outings, but it might bring about the beginnings of change for the better, as some, if not many, gay bashing incidents and forced outings risk doing.

EDUCATING GAY/LESBIAN STUDENTS

We have not yet undertaken a discussion of the implications of the politics of gaydar for schools. Though there are some programs in place in certain schools, the overall climate for lesbians and gays in U.S. schools, according to the Gay, Lesbian, and Straight Education Network (GLSEN) 2001 National School Climate Survey, is unsafe (Kosciw & Cullen, 2002). The survey was an attempt to get a comprehensive picture of what life in schools is like for gay, lesbian, bisexual, and transgendered students. Two-thirds of the 904 respondents said they felt "unsafe," while more than three-quarters reported hearing homophobic remarks from other students. Progressives have sought to help gay and lesbian students succeed as other students do. Both the National Education Association and the American Federation of Teachers have made specific recommendations to help protect the safety of gay, lesbian, bisexual, and transgendered students in schools. GLSEN and the Lesbian and Gay Rights Project of the American Civil Liberties Union also have "kits" designed to help schools address the issue of homosexuality. These kits include recommendations for teaching about homosexuality as part of diversity training. Educators who argue for the inclusion of such diversity often take up the issue of homosexuality in terms of tolerance or equal-rights discourse. We do think, following Sears (1991), that the focus needs to be shifted from labeling gay and lesbian students as "at risk" and instead focus on how gay and lesbian bodies are constructed and (de)valued.

We think, however, that all of these progressive projects are worth pursuing, for they do seek to address the negative stereotypes and the deplorable conditions for gay and lesbian students in schools. But we offer here another project, one that our discussion of gaydar leads us to propose. We have sought in this chapter to problematize the essentialism associated with homosexuality via a discussion of gaydar. This makes our project a "queer" one. If taken seriously, as Susan Talburt (1999) argues, a queer project would shift inquiry (and practices) away from representations of gay and lesbian experiences and toward an understanding of social practices and institutional locations that define gay and lesbian people as such and such and that make them abject bodies in particular locations, such as schools. We think educators must consider how gay and lesbian students become objects of concern, how they respond to discourses that constitute them, negatively or positively, and how these discourses create their voice and experiences Talburt, 1999).

In conclusion, when schools refuse to acknowledge anything but heterosexuality (in its overt and hidden curricula), they collude in the necessity of "gaydar" but only by requiring gay and lesbian students to speak such silence to each other and perhaps by implicitly permitting the gay basher or harasser to also speak such silence. Extending "gaydar" to heterosexuals, in a project that also seeks to understand the production of gay and lesbian identities rather than essentialize them, might mean that schools will face more harassment, but it might also go a long way toward undoing heteronormativity. Until schools explore the power of heteronormativity and how it upholds the silence of homosexuality, they will continue to be complacent in maintaining the need for gaydar as a silence that speaks only to and about abject bodies.

REFERENCES

Anzaldua, G. (1991). To(o) queer the writer—Loca, escritora y chicana. In B. Warland (Ed.), *Inversions: Writing by dykes, queers, and lesbians* (pp. 249–263). Vancouver: Press Gang.

Berlant, L. & Warner, M. (1998). Sex in public. *Critical Inquiry, 24*(2), 547–566.

Butler, J. (1990). *Gender trouble: Feminism and the subversion of identity.* New York: Routledge.

Butler, J. (1989). Foucault and the paradox of bodily inscriptions. *The Journal of Philosophy, 86*(11), 601–607.

Creed, B. (1999). Lesbian bodies: Tribades, tomboys and tarts. In J. Price & M. Shildrick (Eds.), *Feminist theory and the body: A reader* (pp. 111–124). New York: Routledge.

Davis, K. (1997). *Embodied practices: Feminist perspectives on the body.* Thousand Oaks: Sage.

Dhairyam, S. (1994). Racing the lesbian, dodging white critics. In L. Doan (Ed.), *The lesbian postmodern* (pp. 25–46). New York: Columbia University Press.

Foucault, M. (1978). *The history of sexuality. Volume I: An introduction.* (R. Hurley, Trans.). New York: Pantheon Books.

Foucault, M. (1977). *Discipline and punish: The birth of the prison.* (A. M. Sheridan Smith, Trans.). New York: Vintage Books.

Freud, S. (1905/1975). *Three essays on the theory of sexuality.* (J. Strachey, Trans.). New York: Basic Books.

Gamson, J., & Moon, D. (2004). The sociology of sexualities: Queer and beyond. *Annual Review of Sociology, 30,* 47–64.

Grosz, E. (1995). *Space, time, and perversion.* New York: Routledge.

Grosz, E. (1994). *Volatile bodies: Toward a corporeal feminism.* Indianapolis: Indiana University Press.

Harper, P. B., White, E. F., & Cerullo, M. (1993). Multi/queer/culture. *Radical America, 24*(4), 27–37.

Kosciw, J. G., & Cullen, M. K. (2002). The GLSEN 2001 national school climate survey: The school-related experiences of our nation's lesbian, gay, bisexual, and transgender youth. (Report No. UD 035 000). New York, NY: Gay, Lesbian, and Straight Education network. (ERIC Document Reproduction Service No. ED 464978).

Lock, M. (1993). Cultivating the body: Anthropology and epistemologies of bodily practice and knowledge. *Annual Review of Anthropology, 22,* 133–155.

Rupp, L. J., & Taylor, V. (2003). *Drag queens at the 801 Cabaret.* Chicago: University of Chicago Press.

Scott, J. W. (1991). The evidence of experience. *Critical Inquiry, 17,* 773–797.

Sears, J. T. (1991). Helping students understand and accept sexual diversity. *Educational Leadership,* 54–56.

Sedgwick, E. K. (1990). *Epistemology of the closet.* Berkeley: University of California Press.

Sedgwick, E. K. (1985). *Between men: English literature and male homosocial desire.* New York: Columbia University Press.

Seidman, S. (1996). Introduction. In S. Siedman (Eds.), *Queer theory/sociology* (pp. 1–29). Cambridge: Blackwell.

Shildrick, M. (1999). Openings on the body: A critical introduction. In J. Price & M. Shildrick (Eds.), *Feminist theory and the body: A reader* (pp. 1–14). New York: Routledge.

Spivak, G.C. (1988). *In other worlds: Essays in cultural politics.* New York: Routledge.

Sullivan, S. (2001). *Living across and through skins: Transactional bodies, pragmatism, and feminism.* Bloomington: Indiana University Press.

Talburt, S. (1999). Open secrets and problems of queer ethnography: Readings from a religious studies classroom. *Qualitative Studies in Education, 12*(5), 525–539.

Walters, S. D. (1996). From here to queer: Radical feminism, postmodernism, and the lesbian menace (or, why can't a woman be more like a fag?). *Signs, 21*(4), 830–869.

Weiss, G. (2002). The anonymous intentions of transactional bodies. *Hypatia, 17*(4), 187–200.

PART II

METHODOLOGICAL AND
PEDAGOGICAL CONTEXTS

CURRICULUM, CULTURE, RELEVANCE, AND PRAXIS

CHAPTER SEVEN

THE IMPACT OF TRICKSTER
PERFORMANCES ON THE CURRICULUM

EXPLORATIONS OF A WHITE, FEMALE CIVIL RIGHTS ACTIVIST

RHONDA B. JEFFRIES

INTRODUCTION

In a graduate course I teach, Principles of Curriculum Construction, I strive
to assist practicing educators, aspiring school administrators, media special-
ists, and school psychologists to think of curriculum as something larger than
the huge binder they are given from some powerful invisible entity. The
majority of my students are fairly dismayed with this approach as I ask them
to consider performance as more than an evaluation session where preconceived notions of teaching are acknowledged and model lessons are suggested
for emulation. Exploring the broadest context of curriculum and expecting
students to see performance as all things impacting education require them
to move well beyond their comfort zones. The reading list includes such texts
as *Media Messages* (Holtzman, 2000), *Going up the River: Travels in a Prison
Nation* (Hallinan, 2001), *The Ornament of the World: How Muslims, Jews, and
Christians Created a Culture of Tolerance in Medieval Spain* (Menocal, 2002),
and *Political Fictions* (Didion, 2001), among other various readings that to
them seem to have nothing to do with curriculum and schooling. I still
wonder from time to time why I torture them and myself when they might
be more content if I simply asked them to create a vacuous lesson plan,

assemble it into yet another huge binder, and march satisfactorily on with their professional lives into institutions that will appreciate the binder they bring. While some of these students leave the course firmly wedded to the notion that they have the market cornered where curriculum construction and implementation are concerned, many others are grateful for the opportunity to analyze the various aspects of curriculum that directly and indirectly impact learning in classroom settings.

This chapter looks at curriculum in its broadest form and extends my long-standing examination of the trickster figure. It explores the peripheral performances that subtly yet profoundly impact the educational landscape in every way and on every day. The chapter continues a specific exploration of the less prominent female, and more specifically white female, trickster and the impact her influence has had on social institutions that shape classroom curricula in post–civil rights era America.

Benjamin Disraeli first employed the term *trickster* in the nineteenth century to describe lying political opponents within the Whig Party (Hynes, 1993). This review explores the political dimension of the trickster archetype by initially exploring the arguments made in the literature on cross-cultural mentoring, multiculturalism, and diversity education and other works espousing social justice as a means to improve the human condition and examines manifestations of the trickster figure within the historical and political contexts of the contemporary civil rights movement. Using Hynes' (1993) framework for understanding trickster traits—(1) ambiguous and anomalous, (2) deceiver and trick player, (3) shape-shifter, and (4) situation inverter—and how they manifest, the chapter also explores atypical tricksters within the twentieth century's second-wave civil rights movement. Specifically, the chapter focuses on Virginia Foster Durr as a vivid example of one white, female trickster who significantly impacted the curriculum of race, class, and gender at large.

THE POLITICAL DIMENSIONS OF A
MULTIFACETED PERFORMANCE

Viewing curriculum beyond the boundaries of traditional structures and ideals requires a cursory look at some of the frameworks that inform the atypical responses needed to create socially responsive curricula. Specifically, trickster traits can sometimes be achieved in traditional organizational structures via particular methods such as cross-cultural mentoring and the use of diversity education. Crosby (1999) and Thomas and Ely (1996) noted that cross-cultural mentoring relationships improve the personal and professional lives of the individuals involved in the relationship as well as the organizations in which the individuals contribute. Mentoring across culture unites diverse people through developmental experiences that encourage *new lines of questioning* and *unique methods of problem solving*.

There exists a natural connection between the work of all marginalized people, and consequently, seemingly apparent barriers between marginalized groups can be social constructed artifices that only serve to keep the powerless groups at odds with one another. Cross-cultural mentoring can more effectively eradicate racial, class, and gender borders and facilitate program as the groups help each other as marginalized people. At any given time, an individual who holds one or more marginalized designations may have some level of social capital, professional power, or other means of negotiating position to bring about social justice that can be shared among the groups. Similarly, contrary to more conservative theories, the most appropriate method for emerging from oppression is not always for oppressed people to help themselves. While this argument does not infer that marginalized people should assume a victim's mentality and assume that those in traditional positions of power are best suited to enable their causes and provide access, the chapter does suggest that cross-cultural mentoring should be viewed as the method of greatest degrees of freedom.

Difficulty can arise in cross-cultural mentoring relationships according to Johnson-Bailey and Cervero (2004), who cite several issues around which struggle can be found as the issues of race, class, and gender are confronted. Traditional power dynamics that are found within Western society are foundational roadblocks that can deter a productive relationship across cultural boundaries. Their research found trust, hegemony, paternalism, and marginalized groups' reliance on nonlinear, shared power systems among the problems that confound the effective collaboration between agents of diverse perspectives and orientations. Tricksters often facilitate and transition agents away from these cited barriers and are often prepared to shoulder the responsibility and unpleasantness of this provision.

CURRICULUM TRICKSTERS: A REVIEW OF THE LITERATURE

TRADITIONAL TRICKSTERS

Tricksters have been described in a multitude of ways ranging from virtuous to evil and even as one in the same depending on the writer's perspective. One aspect of trickster that has been agreed upon by virtually every writer is that the archetype's performance is never simple and never quite what it seems. Radin (1972) described trickster as existing simultaneously as "creator and destroyer, giver and negator, he who dupes others and who is always duped himself. Tricksters have been recorded in cultures from antiquity to the present and have been noted to transform themselves depending upon the nature of the challenge they face. They are the characters seen struggling with the notion of modernity and are most often depicted as change agent and reformer (Christen, 1998).

The trickster can be found wherever there is a literary or oral folk tradition and characteristically is the protagonist in a plot involving switches in gender, shape-shifing or the mischievous intermingling of the sacred and the profane, performing miracles or violating taboos. The trickster mocks order and takes pleasure in the confusion of boundaries, standing at the cross roads of paradox and ambiguity. An unpredictable master of deception and artifice, the trickster is the simpleton who is fooled and yet at the same time engineers malicious pranks: trickster tales cause laughter in their transgression of sacred beliefs, yet at the same time they focus attention on the nature of those beliefs, highlighting the threshold between order and disorder, sacred and profane, centre and periphery (Wright, 2000, p. 4).

Texts exploring the nature of trickster and her/his ability to reshape curriculum abound. Ellison's *Invisible Man* is aptly critiqued by Reed (1992) where he noted the novel's ability to

speak to present concerns in part because it embodies that conflict, and, at its best, refuses the either/or of separatism versus integration, opting instead for a complex both/and strategy that, among other things, recognizes black and white culture in America as always already integrated, already predicated on occasionally cooperative but generally oppressive, unequal, and agonistic interrelations. (p. 64)

Wright (2000) furthered the exploration of tricksters in text by examining how the figure uses power to transform. In this instance, trickster tests the space of liminality in the theater by enticing the unenlightened audience to explore in a relatively safe venue this space of liminality. Here the audience can explore the imaginary world of the theater and face the cultural structures and confining boundaries reality presents. In this space, a countercurriculum can at least be experienced without the pressure of concern for ramifications.

WOMEN AS TRICKSTERS

It should not be surprising that women and tricksterism has not been as widely recorded as the myriad tales of male character tricksters. Hyde (1998) delineated the patriarchal mythologies that frame most tricksters and noted that even when powerful females assume trickster character traits, the female version is still accompanied by a dominant male who is responsible for much of the tale's action. Lust, hypersexuality, and nonprocreative mating, and other features commonly used to describe trickster behavior have been suggested as an explanation for why a female trickster might have some difficulty managing and maintaining the characteristic of freedom from child-birth and mothering. While the majority of trickster literature focuses on male conceptualizations of the archetype, Jurich (1998) devoted thorough attention to the proliferation of the female trickster and described its presence in folk narrative as central and significant. Jurich's work detailed the emergence of the female trickster from one who is an evil, manipulative, irrational, deviant, one-dimensional, and purely negative creature toward a more fully developed figure equally if not more capable than her male counterpart to affect the fate of her world. In fact, women have acted as trickster for centuries, and classic and popular texts are filled with accounts of women using their intellect and cunning to control and alter outcomes. While there are many studies of tricksters, most have failed to acknowledge the female performance as one of trickster, and it is believed none have dealt with the ways in which the female trickster is constructed in contemporary American life (Landay, 1998).

THE FACES OF DURR USING HYNES'S FRAMEWORK

While this does not suggest that Durr continuously functioned as trickster, it does posit that throughout her life she encountered and exhibited trickster characteristics that shaped her life and influenced behaviors, actions, and work. According to Hyde (1998) no human is capable of continuous trickster manifestations, and there are no modern tricksters because trickster only comes to life in the complex terrain of polytheism. If the spiritual world is dominated by a single high god opposed by a single embodiment of evil, then the ancient trickster disappears (pp. 9–10).

He further cautioned that the death of trickster created a good versus evil dichotomy that oversimplified and masked the moral ambiguities of life. Rather than increasing clarity about moral judgments, the good versus evil dichotomy, as with the black versus white race predicament that dominated the contemporary civil rights movement, simply created a false sense of righteousness. As chaos must exist for us to know structure, the trickster must exist to remind us of our frailties and to urge us toward perfection.

Kutz's (2001) explanation of the trickster is a compelling argument to envision the existence of a contemporary manifestation of trickster functioning in our society:

> Consider the relationship you have with your cat. You and your cat negotiate constantly for "operational space." At the moment, she wants to be fed; you want to read your book. She hints, meows, massages your leg with her body. You continue reading. She leaps up onto your lap, interposing herself betwixt the book and your eyes. You put her back down on the carpet. She springs back, purring. You sigh, put your book down, and get up to feed her, following

her to the kitchen. As you pass by the kitchen window, you happen to glance out and see a kid about to travel on to a better life by falling out of the neighbour's tree. You react by opening the window and yelling at the kid to "hang on." You grab the phone to call your neighbour, and then run out to get a ladder so you can help the kid down. As you look back at the cat, she seems to be smirking at you . . . The unconnected technophile would say of all of this that "coincidence" put this entire scenario together. The mystic might claim that some superforce drove you into the position of being able to prevent a possible disaster. (p. 10)

I, on the other hand, might assign the role of *trickster* to the cat. She did not compel you to become a savior but instead prodded you into activity, which happened to lead you in that direction, the ostensible purpose of which was to feed her but which would also set you in motion for whatever else might happen. In other words, the *trickster* cat simply got you moving and prepared to do whatever came next, leaving it up to you to either go for it or ignore it.

Contemporary trickster performances, as with historical acts, can be seen in humans as well as animals. While some tricksters are more clever than others, and the most skillful tricksters will consistently deny their performance (Kutz, 2001) many acts that are powerful enough to set people in motion can be identified as acts of tricksterism. Hyne's framework for understanding trickster traits consists of the following six characteristics: (1) ambiguous and anomalous; (2) deceiver and trick player; (3) shape-shifter; (4) situation inverter; (5) messenger and imitator of the gods; and (6) sacred and lewd bricoleur or creative problem solver. No trickster embodies all characteristics at all times, nor do some tricksters ever exhibit some of these listed characteristics. While some tricksters master some of the traits of tricksterism, they may only be the recipient of some of these trickster behaviors. The following sections outline via the framework the ways in which Virginia Durr was initially changed by her encounters with trickster-type performances and events and later either continued to be subject to tricksterism and/or began to assume the performance for the work she eventually embraced and achieved for the remainder of her life.

AMBIGUOUS AND ANOMALOUS

During Durr's early years, she lived a life of southern comfort assuming, as most people do, her way of life the norm. Her lack of exposure to blacks in positions other than workers or servants caused Virginia much shock and discomfort after she left the South to study at Wellesley. When she was assigned to share a table in the dining hall with a black student she gracefully declined the opportunity. Virginia stated, "I had been surrounded by black people all my life . . . But to eat with them at the table, this was social equality and it meant breaking a taboo I had been trained in all my eighteen years" (Sullivan, 2003, p. 5). Virginia's refusal to accept her seating assignment incurred the wrath of the house manager, who informed her that she could either sit or depart from the college. While Virginia's immediate concern was how she might function without the social life and intellectual stimulation she had grown to love at college, advanced consideration caused fear of what her father would think of her behavior. She decided that what he did not know would not hurt him, and after sitting beside the dreaded black girl, Virginia realized her shame stemmed, not from associating with a person of color, but from behaving against her family's values. The house manager played trickster on Virginia, and "though this was not a moment of epiphany, a doubt had been planted" (Sullivan, 2003, p. 5). Life played the trick on Durr during the early 1920s when the boll weevil infestation destroyed the family cotton farm and on many southern whites living comfortably in 1930s Birmingham when the steel companies failed. It was at this time that Virginia began to more fully question her position in the world and move from a position of being tricked to using tricks to impact a more socially just order.

DECEIVER AND TRICK PLAYER

Virginia Durr was heavily involved in the legal world and political scene of Washington once her husband, Cliff, accepted a position in the Reconstruction Finance Corporation. Since her sister, Josephine, was married to Hugo Black, a member of the 1926 U.S. Senate, Virginia was quickly immersed into the Women's Division of the Democratic National Committee and was socializing with Eleanor Roosevelt. She renewed a college friendship with Clark Foreman, who held a high post in the Interior Department and was the trailblazer for hiring blacks into the Roosevelt administration. Durr disapproved of Foreman's support of blacks, and his response that she was a "white, Southern, bigoted . . . provincial girl" as well as his "enthusiastic and absolutely believing" endorsement of blacks (Sullivan, 2003, p. 8) displaced yet another cog in Virginia's small-minded wheel of convention. Her rude awakening came when the Special Committee on Civil Liberties headed by Senator Robert LaFollette turned its investigation on antiunion practices and violent and illegal acts committed by businesses and manufacturers to deter labor organizing efforts. Her commitment to the New Deal philosophies, built through her and Cliff's new circle of associates, was tested when she discovered that many of the accused were fathers of her childhood friends. Her investigations led her to Joseph Gelders, a self-proclaimed apolitical University of Alabama professor turned activist in response to the poverty associated with antilabor reform. Gelders enlisted Virginia's assistance in rallying southern support for workers' rights through a conference, and in response, her research revealed the apathetic coverage and misrepresentation the media provided this phenomenon. Durr recalled the conference as "a wonderful sort of love feast because it was the first time that all the various elements from the South had gotten together. And we were not segregated" (Sullivan, 2003, p. 11). It is at this convention that the succession of tricks played on Durr came together, and she was transformed.

SHAPE-SHIFTER

Virginia lost favor with her closest Birmingham friends as her affiliation with New Deal politics became overt, and her friends realized Virginia had shifted in her beliefs about integration. Labeled "an outright traitor, an outlaw," she recalled how painful it was to "see all my friends against me, but I never had a moment's doubt of where I stood" (Sullivan, 2003, p. 12). By the late 1930s, Virginia was socializing and working with blacks on the antipoll tax fight, including Mary McLeod Buthune, whose position and influential black associates dispelled all of Virginia's juvenile myths about black inferiority. She quickly realized she needed the support of these powerful blacks to further her mission of bringing democracy to the south.

Sullivan (2003) further documented Durr's talents in this description:

> A tall, striking woman with a loud, clear voice and an easy laugh, she seemed to command a room effortlessly. Virginia could easily play the part of the Southern belle with her gracious manner and flirtatious blue eyes, but she had a penetrating mind and a disarming directness . . . She spoke in a soft scream happily devoid of the slight whine I had come to associate with Southern voices . . . Mrs. Durr made me feel outnumbered, as though I were being cornered by a roomful of reporters, and she used the direct-question method to all without discrimination, no matter how delicate the subject . . . She was a real spellbinder . . . whose particular charm lay in her enormous curiosity about people, her driving passion to find things out, to know about the details and the motives, to trace big events to their small human beginnings. (pp. 13–14).

SITUATION INVERTER

Virginia's goal of improving the welfare of women, blacks, and those in poverty manifested in her work with Joseph Gelders to introduce legislation banning the poll tax in federal elections. This effort was the start of a thirty-year-long struggle to improve voting guidelines in the South. In the 1940s Durr worked singlehandedly without pay for the National Committee to Abolish the Poll Tax. Her political passions conflicted with the traditional role of wife and mother at that time, and it was noted that Durr was a carefree housekeeper and mother who refused to let the contemporary social expectations for women hinder her professional desires (Sullivan, 2003). In 1944, as chair of the Southern Conference on Human Welfare's Washington group, she lobbied to desegregate public facilities in the nation's capital, joined the Arlington, Virginia, branch of the National Association for the Advancement of Colored People (NAACP), and allied with Luther Jackson, professor at Virginia State College, to increase black and white voters around a progressive political platform. Durr's social engagements encouraged her rather conservative spouse, Cliff, to use his position and influence to assist in her dreams. Eventually, he became as radical as Virginia in his quest for social justice and finally left his post with the Federal Communications Commission (FCC), having sharp disagreements with the Federal Bureau of Investigation (FBI) regarding the anti-Communist loyalty program.

It was at this point that the Durrs relocated back to Montgomery, Alabama, to live in Cliff's family home. Back among the unyielding segregationists, Virginia floundered and found her only solace in the constant correspondence she kept with her circle of like-minded friends. Within those letters she found a space in which she could speak freely about the injustices she had come to know and care for so deeply. The South could no longer contain the reinvented Virginia Durr.

TRICKED AND TRICKED OUT:
REVIEWING THE CONTRIBUTIONS OF VIRGINIA DURR

In many instances the early years of Virginia Durr revealed countless encounters with trickster performances. While she was often the recipient of callous, and perhaps well-intentioned, tricks, those encounters undoubtedly ignited the trickster in Durr. Her ambiguous nature was converted into one of passion that later worked to convert others. Her anomalousness was revealed in the unconventional, eclectic social networking skill that enabled her to build a team around her to assist in affecting change. Ultimately the deception and trickery of her very own southern fathers catapulted Durr out of her ambiguity and into action. She was prepared at this point to act as trickster herself—navigating the borders and often playing both sides to achieve her goals. Sullivan (2003) recorded:

> Time and space conspired to broaden the context of Virginia's meditations of the South. With the start of the Montgomery bus boycott in 1955, she was writing from the front lines of the civil rights movement. Through her letters, she created a rich account of life in Alabama from the last days of segregation through the tumultuous years of the late 1950s and the 1960s. She brought a rare insight to this era, sharpened by her marginal status. While she acknowledged her roots in the South, she completely rejected the racial premises of white Southerners. Her allegiances were with the plight and

struggles of black Southerners. She developed friendships with several black women and men in Montgomery, but social interactions
were limited by rigid racial boundaries ... Virginia lived on the
borders of both communities. (p. 24)

CONCLUSION

This account of a white, female trickster evidences the powerful nature of
trickster performances and supports the arguments made in the literature on
cross-cultural mentoring and multicultural and diversity education and other
works espousing social justice as a means to improve the human condition.
Her extensive background fighting in the political arena for voting rights
positioned Durr exclusively to have a unique clarity on the civil rights issues
that shaped the struggles of the 1950s and 1960s. She clearly understood that
the racial attitudes of the South were grounded in more complex issues than
the weak surface arguments such as intellectual inferiority that were popularized. Durr "shared the view that racial discrimination was primarily a
function of economic exploitation, and that core issues of economic inequality and injustice could be effectively met only by interracial political alli-
ances" (Sullivan, 2003, p. 24).

This exploration argues for a more complex understanding of the trickster mode and begs to view the trickster through less derogatory lenses. Often
compared to a Machiavellian performance, the trickster is commonly misun-
derstood as a corrupt figure that will stoop to any level to wield power over
political events and circumstances. Conversely, these figures often exhibit
creativity and ingenuity beyond the average citizen's comprehension and
suffer ridicule and ostracism. In true trickster fashion, Durr acknowledged
and practiced a philosophy that, while at times challenged and misconstrued,
has furthered a cause more so than any other yet to be explored.

REFERENCES

Christen, K. (1998). *Clowns and tricksters: An encyclopedia of tradition and culture.*
     Denver: ABC-CLIO.
Crosby, F. (1999). The developing literature on developmental relationships. In
     A. Murrell, F. Crosby, & R. Ely (Eds.), *Mentoring Dilemmas* (pp. 3–20).
     Mahwah, NJ: Lawrence Erlbahm Associates.
Didion, J. (2001). *Political Fictions.* New York: Knopf.
Ely, R., & Thomas, D. (2001). Cultural diversity at work: The effects of diversity
     perspectives on work group processes and outcomes. *Administrative Science
     Quarterly, 46*(2), 229–273.
Hallinan, J. T. (2001). *Going up the river: Travels in a prison nation.* New York:
     Random House.
Holtzman, L. (2000). *Media messages: What film, television, and popular music teach us
     about race, class, gender, and sexual orientation.* Armonk, NY: Sharpe.

Hyde, L. (1998) *Trickster makes this world*. New York: Farrar, Strauss and Giroux.

Hynes, W. (1993). Mapping the characteristics of mythic tricksters: A heuristic guide. In W. Hynes & W. Doty (Eds.), *Mythical Trickster Figures* (pp. 33–45). Tuscaloosa: University of Alabama Press.

Johnson-Bailey, J., & Cervero, M. (2004). Mentoring in black and white: The intricacies of cross-cultural mentoring. *Journal of Mentoring and Tutoring, 12*(1), 7–21.

Jurich, M. (1998). *Scheherazade's sisters: Trickster heroines and their stories in world literature*. Westport, CT: Greenwood.

Kutz, B. (2001). *Tricksters: A minddance chronicles essay*. Retrieved October 24, 2003, from http://www.ideatree.net/articles/trksters.htm.

Landay, L. (1998). *Madcaps, screwballs and con women: The female trickster in American culture*. Philadelphia: University of Pennsylvania Press.

Menocal, M. R. (2002). *The ornament of the world: How Muslims, Jews, and Christians created a culture of tolerance in medieval Spain*. Boston: Little, Brown.

Radin, P. (1972). *The trickster: A study in American Indian mythology*. New York: Schocken Books.

Reed, T. (1992). *Fifteen jugglers, five believers: Literary politics and the poetics of American social movements*. Berkele: University of California Press.

Sullivan, P. (2003). *Freedom writer: Virginia Foster Durr, letters from the civil rights years*. New York: Routledge.

Wright, S. (2000). *The trickster-function in the theatre of García Lorca*. London: Tamesis.

CHAPTER EIGHT

HEGEMONIC REPRESENTATION

A CRITIQUE OF THE MULTIPLICITY OF DIXIE

Susan Schramm-Pate

INTRODUCTION

Typically, the social studies cultural narrative presented in American history and government textbooks is one of freedom, progress, peace, democracy, and prosperity with things continually improving. This is significant in view of the fact that a transitory glimpse at the history of the nation's expansion, both here on this continent and abroad, is a compilation of unremitting warfare, conquest, colonialism, subjugation, and economic imperialism. In the American South, keenly contested battles still rage over the notion of "heritage," deeply unsettling what Cameron McCarthy calls "racially hegemonic groups" (1998, p. xi).

As an educator in the South, cultural studies has led me to approach the Confederate battle flag and other Confederate symbols as signifiers around which a symbolic battle is being waged, as "floating signifiers" tied to diverse political projects and open to rearticulation and reappropriation within the social studies curriculum. As symbols, they represent an extraordinary place in terms of what McCarthy (1998) calls the "ethnicization of culture." For progressives in education who believe that schools are a major force for social change and social justice, these symbolic battles can expand curriculum to enable young people to become critical readers of their own identity work.

147

One way to enable students to understand the complexity of Confederate symbols in American culture is to use history as a guide to enable them to negotiate identity and difference in the classroom. A cultural studies approach views curriculum as a terrain on which theory, practice, identity, and culture are built, not as reified or essentialist, but as continuously shifting and reconfiguring itself (Gates, 1995; McCarthy, 1998). Because of this continuous movement and repositioning of terrains, cultural studies theorists argue that cultural groups cannot merely be piled up alongside each other and then studied and analyzed separately but that they must be problematized and destabilized from their steady moorings in separate ports (Bhabha, 1994; Carlson, 2002; McCarthy, 1998; McLaren, 1997; Giroux, 1994; Quantz, 1988). Changing the canon to simply reflect multiple voices and a diversity of perspectives and experiences is also inadequate because that simply, as Gates (1995) aptly noted in his critique of the mosaic metaphor of multiculturalism, presents culture as "fixed in a place and separated by grout" (p. 7).

In *The Uses of Culture*, McCarthy (1998) claims that because cultures are interwoven and interdependent, the definition of "culture" depends in part on the existence and interaction with the "other." Thus, in order to understand *relationships* between cultures, we should recognize the ongoing conversation between cultures. Richard Quantz (1988) notes that "a culture group is constituted just as much by what is outside as it is by what is inside and [that] it is defined as much by those outside of the group as by those inside" (p. 3). When studying culture, Quantz also advises placing "the group into its historical situation enmeshed in asymmetrical power relations" (p. 3). To understand this, he argues that we have to understand history as located in the present. For example, he writes:

> We cannot understand the culture of the rural South . . . without clarifying the part played in the construction of that culture by land ownership patterns, cotton, the textile industry, and late 20th Century corporate capitalism. It is not enough to simply place these things in context as a kind of backdrop to a drama, but we must look at these elements as constitutive aspects of Southern rural culture. (p. 3)

In his book *The Location of Culture* (1994), Bhabha suggests that there is a "third space" within cultures that he calls "cultural hybridity." In this sense, "hybridity" is a site of resistance, a strategic reversal of the process of domination that "turns the gaze of discriminated back upon the eye of power" (p. 37). The process of cultural hybridity thus gives rise to something different, something new and unrecognizable, a new area of negotiation of meaning and representation. Hybridity, then, not only displaces the history that creates it but sets up new structures of authority and generates new political initiatives. Hybridity also moves beyond a simple either/or dichotomy to a "third space," or an in-between space that "carries the burden of the meaning of culture" (p. 38). The importance of the "third space" lies in the ways in which the "politics of polarity" can be explored in order for us to emerge as the "others of ourselves" (p. 39). In order to cross what Bhabha calls "discursive liminal space," we first must deconstruct false oppositions. Discursive liminal space does not separate but rather mediates mutual exchanges and relative meanings. Following this model of liminality into the third space, we can deconstruct the gaze of power and its norms and assumptions.

From the beginning, the South has not been an autonomous space with its own history and culture, but rather a space constructed in battle (Schramm-Pate & Carlson, 2003). The South is a creation of a double consciousness in the sense that the "double" of the South (the North) is always a visible or invisible presence in southern heritage narratives (p. 211). By constructing "The South" in opposition to "The North," the gulf is fixed, the die is cast (p. 11). The South has been made to represent the origins of racism in America, from which it supposedly spread like an infection to the North. Racism has been represented as the result of a deficiency in southern character, one of many. This hegemonic representation of southern character places the North on the moral and cultural high ground. Resentment of the northern "other" and of hegemonic representations of southern culture and identity gets played out though Confederate symbols.

This attitude of doing battle against the North becomes easily commodified and commercialized in the redneck and rebel images and lifestyles. The codification of southern poor whites as "hillbillies," "rednecks," and "trailer trash" conjure up images of blue-collar workers speaking with thick southern accents peppered with poor grammar, whose idea of aesthetically pleasing décor is a Confederate battle flag boldly emblazoned in the back window of a pick-up truck and the "double-wide" mobile home. One manifestation of this stereotype is the unchallenged assumption that the South has an exclusive monopoly on the contemporary display of Confederate symbols and other cultural icons that are associated with bigotry and that these racist, classist, and sexist exhibits are rarely found outside of the South.

The tendency to treat the topic of Confederate symbols simplistically and the canonization of Confederate symbols as being uniquely "southern" is one of the weaknesses that mars current social studies curricula. Here Confederate symbols are narrowly "read" as the definitive property of particular groups based on ethnic origins: the culture and meaning of the white planter class during the antebellum era and its descendents in the "New South," versus the culture and style of minority black southerners and the vestiges of oppression, racism, and cruelty.

Further, the construction of a national identity in America historically has occurred by bifurcating Americans into two identity groups, one northern and one southern, one hegemonic and the other subordinate. In *The*

Symbolic Curriculum: Reading the Confederate Flag as a Southern Heritage Text,
Carlson and I argue:

> In order for northern industrial culture to establish its hegemony
> over the American character, it required its Other, its alterity,
> always interrupting and slowing down the inexorable march of
> progress. So the South has been made to assume this role in
> American public life and public consciousness. It has been unable
> to establish its own identity apart from its controlling alter ego,
> the North. (2003, p. 211)

Plus, the notion that the critique and gratuitous opposition of Confederate
symbols is the exclusive property of the North is illegitimate and not empiri-
cally based. There is instead a buoyant play of ideas and a vigorous dialogue
over themes of authority, privilege, freedom, and culture that override the
binary opposition of North/South.

Within the radical cultural hybridity that is foregrounded in postcolonial
and cultural studies literatures, there is a space for the exploration of difference, not simply as a problem but also as an opportunity for conversation
over curriculum reform and the radically diverse communities we now serve
in the university and in schools. By cultural hybridity I am talking about
what Bhabha (1994) calls "the return of the gaze of the discriminated back
on the eye of power" (p. 112). I am talking about what McCarthy (1998)
calls "the interactive, developmental, bricolage of postcolonial knowledge
production that produces discontinuity and disquiet for the colonizer" (p.
149). Hybridization, in this sense, asserts itself in a radical excess of desires
and interests and chooses humor, satire, and parody as its preferred strategies
of resistance.

Confederate symbols are far more dynamic and wide reaching than
the ways they normally get conceptualized in the popular press and school
curricula. The central aim of this chapter is to provide an intervention into
the debate over Confederate symbols as the absolute "cultural property" of
the South by calling attention to the radical cultural hybridity that has
historically evolved within the reality of human encounters in the contemporary world and the implications of this hybridity for social studies curriculum reform.

The remainder of this paper is a detailed historical account of three
bifurcated signifiers that are almost always universally attached to the Confederate "Old South" in our national narrative. They are the concepts of
'Dixie,' 'blackface minstrelsy,' and the fictional archetype 'Jim Crow.' Prac-
titioners might find these three bifurcated signifiers useful when integrating
into broader classroom investigations a rethinking of Confederate symbols
and the relationships between centers and peripheries.

THE SONG "DIXIE"

The first bifurcated signifier that is commonly attached to the Confederate "Old South" but that originated in the North is the song "Dixie" or "I Wish I Was in Dixie's Land." During the twentieth-century American civil rights movement, both the battle flag of the Confederacy and the song "Dixie" gained a racist cast to them as they were taken up by segregationists. Today, the opening line of "Dixie," "I wish I was in the land of cotton," has become a racially charged symbol of old, white, southern pride and the Confederate flag.

"The South" as a distinct American geographical region became popularly known as "Dixie" as early as 1862 (Sacks & Sacks, 1993). Today the song "Dixie" is strongly identified with the Old South and to hear it played stirs emotions and exposes timeworn rifts across American society. The tune was frequently requested by President Abraham Lincoln before it was adopted as a Confederate anthem and marching song of Confederate troops during the Civil War, and it was played at Jefferson Davis's inauguration as Confederate president in 1861 (Timberg, 1999).

Popularized by northern minstrels who performed in the "blackface" style made fashionable by Al Jolson, the original lyrics to "Dixie" are in the stereotyped voice of African Americans as they supposedly long for a return to plantation life and slavery. Misspellings and dialect (i.e., ethnic pronunciations), however, do not appear in most contemporary versions of the song—as they do in the earlier versions (National Public Radio, n.d.).

The original authorship of the song "Dixie" is contested. According to Howard L. Sacks and Judith Rose Sacks in *Way up North in Dixie: A Black Family's Claim to the Confederate Anthem*, some attribute the tune to Daniel Decatur Emmett, a native of Mount Vernon, Ohio, who wrote early American standards such as "Blue-Tail Fly" and "Turkey in the Straw" and performed in blackface at northern minstrel shows with a group called Bryant's Minstrels and the Virginia Minstrels (1993). Emmett was a talented fiddler, singer, banjoist, comedian, and author of plays and songs for minstrel shows. The rare book manuscript and special collections library of Duke University houses a historic piece of sheet music that credits the title "I Wish I Was in Dixie's Land" to "Dan Emmett as writing and composing the song for Bryant's Minstrels" (National Public Radio, n.d). However, Sacks and Sacks (1993) argue that the song "Dixie" was really a tune passed on to Emmett by a pair of African American brothers, Ben and Lew Snowden, who were born to parents who were slaves. The Snowden family of Clinton, Knox County, Ohio, was an African American family of musicians who performed banjo and fiddle tunes and sang popular songs for black and white audiences throughout rural Ohio from the 1850s to the early twentieth century.

Sacks and Sacks (1993) advance the theory that "Dixie" is a childhood recollection from Mrs. Ellen Snowden and that Emmett learned it from her sons, a pair of black musicians whom he knew from his hometown. Snowden's parents had been slaves in Maryland, but by the 1820s were living outside Mount Vernon, Ohio, not far from where Emmett's family lived.

For many contemporary African Americans "Dixie" is a symbol of racism and slavery. Thomasina Neely-Chandler, an ethnomusicologist and music professor at Spelman College in Atlanta, Georgia, says the most important thing to remember is that "Dixie" is a harmful misrepresentation of Blacks. "It's not the song or the text," Neely-Chandler says, "so much as how it's used in a distorted way to present a particular people with an image that doesn't really represent them" (Jim Crow Museum of Racist Memorabilia). During the civil rights movement the divide over the song deepened. According to University of Mississippi historian Charles Reagan Wilson,

> [Blacks] would sing a song like 'We Shall Overcome' or 'The Battle Hymn of the Republic' . . . But then opponents of integration and black rights would sing 'Dixie' as a kind of counter-song asserting white privilege and white supremacy. (Jim Crow Museum of Racist Memorabilia)

Just as there are differing theories of "Dixie's" origin, there are also differing theories as to its symbolism. For example, some maintain that while Emmett probably penned the tune, he was influenced by the concept of runaway slaves and that the tune embodies a slave idea of paradise. According to musician Mike Petee, Emmett's inspiration for the tune of "Dixie" may have been this imaginary paradise:

> It's New York City . . . It's rainy, it's cold and what minstrels loved to do was tour the north during summer and in the winter they want to go down south. So he's in the north, it's cold, it's dreary, his thoughts go to Dixie, where he wants to be. (Jim Crow Museum)

Howard Stack believes "Dixie" retains a quintessential American quality:

> What it tells us is that black, white, male, female, southern, northern, slave, free, urban, rural—these aren't separate realms . . . The story of the American experience is the story of movement between these realms . . . Understanding the creation and recreation of "Dixie" is that story encapsulated in the words and music of a single song. (Jim Crow Museum)

Chief Justice William H. Rehnquist often includes a rendition of "Dixie" in what he calls his "old-fashioned sing-alongs" (Timberg, 1999). At the Fourth

Circuit Judicial Conference in 1999, which included hundreds of federal judges and lawyers from Maryland, Virginia, West Virginia, North Carolina, and South Carolina, an invitation read, "We hope you will plan to join in singing favorite old songs with the Chief Justice!" (Timberg, 1999, p. B1). Rehnquist stood at the front of the room leading the lawyers and judges as they sang from songbooks such American standards as "The Battle Hymn of the Republic," "America the Beautiful," and "Anchors Aweigh." Many lawyers avoided singing when "Dixie" began. "The song is offensive to African Americans," said Brent Clinkscale, a black South Carolina lawyer at the conference, "I think it's nostalgic of slavery" (as quoted in Timberg, 1999, p. B1).

Others at the conference viewed the song as nothing more than a piece of Americana appropriate for a mostly southern conference. According to George C. Freeman, Jr., a white Richmond lawyer, "I think all this stuff about reliving history is overblown . . . I really think that the past is the past" (as quoted in Timberg, 1999, p. B1). Zoe Sanders Nettles, a white lawyer from South Carolina, approached Rehnquist after the sing-a-long and registered her objections saying, "I really don't think we should sing 'Dixie' " (as quoted in Timberg, 1999, p. B1). Federal Judge U. W. Clemon of Birmingham, who is black, said the song "symbolizes a determination to keep things as they were, that is, to keep blacks in a subservient position" (as quoted in Timberg, 1999, p. B1).

Some contemporary musical performers have tried to make the song "Dixie" acceptable by combining it with other tunes that acknowledge its complex history. For example, Elvis Presley often mixed "Dixie" into his medley with the "Battle Hymn of the Republic" (a song written for the Union during the Civil War) and the spiritual "All My Trials," and jazz singer Rene Marie combined it with Billie Holliday's "Strange Fruit"—a dramatic depiction of a lynching. When George W. Bush spoke at the University of South Carolina's graduation commencement last May 2003, the tune "Dixie" was interwoven in an instrumental medley of "patriotic" songs performed by the school's band. I turn now to the second bifurcated signifier that is associated with the Confederate Old South but that originated in the North, blackface minstrelsy.

BLACKFACE MINSTRELSY

Blackface minstrelsy was a very popular form of American entertainment in the nineteenth century. The name derived from white performers who blackened their faces with burnt cork makeup. In this form of entertainment northern white males masquerading as blacks typically performed songs, dances, and dialect inspired by African Americans living on southern plantations. According to Sellman (n.d.), while American minstrelsy helped create fictional and highly demeaning stereotypes of African Americans, it also captured something of the distinctive qualities of African American humor and song, especially during the late nineteenth century, when a number of African American minstrel troupes appeared.

Blackface minstrelsy was known for its lively songs and dances and for infamous use of outlandish stereotypes and offensive dialect. Examples of these exaggerated stereotypes include characters such as Jim Crow, who in the eyes of white northerners was a naïve, clumsy, devil-may-care, southern plantation slave, who appeared dressed in rags. Another example that represented white northerners' idea of a typical black male was the character Zip Coon or Dandy Jim, who portrayed the northern urban black as an absurd man who wore a blue coat with tails. According to Thomas Hampson's Public Broadcasting System's (PBS) worldwide website called *I Hear America Singing*, Stephen Foster, who was made famous by early songs in minstrelsy, advocated for depicting the black condition in the nineteenth century with compassion and dignity. For example, he eliminated offensive words in his dialect songs and refused to allow his sheet music to portray images that poked fun at Blacks.

According to author Robert C. Toll in his book *Blacking Up: The Minstrel Show in Nineteenth-Century America*, blackface minstrelsy had its origins after the War of 1812, when America underwent many changes including increases in urban population and a desire to distance itself from English culture (1974). Ironically, it was an Englishman, Charles Matthews, who first characterized blacks and used black material in his theater productions. Toll notes that Matthews, who was captivated by black music and dialect during his visit to the United States, began transcribing sermons, lore, songs, and speeches and studying black dialects. After witnessing at the African Theater Company in New York City a black actor's performance of Hamlet's soliloquy become interrupted by an audience that demanded the actor stop the soliloquy and instead sing "Possum up a Gum Tree," Matthews studied the song and included it in his "Trip to America" act (Toll, 1974).

According to Clayton W. Henderson (1986), in *The New Grove Dictionary of American Music*, when minstrel shows first began, their main purpose was just as an entr'acte in theaters or circuses. As their popularity grew, these minstrelsies started to become independent. Henderson (1986) also notes that New York City is the birthplace of the blackface minstrel shows and the place where minstrel shows enjoyed the greatest popularity until the American Civil War ended.

By 1856, the state of New York had ten full time resident companies and twice that many a decade later (Jackson, 1995). New York's ten major minstrel houses that thrived during the 1850s and 1860s included large theaters such as Bowery and Barnum's Museum, showboats that toured around New York, and newly built theaters known as "Ethiopian Opera Houses" (1995). Between 1840 and 1870 numerous duos, trios, and quartets of performers formed troupes and traveled to the White House where they entertained such presidents as Polk, Filmore, Tyler, and Pierce (1995).

In his critically acclaimed book about race, culture, and African American humor, *On the Real Side: Laughing, Lying, and Signifying: The Underground Tradition of African American Humor That Transformed American Culture, from Slavery to Richard Pryor*, Mel Watkins (1994) argues that minstrel shows were the most popular form of entertainment during the nineteenth century, that they had a powerful impact on American culture, and that minstrelsy helped transform American humor and, to a lesser extent, African American popular music. In particular, Watkins notes that minstrelsy served to "codify the public image of blacks as the prototypical Fool or Sambo" (1994, p. 35). In performance, minstrels exuded an energy bordering on the manic, as Toll (1974) vividly recounted:

> They burst on stage in makeup [that] gave the impression of huge eyes and gaping mouths. They dressed in ill-fitting, patchwork clothes, and spoke in heavy "ni**er" dialects. Once on stage, they could not stay still for an instant. Even while sitting, they contorted their bodies, cocked their heads . . . and twisted their outstretched legs . . . [Their] seemingly compulsive movements charged the entire performance with excitement. (p. 40)

Two of the most famous African Americans to emerge from minstrelsy, James Bland and William Henry Lane (a.k.a. "Master Juba"), were praised by English author, Charles Dickens for their unique, lively dances that combined European dance with African tradition to form a distinctive style (Ivey, 2003). Much of the music that was performed by the blackface performers contained melodies that had originated in Great Britain. For example, "Jim Crow" resembles an Irish folk tune, the melody to "My Long Tail Blue" is similar to a Scottish folk song, and "Gumbo Chaff" is identical to the English tune "Bow Wow Wow" (Ivey, 2003). According to Henderson (1986), the Virginia Minstrels originated the popular format in which a quartet would gather around in a semicircle with one man playing a tambourine sitting across from a man playing the bones, while two others whistled, stomped their feet, or shouted along.

Clearly, blackface minstrelsy is the most shameful chapter within the history of American musicals. Not only did it embody racial hatred, but also it showed blacks as naïve buffoons singing and dancing their days away, gobbling "chitlins," stealing the occasional watermelon, and inexplicably expressing their love for "ol massuh." According to Toll (1974), these negative images were "the first example of the way American popular culture would exploit and manipulate Afro-Americans and their culture to please and benefit white Americans" (p. 51). At the same time, Toll noted that "it was the first indication of the powerful influence Afro-American culture would have on the performing arts in America" (p. 51). Although black performers found opportunities in minstrelsy, they also found themselves trapped by its restrictive racial conventions. As Watkins cautioned, "if African Americans adopted many of the epithets and referents of minstrel humor, they did not necessarily accept [its] general racist connotations" (as quoted in Sellman, n.d, p. 6).

The legacy of minstrelsy remains extensive and complex. Long after vaudeville became the principal popular entertainment in major cities of the Northeast, minstrel companies continued to tour the small towns of that region and widely through the South and Midwest (Sellman, n.d). Featuring degrading heavy dialects and perpetuating extreme stereotypes, the shows were intended to invoke a warm nostalgia for the bygone days of plantation slavery. Combined, minstrelsy's musical, dance, and comic legacies shaped performances well into the twentieth century including vaudeville, musical theater, motion pictures, radio, and television. I turn now to a third bifurcated signifier that is commonly attached to the Confederate Old South but that originated outside of the South, Jim Crow.

JIM CROW

In the Reconstruction period closely following the American Civil War, three constitutional amendments (i.e., the Thirteenth, Fourteenth, and Fifteenth) and a fundamental civil rights act were passed to provide rights to former slaves. The Thirteenth Amendment abolished slavery, and the Civil Rights Act of 1866 documented that former slaves were citizens with equal civil rights and that the federal courts had jurisdiction over state courts in cases involving African Americans and other persons of color. The Fifteenth Amendment, ratified in 1870, prohibited the federal and state governments from denying male citizens the right to vote "on account of race, color, or previous condition of servitude" (Patrick, Pious, & Ritchie, 2000, p. 589).

Originally constructed to deal with the rights of former slaves, the Fourteenth Amendment was originally ratified on July 28, 1868, to protect the newly freed slaves from states seeking to nullify their constitutional rights, and it later provided the foundation for civil rights in the midtwentieth century in cases such as *Brown versus Board of Education*. After the Civil War, southern states (i.e., former Confederate states) were required to ratify it in order to be readmitted into the Union.

The Fourteenth Amendment is arguably the most important of the constitutional amendments since it radically changed the definition of the United States citizen and is the source of the clause of due process and equal protection for all citizens. The amendment guaranteed African Americans citizenship and prohibited the states from denying or abridging their fundamental rights by declaring, "All persons born or naturalized in the United States . . . are citizens of the United States . . . No state shall . . . deny to any person within its jurisdiction the equal protection of the laws" (2000, p. 588). Of course the Fourteenth Amendment did not erase the color line between blacks and whites that was drawn by custom and social mores in a myriad of cultural activities and institutions in both the North and the South known as "Jim Crow." In 1896, the *Plessy versus Ferguson* case legitimized Jim Crow laws and the Jim Crow way of life. In 1891, a group of African Americans challenged Jim Crow laws by having Homer A. Plessy, who was seven-eighths white and one-eighth black (therefore, legally black according to the one-drop rule), sit in a white-only railroad coach. According to The Jim Crow Museum of Racist Memorabilia (2003),

> After Plessy was arrested, his lawyer argued that Louisiana did not have the right to label one citizen as White and one as Black for the purposes of restricting their rights and privileges. The United States Supreme Court, by a 7-2 vote, upheld the Louisiana law declaring racial separation as state law constitutional as long as local governments provided legal process and legal freedoms for Blacks equal to Whites. (para 3)

In 1896, the Supreme Court handed down a landmark decision on the meaning of this equal protection clause. In *Plessy versus Ferguson*, the Court ruled that the Fourteenth Amendment allowed a state to segregate Blacks and Whites by providing "separate but equal" facilities for blacks in all institutions, including schools.

According to the Jim Crow Museum of Racist Memorabilia (2003) website, The name *Jim Crow* is often used to describe the segregation laws, rules, and customs that arose after Reconstruction ended in 1877 and after the Plessy ruling and continued until the mid-1960s.

> Jim Crow was more than a series of rigid anti-Black laws. It became a way of life—a racial caste system that operated primarily, but not exclusively, in the South and in border states . . . Under Jim Crow, African Americans were relegated to the status of second class citizens with Jim Crow representing the legitimization of anti-Black racism. (para 4)

In 1959, Stetson Kennedy (1959/1990), the author of the *Jim Crow Guide*, offered these "simple rules" that blacks were supposed to observe in conversing with whites:

1. Never assert or even intimate that a White person is lying;

2. Never impute dishonorable intentions to a White person;

3. Never suggest that a White person is from an inferior class;

4. Never lay claim to, or overly demonstrate, superior knowledge or intelligence;

5. Never curse a White person;

6. Never laugh derisively at a White person; and

7. Never comment upon the appearance of a White female. (pp. 216–17)

Kennedy (1959/1990) also noted that the Jim Crow system was undergirded by the following beliefs or rationalizations:

1. Whites were superior to Blacks in all important ways, including but not limited to intelligence, morality, and civilized behavior;

2. Sexual relations between Blacks and Whites would produce a mongrel race which would destroy America;

3. Treating Blacks as equals would encourage interracial sexual unions; and

4. If necessary, violence must be used to keep Blacks at the bottom of the racial hierarchy.

The Jim Crow Museum delineates the following Jim Crow etiquette standards to illustrate how inclusive and pervasive these norms were:

1. A Black male could not offer his hand (to shake hands) with a White man because it implied being socially equal. Obviously, a Black male could not offer his hand or any other part of his body to a White woman, because he risked being accused of rape;

2. Blacks and Whites were not supposed to eat together. If they did eat together, Whites were to be served first, and some sort of partition was to be placed between them;

3. Under no circumstance was a Black male to offer to light the cigarette of a White female—that gesture implied intimacy;

4. Blacks were not allowed to show public affection toward one another in public, especially kissing, because it offended Whites;

5. Jim Crow etiquette prescribed that Blacks were introduced to Whites, never Whites to Blacks. For example: "Mr. Peters (the White person), this is Charlie (the Black person), that I spoke to you about";

6. Whites did not use courtesy titles of respect when referring to Blacks, for example, Mr., Mrs., Miss., Sir, or Ma'am. Instead, Blacks were called by their first names. Blacks had to use courtesy titles when referring to Whites, and were not allowed to call them by their first names;

7. If a Black person rode in a car driven by a White person, the Black person sat in the back seat, or the back of a truck; and

8. White motorists had the right-of-way at all intersections.

Many southern historians clearly articulate how Jim Crow etiquette operated in conjunction with Jim Crow laws (i.e., Black Codes) (Edgar, 1998). According to Kennedy (1959/1990), when most people think of Jim Crow they think of the laws that excluded blacks from public transport and facilities, juries, jobs, and neighborhoods, not of Jim Crow etiquette.

The Thirteenth, Fourteenth, and Fifteenth Amendments to the Constitution had granted people of color the same legal protection as whites; however, after 1877 and the election of Republican Rutherford B. Hayes, many southern, northern and border states continued restricting the liberties of people of color (Jim Crow Museum of Racist Memorabilia, 2003). Jim Crow states (i.e., Alabama, Florida, Georgia, Kentucky, Louisiana, Mississippi, North Carolina, Oklahoma, South Carolina) passed statutes severely regulating social interactions between the races (Jim Crow Museum of Racist Memorabilia, 2003). Jim Crow signs were placed above water fountains, door entrances and exits, and in front of public facilities, and there were separate hospitals for blacks and whites, separate prisons, separate public and private schools, separate churches, separate cemeteries, separate public restrooms and separate public accommodations. In most instances, black facilities were grossly inferior—generally older, less well-kept, and in other cases, there were no black facilities—no "colored" public restroom, no public beach, no place to sit or eat (Jim Crow Museum of Racist Memorabilia, 2003). In short, the *Plessy* ruling gave Jim Crow States a legal way to ignore their constitutional obligations to their black citizens. For example, typical Jim Crow laws maintained that schools for white children and schools for black children be conducted separately, and even reform schools kept children of color and white children separate (Jim Crow Museum of Racist Memorabilia, 2003).

While teachers who dared to teach in schools, colleges, or institutions where whites and blacks were enrolled as students were merely considered guilty of a misdemeanor and often fined, the Jim Crow laws and system of etiquette for blacks were undergirded by violence, real and threatened. According to the Jim Crow Museum of Racist Memorabilia (2003) website:

> Blacks who violated Jim Crow norms, for example, by drinking from the White water fountain or trying to vote, risked their homes, their jobs, even their lives. Whites could physically beat Blacks with impunity. Blacks had little legal recourse against these assaults because the Jim Crow criminal justice system was all-White: police, prosecutors, judges, juries, and prison officials . . . Violence was instrumental for Jim Crow and the method of social control that supported Jim Crow norms with lynching the most extreme forms, lynchings were public—often sadistic—murders carried out by mobs . . . [In] 1882 when the first reliable data were collected and 1968 when lynching had become rare, there were 4,730 known lynchings including 3,440 Black men and women. In the mid-1800s,

Whites constituted the majority of victims (and perpetrators); however, by the period of Radical Reconstruction, Blacks became the
most frequent lynching victims ... Lynching was used in southern
and border states to keep newly freedmen "in their places." (paragraph 5, retrieved October 5, 2003)

How did the name *Jim Crow* become associated with these so-called
"Black Codes" and "Black Etiquette," which took away many of the rights
that had been granted to blacks through the Thirteenth, Fourteenth, and
Fifteenth Amendments? Clues can be traced to northern blackface minstrelsy. White entertainer Thomas D. "Daddy" Rice caused a nationwide
sensation in the 1820s when he donned burnt cork to perform the song
"Jump Jim Crow" during the intermission of a popular show. According to
Watkins (1994), Rice based his Jim Crow sketch on a song and dance he had
seen performed, in the words of Watkins, by a "crippled and deformed black
stable groom" (p. 40). The verse and chorus of the song were simple:

> *Come listen all you gals and boys,*
> *I'm going to sing a little song,*
> *My name is Jim Crow.*
> *First on de heel tap, den on the toe*
> *Eb'ry time I wheel about I jump Jim Crow.*
> *Wheel about an' turn about an' do jes so.*
> *An' eb'ry time I wheel about, I jump Jim Crow.* (Kenrick,
> retrieved October 5, 2003)

According to Watkins (1994), Rice dressed his Jim Crow character in
the long blue coat and striped pants associated with another popular stereotype, the stage "Yankee." Rice's Jim Crow song-and-dance routine was an
astounding success that took him in 1832 from the northern American cities
of Cincinnati, Pittsburgh, Philadelphia, and New York to European cities
such as London and Dublin (Watkins, 1994). His Jim Crow character, along
with counterparts Jim Dandy and Zip Coon, became a standard in the show.
Rice's subsequent characters played to receptive white audiences that enjoyed the racist portrayals of blacks as "Sambos," "Coons," and "Dandies"
that sang and danced like grinning fools (Watkins, 1994). According to the
Museum of Racist Memorabilia (2003) website:

> By 1838, the term "Jim Crow" was being used as a collective racial
> epithet for Blacks, not as offensive as ni**er, but as offensive as
> coon or darkie. Obviously, the popularity of minstrel shows aided
> the spread of Jim Crow as a racial slur ... By the end of the 19th
> Century, the words Jim Crow were less likely to be used to derisively
> describe Blacks; instead the phrase Jim Crow was being used to

describe laws and customs which oppressed Blacks (paragraph 2, retrieved October 5, 2003).

Inspired by Thomas Rice's solo efforts, four White men calling themselves "Dan Emmett's Virginia Minstrels" debuted at a blackface revue at New York's Bowery Amphitheater in 1843. According to Kendrick (1996), this is the first known troupe to offer a full evening of blackface entertainment. Touring Europe and the United States, in addition to performing "Jump Jim Crow," they introduced songs such as "Blue Tail Fly" and "Polly Wolly Doodle." As a result of Rice's travels and of the traveling Emmett troupe "Jim Crow" became more than a popular song, it became a by-word for legalized racial oppression. As Richard Wormser (2003) wrote:

In 1828, Jim Crow was born. He began his strange career as a minstrel caricature of a black man created by a white man, Thomas "Daddy" Rice, to amuse white audiences. By the 1880s, Jim Crow had become synonymous with a complex system of racial laws and customs in the South that enabled white social, legal, and political domination of blacks. Blacks were segregated, deprived of their right to vote, and subjected to verbal abuse, discrimination, and violence without redress in the courts or support by the white community. (p. xi)

The notion that God supported racial segregation was perpetuated through clergymen of various Judeo-Christian religious institutions, as well as laymen who reinforced the notion that whites were the "chosen" people, and blacks were cursed to be servants. Social Darwinists, at every educational level, buttressed the belief that blacks were innately, intellectually, and culturally inferior to whites. Miscegenation statutes, intended to prevent racial interbreeding, led the list of Jim Crow Laws and further illustrate that racism existed nationwide. According to Susan Falck (2003) in *Jim Crow Legislation Overview,*

At least 127 laws prohibiting interracial marriage and cohabitation were passed between 1865 and the 1950s nationwide, with 37 percent of the statutes passed outside the South . . . Punishment for miscegenation in state statutes was still in force in the 1960s in Delaware, Florida, Indiana, Maryland, Mississippi, and North Carolina. (Retrieved October 12, 2003)

Southern and northern heritage was linked to a cultural politics of establishing bloodlines and "purifying" the white race. Clergymen and prosegregation politicians in both the North and the South gave eloquent speeches on the great danger of integration: the mongrelization of the white race. Added evidence that Jim Crow existed nationwide is evident in education laws of the era. States outside the South enacted 23 percent of the laws that authorized segregated schools, and seven of the twelve laws required race to be considered in adoption petitions that were passed outside the South (Falck, 2003). Although the 1954 United States Supreme Court decision in *Brown versus Topeka Board of Education,* formally made segregation illegal, historian C. Vann Woodward estimated that 106 new segregation laws were passed nationwide between the *Brown* decision and the end of 1956 (Falck, 2003). While, not surprisingly, the South legislated the greatest percentage of these Jim Crow laws with 78 percent, other sections of the nation were involved: The West had 13 percent, the Midwest had 6 percent and the Northeast had 3 percent (Falck, 2003).

CONCLUSION

Not only do Confederate cultural icons bifurcate borders delineated by race, class, gender, and the Mason Dixon Line, but bigotry does as well. My principle concern in this chapter, has been to argue that the North/South binary must be decidedly interrupted in order to investigate issues of culture and identity and to provide three examples of powerful signifiers that could be interwoven into the curriculum to enable students to begin to deconstruct the binary and the national discourses that define the "South." If we consider the North and the South as fixed and separate, we have neglected both the historical and the contemporary heterogeneity of human interactions and lives.

Cultural studies provides arenas in which cultural hybridity can be displayed in curriculum, and even flaunted, through tropes such as the caricature, tragedy, and melancholy of Dixie, blackface minstrelsy, and Jim Crow. To understand Confederate symbols more broadly, we must broaden our understanding to include processes of globalization (big business in the New South) and hybridity (new possibilities for North and South—bound together for better or worse).

McCarthy (1998) argues, "The complexities of this world must not be masked but addressed and confronted in the multicultural world that rages into the 21st century" (p. 160). In this sense, proponents of multicultural education must cease to understand culture and identity in static and atheoretical terms but instead must highlight the complex interpretation of cultures. By deconstructing the contemporary bifurcation of Confederate symbols and other cultural icons of Dixie, we may eventually craft a different, more inclusive version of southern history and examine how that new vision has competed with more traditional perspectives.

In this chapter, I attempted to complicate that part of American culture's careful construction that is situated within the categories of Dixie, blackface minstrels, and Jim Crow. By working toward breaking down the Yankee/ Rebel dichotomy, we may begin to understand how meanings and symbols of culture have no primordial unity or fixity. That is to say, Confederate symbols can be appropriated, translated, rehistoricized, and read anew, and we can challenge, as Bhabha notes, "our sense of the historical identity of culture as a homogenizing, unifying force, authenticated by the ordinary Past, kept alive in the national tradition of the People" (p. 37).

REFERENCES

Bhabha, H. (1994). *The location of culture*. New York: Routledge.

Carlson, D. (2002). *Leaving safe harbors: Toward a new progressivism in American education and public life*. New York: RoutledgeFalmer.

Edgar, W. (1998). *South Carolina: A history*. Columbia: University of South Carolina Press.

Falck, S. (2003). *Jim Crow Legislation Overview*. Retrieved October 12, 2003 from http://www.jimcrowhistory.org/resources/lessonplans/hs_es_jim_crow_law.

Gates, H. L. (1995). Multiculturalism: A conversation among different voices. In D. Levine, R. Lowe, B. Peterson, & R. Tenorio (Eds.), *Rethinking Schools* (pp. 7–9). New York: New York Press.

Giroux, H. (1994). Doing cultural studies: Youth and the challenge of pedagogy. *Harvard Educational Review*, 64 (3), 278–308.

Hampson, T. (n.d.). Hear America singing. *Daniel Decatur Emmet & the American Minstrel, 1815–1904*. Retrieved June 8, 1999 from http://www.pbs.org/wnet/ihas/icon/emmet.html.

Henderson, C. W. (1986). Music. *The New Grove Dictionary of American Music*. Volume 3. New York: MacMillan Press Limited London Groves Dictionaries of Music, pp. 245–247.

Ivey, J. D. (2003). Blackface minstrelsy. *Antebellum America 1794–1865*. Retrieved October 5, 2003 from http://www.uncp.edu/home/canada/work/allam/17841865/music/music4.htm.

Jackson, K. (1995). (Ed.). *The encyclopedia of New York City*. New Haven, CT: Yale University Press.

Jim Crow Museum of Racist Memorabilia. *What was Jim Crow?* Retrieved October 5, 2003, from http://www.ferris.edu/news/jimcrow/what.htm.

Kennedy, S. (1959/1990). *Jim Crow guide: The way it was*. Boca Raton: Florida Atlantic University Press.

Kenrick, J. A. History of the musical minstrel shows: *"That shuff-a-lin' throng."* Retrieved October 5, 2003, from http://www.musicals101.com/minstrel.htm.

McCarthy, C. (1998). *The uses of culture: Education and the limits of ethnic affiliation*. New York: Routledge.

McLaren, P. (1997). Decentering whiteness: In search of a revolutionary multiculturalism. *Multicultural Education*, 5(2), pp. 4–11.

National Public Radio. "Dixie: Present at the creation." Retrieved November 11, 2002, from http://www.npr.org/programs/morning/features/patc/dixie/index.html.

Patrick, J. J., Pious, R. M., & Ritchie, D. A. (2000). *The Oxford Essential Guide to the U. S. Government*. New York: Berkley Books.

Quantz, R. A. (1988). *Culture: A critical perspective*. A paper presented at the American Educational Studies Association. Toronto, Canada.

Sacks, H. L., & Sacks, J. R. (1993). *Way up north in Dixie: A black family's claim to the Confederate anthem*. Washington, DC: Smithsonian Institution Press.

Schramm-Pate, S. L., & Carlson, D. (2003). The symbolic curriculum: Reading the Confederate flag as a southern heritage text. In G. Dimitriadis and D. Carlson (Eds.), *Promises to Keep: Cultural Studies, Democratic Education, and Public Life* (pp. 203–225). New York: RoutledgeFalmer.

Sellman, J. C. (n.d). Africana.com ARTS Entertainment & Inspiration—*Minstrelsy*. Retrieved November 11, 2002, http://www.africna.com/Articles/tt_200.htm.

Timberg, C. (July 22, 1999). Rehnquist's inclusion of "Dixie" strikes a sour note. *The Washington Post*, p. B1.

Toll, R. C. (1974). *Blacking up: The minstrel show in nineteenth-century America*. New York: Oxford University Press.

Watkins, M. (1994). *On the real side: Laughing, lying, and signifying: The underground tradition of African American humor that transformed American culture, from slavery to Richard Pryor*. New York: Simon & Schuster.

Wormser, R. (2003). *The rise and fall of Jim Crow*. New York: St. Martin's.

CHAPTER NINE

WORLD LANGUAGE OTHER THAN
ENGLISH PROGRAM (WLOE)

CONFRONTING DIVERSITY THROUGH READING, WRITING, AND DISCUSSION

RICHARD R. LUSSIER

INTRODUCTION

On August 28, 1963, on the Mall in Washington, D.C., Dr. Martin Luther King enunciated a vision of racial harmony and peace that has yet to be fully realized in the United States and that, unfortunately, has been challenged by a recrudescence of racism in the thinking of many in the dominant Anglo-Saxon culture of our society (hooks, 2000). There is a tendency to blame people of color and working-class poor people for their predicament and to believe that, if only they would accept white, middle-class values and work harder, then all of our problems would be solved (McLaren & Sleeter, 1995; Spring, 2002). In the more rural parts of our country, cultural battles over the Confederate flag or the immigration of Mexicans are being fought in the name of "southern" or American heritage (Horvitz, 1998).

Symbols such as the flag and how they are used in our culture to represent values and heritage are indicative of who has the right to determine fundamental civic meanings and what their contents should be. There is considerable controversy over what we teach our young people about the meaning of U.S. history, our diverse and pluralistic society, and how to behave appropriately as citizens (Apple, 2000; Nash, Crabtree & Dunn, 1997; Ross, 1997). The acrimony of the conflict over the content of the moral, social, and political curriculum of the public schools should not surprise us in view of the power of these institutions, attended by 90 percent of American youth, to inculcate values, attitudes, and beliefs (Spring, 2002). Spencer's nineteenth-century curricular question, "[W]hat knowledge is of most worth?" (essentially nonscientific and begging for a subjective, value-laden response that is inherently controversial, but still worth asking) must be supplemented by Michael Apple's query, "Whose knowledge is of most worth?" (Apple, 2000) For example, whose version of slavery, secession, our many wars, the development of capitalism, and so on, will be taught to our young people and for what purpose? One may not agree with the judgments of textbook critics such as the Gablers in Texas (Apple, 2000), who emphasize the importance of interpretation in the presentation of curricular materials to students.

Recently in a very rural South Carolina high school, I conducted a pilot study of students' attitudes, values, and beliefs regarding diversity in their demographically changing school district. Where once the community was 70 percent rural white and 30 percent African American, the Hispanic population has recently burgeoned, changing the demographics of this high school to 45 percent African American, 5 percent Hispanic, and less than 50 percent white. In 2004, fully 20 percent of the population of the county's four schools are Hispanic, mainly from Mexico and Guatemala. My pilot study revealed that white students in particular were having difficulty adjusting to increased diversity and were deeply resentful of rules recently put in place to ban Confederate symbols from the school. They sensed in an inchoate, but very real, way that their traditional assumptions about life in their community were now under threat from increased diversity. Many white students called for shipping the Mexican population back across the border and for a reinstatement of the symbols of the Confederacy to prominence within the school (e.g., the establishment of Confederate Memorial Day on May 10, complete with flags, honor guard, and a schoolwide assembly). The study revealed the need for helping all students cope with diversity and change by dealing directly with these issues as part of the curriculum. Activities designed to teach students to "dialogue across differences" (Burbules & Rice, 1991) were used to help students deal with their feelings and values in a way that enabled them to value themselves as well as others. Failure to deal with these issues through mere suppression of such things as Confederate regalia could conceivably work to keep the pot simmering, leading potentially to an interracial explosion.

The ideological issues underlying diversity education in a public school do not lend themselves to the same kind of scientific analysis as in the study of physics (in which the questions posed are empirical rather than normative); they constitute, rather, the hotly contested terrain of competing values, attitudes, and beliefs (Aronowitz & Giroux, 1991). The question, however, is not simply one of whose values shall prevail, as if the school were a battleground with victors and vanquished, but rather if and how competing value orientations can coexist, influence one another, and serve as useful material for teaching students about the arduous process of democratic micropolitics, that is, the direct, daily negotiation of difference that they will often face as adults. Will students deal effectively with difficult issues, or will they simply run back to the comforting company of the likeminded, thereby losing an opportunity to work in a civically responsible way with those who are different, with those who may disagree completely with them? What is at issue here is nothing less than the preservation and the deepening of substantive democracy (Gutmann, 1997; Lisman, 1998) within our vast, procedurally democratic republic. Will students always be only spectators, or will they occasionally get to play in our political game?

As nationalism and jingoism at home experience a renaissance in the wake of the collapse of communism and the end of the cold war between East and West, the place of the school as the "public square" (Sears, 1998; Sears & Letts, 1999) in which different social stakeholders learn to talk to one another substantively and in a civil tone is of crucial importance if we are to minimize social strife or obviate it altogether. When white tenth- and eleventh-grade students are able to ask in all seriousness why they must attend school with black people—sometimes within earshot—it becomes obvious that there is still a serious racial problem in South Carolina. What should educators do, if anything? Should they turn a blind eye or simply repeat the usual bromides about equal educational opportunity for all? Alternatively, should they not forthwith engage our impressionable young people who have these questions in substantive dialogue as a step in the direction of Dr. King's vision of building the "Beloved Community" in and through the schools?

How educators deal with students' perceptions of others who form recognizable linguistic, social, ethnic, racial, and religious minorities within schools is of the greatest consequence for American society (Banks, 1996, Gay, 2000, Howard, 1999; Nieto, 1999). It is not enough to expect that with more education and increased academic achievement as defined by standardized measures of success that young people will develop tolerance—perhaps even acceptance—of those who differ from them in any significant way. Indeed, some of the world's greatest war criminals have been well-educated men. For example, Radovan Karadjich was educated as a psychiatrist and lived among his Muslim neighbors peacefully in Sarajevo until the Yugoslav federation fell apart. He subsequently joined other Bosnian Serbs in an effort to exterminate Muslims in a campaign of "ethnic cleansing" directed at crushing the independence of the multinational Bosnian state in 1992 (Malcolm, 1994). How could one so well educated commit such a crime?

The problem before us is educational in the broadest sense of the term: if we wish to develop multicultural understanding in our young people, we must immerse them in cultural diversity while they are in school (Lindsey, Robbins, & Terrell, 2003). And that means more than the occasional in-school celebration of Black History Month or the Cinco de Mayo (Nieto, 1999). The values of pluralism, tolerance, acceptance, and democracy must be consciously taught and simulated for practice within the microcosm that is the school. As Solomon once said in the Book of Proverbs, we must "train up a child in the way that he should go: and that when he is old, he will not depart from it" (Proverbs 22:6). The subjective problems inherent in this approach have been fully explored in the process of conducting this research.

SETTING

The school where the present research was conducted is located in a rural and agricultural county where dairy and poultry farming, logging, trucking, and light manufacturing occupy most of the parents of my students. The usual rustic pastimes of hunting, fishing, and customizing trucks dominate the conversations of most of the boys. Girls are more apt here to be con-cerned about family life. Football and other sports are also pretty big draws for the time and attention of the community. When the new high school facilities opened in 2001, the community insisted on retaining the tradi-tional football stadium next to the old high school downtown rather than using a brand-new field at the new facility located three miles outside of town on a two-lane U.S. highway.

Gender roles for both boys and girls here are traditional, clearly de-fined, and socially enforced. The expectation for most of the students has been that their education would serve, not to challenge their way of life, but to preserve it and to make it possible for them to stay close to home, as have their parents. (It should be noted that this is not necessarily a bad thing [Theobald, 1997]).

But two recent developments have upset the applecart in this rural county: the rise of more rigorous state curricular standards (complemented by a fearsome, new battery of state examinations) and the advent of a large Hispanic population now estimated to be more than 11 percent of the total county population where previously there was none a scant fifteen years ago. Now the county seat has three Mexican restaurants, a Catholic church, and a visible Hispanic presence all over downtown every day. Needless to say, not everyone is thrilled with the change.

Prior to 1970, this county was entirely traditional, completely segre-gated, relatively poor and uneducated compared to the rest of South Caro-lina, monolingual, and almost completely protestant. It was possible to live and die in the comfortable complacency of a community that neither sought change nor expected it any time soon. But, as the economy changed in South Carolina requiring a better-educated workforce, the school district attempted to cope with state mandates by introducing more rigorous college-preparatory curricula, deemphasizing vocational education, and working toward full integration of the schools with a massive building program that culminated in the opening of a new educational complex housing the high school and the now integrated middle school (previously, the eastern part of the county—almost completely white—maintained a K–8 school that was 99 percent Caucasian, while the black population and the county-seat whites went to middle-school in an old building in very bad repair). The unexpected Hispanic population explosion in this county only further destabilized citizens' expectations of what life should be in the county and how the schools should prepare students for it.

It was not uncommon for me to hear high school students complain about their beautiful, new building and compare it to an unfamiliar jail with tons of rules, lots of academic work to which they were unaccustomed, and new expectations for their lives that they consciously rejected. "We didn't need this building!" and "School shouldn't be 'all that'! After all, this is only (fill in the county's name)!" The kids are often as conservative as, if not more than, their parents. But when the kids started complaining that they "shouldn't have to learn Spanish" since "people who come here should learn English first," often (among the white students) buttressing their rejection of cultural difference with ostentatious displays of the Confederate battle flag on t-shirts and elsewhere, I decided to make room in my world-language-other-than-English curriculum for the discussion of the stresses involved in dealing with increasing cultural diversity in a demographically unstable school district.

The methodology I employed for this study was a form of qualitative action research into the values, attitudes, and beliefs of my students concerning cultural diversity that involved essentially three measures, two subjective and one objective, in order to achieve the kind of triangulation that would yield fairly consistent results and shed light upon the question as to why students answered as they did. (Carspecken, 1996).

Since the WLOE (world language other than English) program was fundamentally geared toward second-language acquisition as the primary focus of instruction, discussions of cultural values such as we did this semester were ancillary in nature, but, I believe, necessary to help students cope with steadily increasing diversity within their profoundly conservative, rural community.

CONFRONTING DIVERSITY THROUGH READING, WRITING, AND DISCUSSION

Some of the groundwork for this project had been laid with this cohort of students in 2001–02. Most of my students are juniors who began French and Spanish as sophomores without the expectation that it would be a significant academic challenge. As they discovered that it would not be an easy, automatic good grade with little homework, a number of my students rebelled against having to take a world language other than English. Comments to the effect that Hispanics should have to learn English rather than my Anglo-Saxon students having to learn Spanish were common. It can be argued that, while WLOE instruction interested a plurality of my students who were delighted to learn about other cultures, a large segment (at least one-third) retreated into a sort of rural xenophobia and ended up less accepting of Hispanic culture after taking Spanish than before. During the course of the past year and half that I have been working in my school, I have heard this repeatedly.

Still, the confrontation with diversity and the values of tolerance and acceptance were, on balance, good for these kids. I know this by the way my classes reacted to instruction on a daily basis. A number of students appeared to have found their voices and broken cultural barriers by talking to and befriending students whose background differed from theirs. My class strongly emphasized that this was okay and to be encouraged. I have a banner over my white board saying, "Diversity: it's all good!" There were maps of French-speaking Africa, posters featuring sites in Hispanic and francophone countries, as well as a standing Kwanzaa display under the image of Dr. Martin Luther King. Needless to say, some of my students were bewildered by these images in the classroom of a white teacher who made no secret of his membership in the NAACP.

During the course of the year, I discussed with students concepts of nationalism and what symbols such as the U.S. and rebel flags have historically meant. We spent considerable time discussing Mexico's tortured relationship with the United States and the reasons for continued Hispanic immigration into the United States. Students studied the Mexican-American War (1846–48), the Annexation of Texas, Manifest Destiny, and the social construction of ethnic identity. We also utilized a prepackaged program from the Southern Poverty Law Center (SPLC), A Place at the Table (1995), which included a video in which teenagers of various backgrounds discuss their struggle for identity in America and their aspirations for the future. Students read an article provided by SPLC entitled, "A Tale of Two Schools" in which the desegregation of California schools in the forties was presented and discussed.

Reading this article together in class and discussing it turned over a few rocks to reveal some unexpected unpleasantness as students from the eastern, virtually all-white end of the county reacted negatively to the Winchester and Brown decisions. Two years ago, their 98 percent white elementary school (K–8) was desegregated by merging the middle-school grades with those of the formerly majority-black middle school in the county seat while busing into the school a large contingent of blacks and Hispanics in order to achieve a 65 percent white/35 percent minority ratio in the school in grades K–5. A new wing was added to the building to accommodate the newly diverse school population. The local community resisted this tooth and nail, but ultimately had to bow to the wishes of the Justice Department and the school district. Resentment, however, still runs deep.

My fifth-period French II class had a large contingent of white students who went through the formerly majority-white elementary school and reacted negatively to the article on desegregation in California. "Why do we have to go to school with people we don't want to have with us?" was a common question. Students expressed the view that community schools should not have to bus students in from other parts of a school district to achieve any kind of integration if the local community is opposed. And we are not talking here about long bus rides. This elementary school is fifteen minutes from the county seat.

Furthermore, this integration began to take place at a time when Confederate symbols all over South Carolina (and particularly atop the State House) were under attack. White students began to sport t-shirts featuring the Confederate Battle Flag to express their solidarity with what they took to be traditional, rural white culture in our county. The high school then banned displays of any and all Confederate regalia three years ago in an effort to reduce racial tension. Pent up resentment on the part of white students, however, had been building up ever since "the flag" came down from atop the South Carolina State House in July 2000.

One of the objects of my attention to diversity in class was to defuse this tension through multiracial, multicultural dialogue and to use WLOE classes as a safe space for the reasoned discussion of controversial cultural issues. Although the county is almost 40 percent minority, the cultural hegemony exercised by the diminishing white majority is invisible to itself; white people often feel that their culture is under siege as they attempt to cope with the banishment of their traditional symbols, real integration of the schools, the increasing use of Spanish everywhere, and rising academic expectations for a largely working-class population that has never before seen the need for "city standards" in education. Getting white students to identify the white aspects of the common culture and thereby get a sense of their pervasiveness was difficult, but it is a task, I believe, that is necessary if educators are, first, to alleviate their sense of grievance and oppression and, second, to develop the skills of cultural negotiation that will allow all members of the school community to value themselves and those whom they perceive to be different (Dimitriadis & Carlson, 2003).

WRITING ESSAYS ABOUT CULTURAL DIVERSITY

Prior to showing students the film from the SPLC in mid-October 2002, I had students write a composition in English (except in AP Spanish where the requirement was to use Spanish) on diversity. The essay topic on which they wrote in class in silence for an entire period on October 1, 2002, was as follows:

Explain your attitude toward diversity in our school. Consider the cultural changes that have occurred as a result of the influx of

Hispanic students into our school. Are these students well treated? If not, what should be changed? Has the study of a foreign language helped you to understand people who are different from you culturally? What have you learned in your foreign-language class about other cultures that you did not know before you started taking French and Spanish? Are you more or less accepting of diversity now? Address these and other issues in about 200 words in English.

The substitute who gave my students (about one hundred spread out over six classes) this assignment was startled by the reaction of some of the white students. She reported at the end of the day as follows:

Word of warning. I think most of your white students are being raised up to think black students are lower than them. From the way they were talking and whispering it may come out in their papers. They were very productive though.

And indeed, it did come out in their papers. But not all students expressed racial or cultural intolerance. I would estimate that 30 percent of my students were quite accepting of diversity (these also tended to be the ones who enjoyed WLOE study); another 35% were indifferent, and 35 percent were actively hostile to cultural diversity.

I will now provide you with a few examples of what my students wrote along with my commentary. Keep in mind that students had been hearing the message of acceptance of cultural diversity in my classes for over a year and had had plenty of time to develop opinions about it. This group was mostly juniors with a few tenth and twelfth graders, also.

Since I have been taking Spanish I can see how hard it is for Hispanics to learn English. You really have to want to learn another language to be able to speak it decently. I am the same on accepting diversity. It is fine with me.

This student expressed a typical opinion for those among my enrollment who had been enjoying the experience of learning another language. This sentiment was echoed by the one student in my Spanish I enrollment last year who placed first on the National Spanish Exam in March of 2002 and got third place in the entire country. She stated:

It makes me sad to see some people who steadfastly refuse to accept diversity. Many people seem to feel that they are better than people who are different from them. I wish that they would realize how much different cultures could learn from each other. When people promote discrimination and racism, they are only hurting themselves and others. The world would be much better if people would learn to be more accepting.

These views were decidedly in the minority in my school, however. More typical of the ambivalence many of my students were feeling are the following:

> Diversity is good. I think we should treat everyone . . . equally no matter what color you are. There are limits though. I don't want to date someone that isn't my color or race because frankly, I do think God made us different for a reason.

Traditional religious and cultural values were often at war with students' experience of diversity in our school as they attempt to cope with their demographically unstable school environment. The student quoted above came from the formerly all-white elementary school at the eastern end of the county. Her first experience of blacks and Hispanics was in the ninth grade at the county high school. Her colleague and friend in the same class (also from that elementary school) echoed her feelings:

> I am not one who willingly accepts change. I don't always like having to make accommodations for people (such as Hispanics). However, I am trying and will continue to try until I, or the rest of the world, changes.

Similarly, this otherwise bright student—whose parents were members of the Sons of Confederate Veterans—had difficulty coping with difference:

> Recently, in the past ten years or so, a new influx of people, Hispanic, have come into the county and their children into our schools. I feel that this is good for the community, but in my opinion, because I frown at change, I don't care for it much. I don't hate them or even not being friendly towards them, but I am too much like my mom and dad. I don't like change.

Like the previous two students, this one also came from the all-white elementary school. His first experience of real diversity was in the ninth grade. He loved to read and devoured novels of "alternative southern history" in which the main premise was that the South had won the "war between the states."

Another white student from the same elementary school had a different take on cultural matters:

> If we discriminate against their [Hispanic] culture, aren't we being very hypocritical in making them think one thing but treating them

completely opposite? If America doesn't show these cultures respect, then we aren't living up to our word and our potential.

Some students found Spanish useful in their everyday life, as this student observed:

> My father owns a trailer park around [name of town], and he rents to a lot of the Hispanics who speak no English. Occasionally, they will come to the house, and my dad will hand me the phone, so I can retrieve the information needed. That experience in particular has made me aware of how important and useful Spanish is whether you're a rich person or a janitor. I definitely have a greater respect for diversity more so now than ever. I'm very fascinated with the Hispanic culture and am very excited to continue my study of Spanish.

Besides the utility of learning a second language for everyday life, the following student sees the importance of cultural understanding, as well:

> Since beginning Spanish I last year, I have learned many new things about the Hispanic culture. For instance, I used to think that it was rude for Hispanics to stare at you, but now I know that eye contact is a major way that they convey friendship. Also, I wondered why some Hispanics get offended when someone call[s] them "Mexicans." I now understand that not all of the Hispanics in [name of town] are immigrants from Mexico. I would be mad too if I went to another country and they called me an "Englishman" when I am clearly an American. I am also glad that we not only discuss the Spanish language but the culture as well. What good would it be to learn a foreign language if you didn't know anything about the people who speak that language?

Students of mixed heritage also saw the importance of intercultural understanding to the development and maintenance of a healthy school ecology. One was quick to point out that racism against Hispanics did not originate exclusively with rural whites:

> The only problem I have with the influx of Hispanics is the inappropriate trouble it has caused. I am a quarter Mexican, and it kind of hurts to hear how Latinos are put down just because they are misunderstood. I also don't understand how the Black population of [name of town] can treat the Hispanics so poorly . . . High school students are worse than adults about racism despite the foreign language classes . . . Most students approach foreign language as un-

needed and unimportant. They don't care about learning another culture. They only want to push the Hispanics away to make [name of town] what it once was. People are scared of change.

As some of my black students explained during the focus groups, their sometimes-negative attitudes toward Hispanics stemmed from their fear that the new arrivals could be taking from them what little they already had. As with the white students, contact with Hispanics in class can help to break down barriers of fear and misunderstanding, as had been the case with my French I class where there were six blacks, eight Hispanics, and four whites.

Other students expressed fear concerning the pace of change or the belief that cultural separateness does not violate our commitment to political equality in the United States:

> The school is offering courses in foreign language to all people in an effort to make students more acceptable to other cultures. Nothing else should be done. The students should try to blend in when they feel comfortable to. If you forcefully make people integrate, people will feel uncomfortable and try to keep to themselves. Consequently, this could possibly cause people to reject a culture . . . I believe that we are different for a reason. This, as well, should not be forgotten. We can be separate and still be equal.

Both of these students, in spite of my discussion of *Plessy versus Ferguson*, still considered separate but equal a reasonable doctrinal position in spite of the fact that more than fifty years had passed since the historic *Brown* decision declared it to be in violation of the Fourteenth Amendment and, therefore, unconstitutional. Many other students, however, were far less charitable than these two. I will now explore some of the essays that were less accepting, indeed, downright hostile, to diversity. For many of these students, the issue of the Confederate battle flag loomed large in their thinking, and they bitterly resented the school rule that forbade students from wearing any Confederate regalia (e.g., rebel-flag t-shirts and belt buckles) in school.

> Every day I see Caucasian people. I know and respect this culture because it was what I was brought up in. I've grown up learning my southern culture, and I'm sorry to say I've adopted the feelings that most southern "rednecks" have to other ethnicities. Due to my bringing up, I have various unconscious feelings toward blacks. Some blacks complain and try to start fights with people just because they think they have that right since their people were discriminated against. To me, these people are niggers. [Note: the word *nigger* was used seven times in the ninety-five essays written]

Nevertheless, later on she said, "If you can understand a group of people it helps you change your feelings about them." Other students were more forthrightly southern nationalist in their views:

> We are deeply rooted to our southern heritage. In schools, this causes a problem. Our district will not acknowledge the wishes of the white students. If anyone is discriminated against here, in this school, it is the southern white loyalists. In this school, we honor African American month and Hispanic month. Nothing is done to honor our grandfathers of the South that means so much to over half of the student body. Last year, the students rallied to honor the Confederacy on Confederate's Day, one day. Everyone was sent home and punished. Since the district will not even consider our wishes, we felt we had to take the matter into our own hands. It could have been avoided, easily. The school seems to forget this school is in the heartland of the Old South. No one in this school is racial. We are just loyal to our ancestors, people who we loved dearly.

This young lady (who eventually wanted to teach school here in the community) referred to the attempted pro-Confederate Memorial Day protest on May 10, 2002, that was quickly suppressed by the school administration. We did not allow students to come to school that day dressed in Confederate symbols. Some of the students who walked in that day had loud rebel messages on their t-shirts, and we made them either go home or turn them inside out. We as a school never pretended that students had as great a right to self-expression within the building as they would have had off school property. The district maintained that the school was neutral territory and that inflammatory symbols were unacceptable since they potentially constituted a material disruption of the educational process. Still, this person clearly expressed the resentment that many of our southern-heritage whites were feeling.

This sense of grievance utterly ignored South Carolina's baleful history of secession, disunion, reconstruction, Jim Crow, segregation, the Klan, and so on. Since this view had been expressed a number of times and was the object of serious discussion by a large number of our Caucasian students, it should be addressed within the curriculum of the school. Moreover, the appropriate sites for these discussions are English, social studies, and WLOE classes. WLOE classes are particularly important since the community in which these students lived had been experiencing serious demographic stress as a result of the increasing influx of Hispanics into the county and its schools. Students need to be taught how to cope with diversity (Schramm-Pate & Lussier, 2004).

The mix of strategies in which I engaged in my classes included discussion, essay writing, polling, some lecture, and the focus-group technique. As you can see from the foregoing discussion of students' essays and readings, the focus group, while culminating students' experience of coping with and dealing with diversity in the classroom, was not the primary activity in which students engaged. Indeed, the writing phase, because it involved being able to tell me, the teacher/reader, what was on students' minds in relative privacy, was essential as a subjective measure of where to take subsequent discussions and classroom activities—such as preparing the questions with which students would later grapple face to face in the focus groups.

Before we leave this section of excerpts from students' essays, I will cite some of the more controversial statements made by southern-heritage white students. These statements, while not reflective of the majority of students' considered, written statements (do not forget that my student cohort was about 40 percent minority overall), represented the opinions of at least one-third of the southern-heritage whites. Regardless of what we may think of them, these views need to be dealt with in order to defuse potential conflict in our school and to alleviate these students' abiding sense of grievance in the wake of change in their community and the new linguistic, cultural, ethnic, and social diversity with which they had to cope. Remember that the county is a multiracial community in which the majority of white, black, and Hispanic students come to the public schools rather than fleeing to private institutions as has happened in so many places across South Carolina. Diversity training, of which this study was one small step, might be able to help students cope with change. Figuratively, therefore, I am walking on eggs when dealing with statements such as the following in my students' writing:

> Another thing I don't get about black people is that they can call each other a nigger, but they get ticked off if a white person calls them one. I just don't get it. Caucasian and black people have different opinions on a lot of things. The main thing is the Confederate flag. Some black people act like it's a crime if a white person wears a Confederate flag shirt. I don't see why they get so mad. I have been taught "Heritage not Hate." Foreign language classes are helping our diverse culture understand each other a little better. But in my honest opinion, I don't believe we should have to learn their language. They are coming to the United States . . . It is good to see that the United States is accumulating new cultures. But the new races should not get out of hand.

What this student gave with one hand, she took back with the other, reflecting the ambivalence of a large number of my students on these issues. While it was heartening to hear that WLOE classes helped diverse cultures understand one another, this student did not understand why black students get so upset when white people use the "n" word or see a rebel-flag t-shirt. Her opinions were echoed in the following excerpt from another student's essay:

I was raised in the country by two country and redneck parents. During my childhood the word *nigger* was used quite frequently to refer to black people, but it wasn't because they were black. My parents called the majority of them that because of the kinds of things they were involved in. Dad had lots of black friends. He just did not approve of the way most them acted . . . When it comes to the Confederate flag I think people against it are stubborn, uneducated fools. People are spoon-fed lies and refuse to believe anything else. Slavery was in the U.S.A. for over a hundred years. The Confederate flag only flew four years over slavery.

This summarizes quite well the views many of my white, male students expressed to me orally and in writing over the three years that I taught high school in this county (2001–04). I think it is important to note here the role parents play in forming students' opinions on these issues; although a number of white parents expressed dismay to me personally during parent conferences concerning their children's views on these issues. These parents appeared to be embarrassed by the cultural level their children have embraced. "I don't know where she gets it!" one exasperated parent said to me when we discussed her daughter's run-ins with the administration over Confederate symbols on her clothing.

White boys in general tend to associate the rebel flag with being tough and "country." Since this is the age at which young males are testing their mettle as men among men, toughness and engagement in "manly" pursuits such as hunting, fishing, sports, mud-bogging (i.e., driving powerful, jacked-up pick-up trucks through a muddy field without getting stuck), and so on, as well as hanging out with the guys and working on vehicles are important elements in their socialization. I had often asked these boys if it is possible to separate the rebel flag in their minds from the less controversial aspects of rural male identity formation: do you have to wear a rebel-flag t-shirt to be tough? Why not just wear things that say the name of our school, or the Gamecocks (assuming you are a University of Carolina fan, as I am!) or wear hunting pants, a t-shirt with a deer, and boots?

I think a number of them understood what I was saying but were unwilling to buck the consensus of their peer group. That is also understandable. Nevertheless, we still had to find ways in school to channel the male identity formation process in socially constructive directions. Traditionally, schools have done this with sports (and vocational training such as automotive technology). More work, however, needs to be done in the classroom so that students can work out their feelings and thoughts individually and in private in order to lay the foundation for positive social behavior as adults. Silence concerning controversial issues simply allows the pot to bubble and boil unattended until it overflows and results in severe social disruption in the schoolhouse.

The last excerpt of this kind is one of the most inflammatory that I have read, but it is representative of what white students had been saying to one another in our school and I quote it at length:

> Since I have been raised up out in the country and basically around all whites, I have a strong opinion about diversity. I don't see how the blacks can call us white people racist, when they are too. They get mad when we call them a nigger but is it right for them to call us a cracker or white trash? One reason I have a problem with diversity is because my family has never really been associated with blacks. The thing that makes me mad is the blacks (most of them, but not all) don't try a lick in school, and when they graduate, if they do, they go get on welfare. They are basically living for free, while us whites, a few blacks, and Mexicans work. I hate when the blacks bring up something about the Confederate flag. That is a bunch of bull. If they would take ten minutes to research the history behind the flag, they would feel stupid for acting like they do about it. The Confederate flag don't mean slavery or hate. There were black people who fought in the Civil War also. That flag represents all soldiers in the war, not just the whites. To me I can't understand why they are so down on the Ku Klux Klan, when the NAACP is the same thing. I feel like the NAACP should mean "Niggers Against All Caucasian People." The reason I feel this way is because they are trying to down the White people, like taking the Confederate flag off the State House . . . In a way, foreign language has given me a better view of Hispanics. I think learning a little Spanish has helped me to appreciate their culture. I guess diversity is something for the most part I don't like.

At the bottom of the paper she drew a rebel flag—something I have seen on many white students' papers but about which I said nothing since it was not "in the face" of my black and Hispanic students. As you can see, the above essay is full of stereotypes and misperceptions concerning minorities (e.g., the idea that the majority of blacks are on welfare; whites continue to be the overwhelming majority of welfare recipients in the United States, a fact that I stated in her class at least once or twice). There was also a complete unwillingness to interrogate the meanings associated with the rebel flag from diverse perspectives. Equally disturbing was this student's attitude toward the NAACP and the Klan. Since this student was reasonably bright, I can only conclude that she and her colleagues have come through our county's social studies and English classes without having critiqued their assumptions concerning U.S. history, citizenship, or cultural/ethnic diversity. This student, along with many of her peers, harbored a deep resentment of all attacks on the rebel banner as an attack upon herself and her culture. As

I had heard a number of white students say concerning the county's minorities, "They're just taking over!!"

Needless to say, my black and Hispanic students, whose essays I did not quote here, evinced a very different set of attitudes concerning diversity and often felt left out of the cultural mainstream or silenced altogether. The black female students tended to be a bit more voluble on these issues, but one comment kept recurring in their essays, discussions with me, and in the focus groups: "We just don't say anything when they [the white kids] talk and say stuff we don't like." Rather than being a vociferous, insistent, grievance-ridden minority, blacks in our school tended to let people talk and just said nothing back since they considered it to be useless. It is the county's white population that seemed to be nursing an abiding sense of grievance and hurt pride. This needs to be dealt with in the schools across the curriculum in a way that will become as culturally affirming for them as for our two minority populations.

POLLING STUDENTS

In addition to the foregoing, I had students take a poll in October concerning the issues raised in class and in their essays. The results were quite illuminating and revealed some serious inconsistencies in our students' collective sense of what is right and wrong concerning cultural and ethnic diversity in the community and in the high school. Ninety-eight students out of my enrollment of one hundred one responded to the sixteen questions I posed, the results for which are listed after each item:

Opinion Poll on Diversity

DIRECTIONS: *Write an A if you agree with the statement, N if you are neutral (no opinion or not sure), or D if you disagree. Do not sign your name or write any comments.*

1. I support continued Hispanic immigration into our county.
39A—35N—24D

2. I am glad that our school has a diverse population.
70A—24N—4D

3. I support racial integration of the public schools.
56A—27N—15D

4. I like hearing Spanish spoken in the halls of this school.
34A—38N—26D

5. Having Hispanic people here gives me an opportunity to learn about another culture and another language.
79A—9N—10D

6. I think all Americans should learn a world language in addition to English.
45A—28N—25D

7. This school should teach students to get along with one another regardless of racial, ethnic, or religious background.
82A—10N—6D

8. I support the school rule that prevents students from wearing Confederate symbols.
27A—27N—44D

9. I believe that America has a responsibility to help people who have suffered discrimination.
57A—32N—9D

10. School should teach students to think critically about issues rather than just memorizing many facts.
66A—24N—8D

11. I believe that diversity is a good thing for our school.
71A—25N—2D

12. My education should prepare me to deal with diversity in my community, my country, and in the world.
78A—19N—1D

13. We should not discriminate against American Muslims because of 9/11.
64A—23N—11D

14. We need to protect the rights of women to equal treatment under the law.
83A—11N—4D

15. Learning a world language other than English is important to me.
53A—25N—20D

16. Everyone should have the same rights; no one is better than anyone else is!
90A—6N—2D

As you can see from these results, there are a number of inconsistencies reflective of students' ambivalence concerning the issues at hand. Only thirty-nine students said that they supported continued Hispanic immigration while twenty-four were opposed. The rest would not commit themselves. Nevertheless, seventy students were "glad" that our school has a diverse population. Only four disagreed. Still, only fifty-six supported racial integration while twenty-seven were neutral and fifteen opposed.

Concerning the use of Spanish, only thirty-four liked hearing Spanish in the halls of our school, and the largest group (thirty-eight) was neutral on this question. Still, seventy-nine felt that having Hispanics here gives them the opportunity to learn about another culture and language. Only forty-five, however, felt that Americans should learn a world language other than English. While most students recognize the opportunity to learn, not all are willing to do so.

On general questions of values such as having the school teach students to get along, to think critically, and prepare students to deal with diversity in the wider world, students registered healthy majorities in favor. Fully ninety students believed that "everyone should have the same rights." In addition, fifty-three students felt that learning a world language other than English was important to them. This is particularly encouraging to me since my classes are not easy, and not all students have appreciated the academic challenge I provide for them. Nevertheless, when it came down to specific applications of values supportive of diversity, students were far more ambivalent.

Only twenty-seven students out of ninety-eight respondents supported the school rule that bans the display of the rebel flag (and anything else inflammatory, for that matter). Forty-four are opposed to it. This is after much on-and-off discussion in class of why schools restrict students' political speech far more than would be consistent with their First Amendment rights off school property. As one of my white male students expressed it, "I don't care what you think about the rebel flag. It should never have been taken down from the State House dome, and I am never going to change my mind on the subject!" This rejectionist attitude is common among those whites who strongly identify with a traditional, rural South Carolina lifestyle. There is a complete unwillingness among a large number of these students to see what blacks and others see when they behold the rebel flag in a position of sovereignty—or any place else, for that matter. It goes to the heart of the question of who has a right to be in South Carolina and consider him/herself a South Carolinian, particularly since the rebel flag is unrepresentative of so many of our citizens.

In the course of my teaching, I usually throw out questions such as this for students to think about whenever they spontaneously bring up cultural topics before, during, or after class. The goal is to get them to think for themselves and consider issues from a variety of angles. "What are you saying to me, personally," I ask them, "when you wear a rebel flag? How do you expect to be interpreted?"

Considering seventy-one students believed diversity to be a good thing, eighty-two believed that we should actively teach them to get along with one another, and seventy-eight believed that their education should prepare them for a wider world of difference, these are questions that must be posed, discussed, written about, mulled over, and presented to students in order to show them that we take what they think seriously enough to address it as part of the curriculum on a daily basis.

FINALLY, THE FOCUS GROUPS

As you can see from the foregoing, much groundwork had been laid in my classes prior actually to holding formal focus-group sessions in class. In fact, they are almost anticlimactic. Nonetheless, careful, painstaking preparation must go into this process in order to prevent conflict and, instead, foment the kind of "dialogue across difference" (Burbules & Rice, 1991) that will teach students to engage in democratic micropolitics at the classroom level. As students engage in productive talk in a structured environment with one another, they learn how difficult it is to confront others who, for them, represent difference and work out settlements that are mutually satisfactory to all participants. Yet it is precisely this sort of discussion (as opposed to debate, which, in large measure, I consider to be counterproductive in a high school precisely because it sets up irreconcilable opposites and posits the existence of winners and losers) in which students do not have much practice in high school. As I worked on this project, my goal ultimately was to establish a framework for diversity training across the curriculum in high schools that would feature the activities in which we had been engaged in my classes up to this point, culminating in focus-group discussions followed by metacognitive activities.

The groundwork having been laid, I made a list of questions arising from students' concerns expressed orally, in writing, and in their poll conducted in October. These questions, plus my commentary on their reactions to each, follow. At the end of this section, I have transcribed a short segment of one of my classes "dialoguing across their differences" followed by a brief conclusion.

On Friday, November 1, 2002, each of my six classes considered the following questions—some at length, some hardly at all—according to their interests. My classes were divided into diverse groups of three that went to the front of the room and sat in six or seven chairs for approximately fifteen minutes apiece. (In compliance with district policy, we did not videotape the proceedings. They were, however tape-recorded so that I could make reference to what students said later. I will not, however, release the tapes to anyone or ever play them out of school. I asked students not to identify themselves personally while the tape recorder was running.)

At one point, the principal walked in to encourage the students as they were grappling with their differences over the rebel flag, immigration, culture, et cetera. He listened to them talk and then praised them for their courtesy, thoughtfulness, and bravery in dealing with difficult issues. The students beamed, and several told me later how much they appreciated his comments and attention to what they were trying to do.

I handed out to students a copy of the following questions (minus the commentary!) the day before the discussion in order to give them a chance to think about what they wanted to talk about.

Handout Sheet:

2002 WLOE Focus Groups on Diversity

Ground Rules: Take turns, show respect for others as you express your opinions, attempt to understand the other points of view. Do not debate or argue. Do ask one another probing questions. Always maintain your cool, but feel free to express your opinion respectfully. Try to analyze your own point of view critically.

Possible Questions Arising from Your Compositions:

1. Has taking a WLOE helped you to understand people who are different from you? How?

Students basically agreed that WLOE had helped them understand a different culture. Black students were particularly pleased to see people of color represented in curricular materials, particularly in French class. I make it a point to stress "la négritude" in French culture and in West African countries that speak French. All students felt that WLOE was useful, but several expressed the belief that WLOE should not be "all that," i.e., all that much work.

2. Should students be required to take a WLOE for college admissions?

A number of students reacted negatively here. They did not believe that a world language should be an admission requirement because "this is America," and "we speak English here." I asked them to consider the wide diversity of native and immigrant cultures to this continent over the centuries.

3. Should people be required to know English before they come here? Why?

The majority believed that people should be required to know English before immigrating since they felt that the burden of communication should be on the newcomers, not on those who were here "first." I asked them why their ancestors did not learn the various Amerindian languages that were spoken here prior to and during the European settlement of this continent?

4. What are the advantages and disadvantages of living in a diverse society?

Most students actually agreed that being able to cope with cultural differ-ence was an important social skill. They also felt that they should be able to be as judgmental about ethnic groups as they wanted. They based this on their democratic right to have whatever opinion they wanted about any and everything. I conceded their right to their own opinions although not to their expression when and wherever they chose. We agreed to disagree here.

5. Do you like diversity, or are you more comfortable being only with people like you?

Many students were uncomfortable with diversity. They felt that they needed to be able to handle it when they came across it but not that they should have to deal with it constantly, such as when they run into His-panics downtown.

6. Why do you think that the Supreme Court said in its 1954 *Brown* decision that "separate but equal" is really unequal?

Students did not directly address this question since they perceived it to be an academic question with a right or wrong answer. In addition, a num-ber stated that they did not like the results of the decision.

7. Should the school curriculum include more about minority and world cultures? Is the curriculum we now have "too white," bal-anced, or too minority-oriented?

Students had trouble understanding this question, supporting my conten-tion that white cultural hegemony in this country is basically invisible to the white majority who usually take for granted their culture as the sub-stance of what it means to be American. Most felt that their classes have been addressing multicultural issues and that minorities are well repre-sented in their learning.

8. Do we celebrate enough minority holidays and customs (e.g., Kwanzaa, Martin Luther King Day, Cinco de Mayo, etc.?)

We do none of these things right now. The question I posed to the students was how do we get to a point where we can have such celebra-tions with assemblies and other observances in school without alienating one group or another? Black students (vide dialogue below) felt that

MLK Day already represented diversity and respect for everyone's human rights, but whites countered that they were not permitted to have Confederate Memorial Day or display the rebel flag and that this disrespected their heritage. I invited students to "unpack" the symbol of the Confederate flag and think about what it means, not just to whites, but also to everyone. Then I asked them if there were not a way to have a Confederate Memorial Day observance that would not be offensive to minorities and yet would honor the soldiers who fought for South Carolina. Interestingly, whites acknowledged that there was probably no way to do this.

9. The Constitution says that citizenship is defined by birth or naturalization. What does it mean to be an American?

Students had trouble with this one, too. White students basically defined it in terms of their own culture, thereby establishing southern, white ethnic hegemony to which all would be invited who accepted its terms, which included "respect" for Confederate heritage. Blacks usually saw things quite differently, and more inclusively, frequently referring to the words of Martin Luther King's dream speech. I was struck (and pleased) by the passionate commitment all black students (and a few of the whites!) displayed for the values of diversity so forcefully expressed by Dr. King almost forty years ago. For them, he expressed the essence of what it should mean to be American: an idea of citizenship rooted in our common humanity rather than a specific ethnic heritage such as that which is advocated by many southern-heritage whites.

10. What is the difference between civic versus ethnic nationalism? What does the U.S.A. represent, and why?

Students understood the distinction that I had made for them a number of times on this subject, and they agreed that the U.S.A. represented the concept of civic, as opposed to ethnic, nationalism. Being American means participation in a common community of democratic republican values, not in a particular ethnicity of blood and soil.

11. Do you support continued Hispanic immigration into our county? Under what circumstances?

Students were divided on this issue. A number of them expressed the fear that they were being "swamped by Mexicans." Others spoke up in favor of legal immigration.

12. To what extent does the Confederate flag represent heritage?

Students discussed this one at length and basically divided along ethnic lines. A few black students expressed support for whites so that they could wear whatever they wanted. For some of the girls, the problem was the very idea of a dress code. I invited them to think of what the situation here might be if we literally had no dress code.

13. Why do blacks object to the rebel flag?

Most agreed that blacks objected because of slavery, segregation, Jim Crow, the Klan, and so on, but the whites felt that blacks were mistaken because the symbol, they said, did not mean anything discriminatory to them. Most black students were adamant in their support of the school rule against the rebel flag, which they took to be a personal insult and an invitation to fight in school.

14. Should students be able to wear whatever they want?

See number 12 above.

15. Should we celebrate Confederate Memorial Day?

The white students were in favor, blacks against. No one believed that the day could ever be celebrated since its message and symbols were offensive to people of color.

Here is a sample dialogue from November 1:

STUDENT A: *I look at the Confederate flag as a southern tradition. Going hunting, fishing, and stuff. The flag reminds me of mud-bogging, fishing, and good times with friends. I never really look at it as racism. But some black people look at it as a bad symbol, but most white people don't. It's just a small percentage that think of it like black folk do, and that messes it up for everybody.*

STUDENT B: *A doesn't see it what we see [as black people].*

STUDENT A: *But B won't get over it.*

STUDENT C: (talking about Hispanics) *I don't support Hispanic immigration. Already about a million of 'em over here.*

STUDENT D: *I don't support it, either, because I rode through town the other night, and all I seen on every street corner was Mexicans.*

STUDENT E: (back to the flag) *The flag has been used to express hatred toward black people. You can't deny that!*

STUDENT D: *Some white people want to start stuff, and for them it means hate. But not for me. Like Student A said, it means heritage. Huntin', fishin', out in the woods with the boys shootin' things. (A number of white boys nod their heads in agreement.)*

STUDENT F: *To them it means something good, to us [blacks] something else. But I just keep my mouth closed. Confederate Memorial Day isn't for everybody, but Martin Luther King Day, it's for everybody.*

STUDENT D: *Both days should be celebrated.*

STUDENT F: *But the problem is that Confederate Memorial Day offended the back race. Martin Luther King is all about equality. But Confederate Memorial Day is about slavery for some whites.*

As one of my black, female students said in a later class period, the rebel flag, "says you don't like black people."

CONCLUSION

As my students experienced during the micropolitical focus-group sessions, doing democracy face to face is difficult. It is much easier to sit in the atrium of the school at a table with your friends and solve all problems from the perspective of your in-group. However, when you are forced to dialogue with others who are different and whose values you know are significantly divergent from your own, you must make a special effort to be careful about how you say what you say, so that your words result in understanding of views over which there is disagreement, rather than hurt, anger, and rejection. You learn to talk to people effectively who disagree with you, and you eventually get some things done.

In a community such as ours that is experiencing rapid change while trying to hold onto time-honored tradition, it is incumbent upon the public schools to teach students how to dialogue across their differences so that they will know how to do so with understanding and compassion when they take their places in society as contributing adults. In the process, they will improve basic reading, writing, reasoning, and discussion skills as they grapple with important issues to which there are no easy answers. This strikes me as far better than the imposition of silence and the relentless drill and recitation of low-level facts and skills that often characterize secondary-school instruction in language and social studies. Teaching kids how to think about real-world problems such as they have been trying to do in my class, being challenged—and sometimes angered in the process—this should be one of the fundamental goals of secondary education as we prepare our students for college and/or the world of work.

REFERENCES

Apple, M. W. (2000). *Official knowledge*. (2nd ed.) New York: Routledge.

Aronowitz, S., & Giroux, H. (1991). *Postmodern education: Politics, culture and social criticism*. Minneapolis: University of Minnesota Press.

Banks, J. A. (1996). *Multicultural education: Transformative knowledge and action*. New York: Teachers College.

Burbules, N. C., & Rice, S. Dialogue across differences: Continuing the conversation. *Harvard Educational Review* 4(61), 393–416.

Carspecken, P. F. (1996). *Critical ethnography in educational research*. New York: Routledge.

Dimitriadis, G., & Carlson, D. (2003). *Promises to keep*. New York: Routledge-Farmer.

Foner, E. (2002). *Who owns history?* New York: Hill & Wang.

Freire, P. (1970, 1998). *Pedagogy of the oppressed*. New York: Teachers College.

Gay, G. (2000). *Culturally responsive teaching*. New York: Teachers College.

Gutmann, A. (1999). *Democratic education*. (2nd ed.) Princeton, NJ: Princeton University Press.

hooks, B. (2000). *Where we stand: Class matters*. New York: Routledge.

Horvitz, T. (1998). *Confederates in the attic*. New York: Vintage Books.

Howard, G. R. (1999). *We can't teach what we don't know: White teachers, multiracial schools*. New York: Teachers College.

Janks, H. (2001). Identity and conflict in the critical literacy classroom. In B. Comber & A. Simpson (Eds.), *Negotiating critical literacies in classrooms* (pp. 137–50). Mahwah, NJ: Erlbaum.

Linsey, R. B., Robins, K. N., & Terrell, R. D. (2003). *Cultural proficiency: A manual for school leaders*. Thousand Oaks, CA: Corwin Press.

Lisman, C. D. (1998). *Toward a civil society*. Westport, CT: Bergin & Garvey.

Malcolm, N. (1994). *Bosnia: A short history*. New York: New York University Press.

McLaren, P. L., & Sleeter, C. (Eds.). (1995). *Multicultural education, critical pedagogy, and the politics of difference*. Albany: State University of New York Press.

Mellor, B., & Patterson, A. (2001) Teaching readings? In B. Comber & A. Simpson (Eds.), *Negotiating critical literacies in classrooms* (pp. 119–34). Mahwah, NJ: Erlbaum.

Nash, G. B., Crabtree, C., & Dunn, R. E. (2000). *History on trial: Culture wars and the teaching of the past*. New York: Vintage Books.

Nieto, S. (1999). *The light in their eyes*. New York: Teachers College.

Ross, E. W. (Ed.). (1997). *The social studies curriculum*. Albany: State University of New York Press.

Schramm-Pate, S., & Lussier, R. (2003, December–2004, January). Teaching students to think critically: The Confederate flag controversy in the high school social studies classroom. *The High School Journal*, 2(87), 56–65.

Sears, J. T. (1998). *Curriculum, religion, and public education*. New York: Teachers College.

Sears, J. T., & Letts, W. J. (1999). *Queering elementary education*. New York: Rowman & Littlefield.

Spring, J. (2002). *American education*. Boston: McGraw-Hill.

Strike, K. (1998). Dialogue, religion, and tolerance: How to talk to people who are wrong about (almost) everything. In J. T. Sears & J. C. Carper (Eds.), *Curriculum, religion, and public education*. New York: Teachers College.

Tanner, D., & Tanner, L. (1995). *Curriculum development: Theory into practice*. Englewood Cliffs, NJ: Merrill.

Theobald, P. (1997). *Teaching the commons: Place, pride and the renewal of communuity*. Boulder, CO: Westview.

Theobald, P. (1995). *A Place at the table* (video and readings), Teaching Tolerance Project, Atlanta, GA: Southern Poverty Law Center.

CHAPTER TEN

THE CINCINNATI FREEDOM CENTER

IMPLICATIONS FOR A MORE EMANCIPATORY PRAXIS

ADAM RENNER

INTRODUCTION

Approximately three miles from the Ohio River, driving north along I-75, a spectacular view of downtown Cincinnati and its waterfront unfolds in a dramatic panorama. In addition to distinctly designed tall buildings punctuating the horizon, two unmistakable features of this scenic view immediately draw one's attention: Paul Brown Stadium, home of the infamous Cincinnati Bengals, and Great American Ballpark, home of the slightly less infamous Cincinnati Reds. Ironically, or perhaps not, between these two monstrous monuments to competition and capitalism, the National Underground Railroad Freedom Center emerges as both uniquely styled building and hybrid symbol.

Launching from Homi Bhabha's (1994) concept of 'cultural hybridity,' this chapter explores the building and symbolism of Cincinnati's new Freedom Center as a potential site of resistance and a possible place where a new negotiated understanding (and/or reconciliation) of race and racism may arise. Using the Ohio River as a historical and problematic division of North and South, I navigate this river as a fluid and liminal space over which the Freedom Center stands sentry from its northern banks. As a more critical discursive practice, I mean to position the Freedom Center and the river in a third space, attempting to make new sense of them by asking probing questions. These questions are intended to provide a starting point for a more constructive and critical social studies pedagogy.

191

I begin this chapter with a description of the Freedom Center, its architecture, and its purpose and promise for visitors. Next, I examine its interesting physical positioning both generally in Cincinnati and particularly between the two stadiums. Making this examination a sample of what is possible when studying and/or using the Freedom Center, concrete curriculum suggestions follow for high school teachers. I offer not only how it can be incorporated into theoretical study in the social studies classroom through both field trip experiences and educational materials produced by the Freedom Center but also how the Freedom Center can enhance service learning experiences tethered to these classrooms. Finally, I propose that the Freedom Center and the majestic Ohio River that flows before it offer a much needed location for transgressing boundaries of race and racism and may open up a third space for an emancipatory dialog and activism among our students.

THE UNDERGROUND RAILROAD

Although the precise origins for the name *Underground Railroad* cannot be determined, its meaning and use for men, women, and children who were enslaved in the midnineteenth century are well known in the United States. Organized initially in the 1830s due to increasing southern white violence to black families, slave resistance, and aggressive northern abolitionism, and later better systematized after the passage of the Fugitive Slave Act in 1850, the Underground Railroad provided a more deliberate but no less dangerous passage to the North. It was not an easy journey. Disease and pursuing slaveholders often claimed the lives of many fleeing along the "railroad." Ontario, known as Canada West at the time, provided the ultimate Underground Railroad destination since slavery was made illegal in the British Empire after 1833. While many "freedom-seekers" set out and completed their self-emancipatory journey unaided, the more systematized Underground Railroad offered a chance for people to come together toward a common goal: a solidarity-building opportunity for abolitionists, northern and southern alike, and enslaved African-Americans to work together toward freedom and humanization during one of our nations' most despicable eras (Hine, Hine, & Harrold, 2003)

The Underground Railroad, then, served as a light in the darkness, a symbol of hope and reconciliation in the face of apartheid, terrorism, and genocide. The National Underground Railroad Freedom Center in Cincinnati, Ohio, now seeks to remind us of this flame and to provide a sobering reminder of our xenophobic history.

THE NATIONAL UNDERGROUND RAILROAD FREEDOM CENTER

According to a National Underground Railroad Freedom Center (NURFC) brochure,

Through a powerful blend of compelling history, contemporary design and high-impact interactive displays, the National Underground Railroad Freedom Center will show the importance of looking back in order to clearly see tomorrow. Because it was during one of America's darkest periods that the beauty and heroism of the human spirit shone brightest . . . when people of all races, backgrounds and beliefs worked together as part of the Underground Railroad, risking their homes, their families and their lives to help each other escape from slavery and establish freedom for everyone. That same spirit led to the American Civil Rights movement, the call for equality in South Africa, the toppling of the Berlin Wall and the stand for freedom in Tiananmen Square. We have seen what individuals have accomplished by speaking up and joining together not so long ago. Imagine what the power of our voices joined together can accomplish today.[1]

The physical construction of the Freedom Center, unique and impressive was designed by Walter Blackburn of Blackburn Architects of Indianapolis in cooperation with BOORA Architects of Portland, Oregon. Its wavelike design and shimmering brown color are natural extensions of and connections to the Ohio River. The Freedom Center is comprised of three interconnected buildings. It contains a teachers' resource center; the John Parker Library and Family Search Center; immersive interactive exhibits, designed by Jack Rouse Associates of Cincinnati (including the Suite for Freedom, Slave Pen, Escape! Freedom Seekers and the Underground Railroad, Brothers of the Borderland, From Slavery to Freedom, Everyday Freedom Heroes, the Struggle Continues, Reflect/Respond/Resolve, and Freedom Flows); two theaters; a gift shop; and a café.

Theoretically constructed around the pillars of Courage, Cooperation, Perseverance, and Freedom, the Freedom Center boasts of programs that unite music and art, education, history, contemporary life, and outreach. According to the Freedom Center visionaries, "Our goal is to help shape tomorrow's leaders with lessons of courage, cooperation, perseverance, and freedom" (NURFC). In conjunction with a burgeoning network of freedom stations across the country, they add, "the Freedom Center feature[s] engaging web-based curricula, dynamic in-classroom materials, national programming, a teacher resource center, classrooms, training, and conferences" (NURFC). All three buildings, or pavilions—Courage, Cooperation, and Perseverance—are sleekly designed, remarkably adorned, and user-friendly. What the architects sought and the visionaries imagined certainly came to fruition.

This said, there are noteworthy ironies and critiques that could be offered about the Freedom Center, which have both *particular* and *general* implications. In the next two sections I explore these problems before discussing how one might more critically use the Freedom Center as a resource in secondary social studies classrooms.

AN IRONIC POSITIONING OF THE CENTER, *PARTICULARLY*

As I stood on the concrete slab between Paul Brown Stadium and what was Riverfront Stadium (which would become Great American Ballpark) for the groundbreaking ceremony of the Freedom Center in the summer of 2002, I was struck immediately by its positioning between these two giants of greed. I considered how these professional monstrosities were and would be constructed at great taxpayer expense, particularly to the economically disenfranchised and underrepresented of Cincinnati. These stadiums represent sites that most of these same disenfranchised will hardly ever access, except, perhaps, as underpaid, overworked employees. Many of the stories of the ancestors of these same disenfranchised are intimately intertwined with the building that would stand between the Paul Brown and Great American Ballpark Stadiums. Questions for reflection and discussion rapidly revealed their possibilities: Who bears most of the tax burden for these *city* stadiums? And who generally attends events at these stadiums? City or suburban (county) residents? How was the Freedom Center financed?[2] What connections can we draw between injustice based on race *and* class? What other connections can we draw among these three buildings? Who plays in these stadiums, and how did *they* get here? Who manages/owns these teams and facilities and how did *they* get here?[3]

AN IRONIC POSITIONING OF THE CENTER, *GENERALLY*

As I stood on the concrete slab, facing the Ohio River on the evening of June 17, 2002, during the ground-breaking ceremony, I could almost feel the heat from the racially hot city of Cincinnati behind me. The positioning of the Freedom Center in Cincinnati is both promising and problematic. In a number of ways it is an obvious placement, given that Cincinnati was a critical destination along the Underground Railroad, representing "free" territory. Additionally, Cincinnati is home to the Harriet Beecher Stowe House, which operates as a cultural and educational center, promoting black history. Articulating Cincinnati's historical symbolism as a gateway to freedom in the North, though, with its more recent racial tensions and riots (Anglen, Alltucker, Bonfield, & Horn, 2001; Burton, 2001; Moloney, 2001; Osborne, 2001), this positioning on the northern banks of the Ohio River provides an interesting and contested site for negotiation and theoreticization.

Cynically, the Freedom Center may provide a superficial bandage for a gaping racial wound that is symbolic for many urban centers across this nation. More charitably, though, it may provide an ameliorative site for more conciliatory dialog and future humanizing possibilities. The river before it may provide the much needed baptismal font of rebirth into this emancipatory third space. Questions to consider for social studies classrooms include: What role did Cincinnati play in the freeing of enslaved Africans?

How did local and national papers treat issues of race during the second half of the nineteenth century? How does this treatment compare or contrast with today? What did "freedom" mean for the enslaved Africans? What opportunities existed on the north side of the river that the south side did not offer? What was still lacking? Has that been rectified in the years since the nineteenth century?

Departing from this critical analysis and theoretical questioning, I now move to the more practical phase of this chapter to consider the Freedom Center's usefulness for high school classrooms.

THE FREEDOM CENTER AS LIMINAL LEARNING SPACE FOR HIGH SCHOOL CURRICULUMS: PROMOTING A MULTICULTURAL/ANTIRACIST SOCIAL STUDIES AGENDA

I begin from the premise that multicultural/antiracist pedagogical practices are preferred in a more critical social studies curriculum. Simply indicating that one desires multicultural/antiracist education provides no actual clarity, of course, to this contested arena. According to many critical educators (Kincheloe & Steinberg, 1997; Giroux, 1994; Sleeter 1996; McLaren, 1994; 1997), multicultural agendas range anywhere from a conservative (essentially monocultural) multiculturalism on the right to radical, critical (Kincheloe & Steinberg, 1997), insurgent (Giroux, 1994), resistant (McLaren, 1994), and revolutionary (McLaren, 1997) "multiculturalisms" on the far left. There are certainly multiculturalisms in between, but, suffice to say, I advocate for the more radical project of multiculturalism that Christine Sleeter (1996) claims "is a form of resistance to oppressive social relationships . . . [a] resistance to white supremacy and also (for many) to patriarchy" (p. 10), and that Peter McLaren (1994) argues, in his particular development of *resistance multiculturalism*, is a

> refus[al] to see culture as non-conflictual, harmonious and consensual. Democracy is understood from this perspective as busy—it's not seam-less, smooth or always a harmonious political and cultural state of affairs. Resistance multiculturalism doesn't see diversity itself as a goal, but rather argues that diversity must be affirmed within a politics of cultural criticism and a commitment to social justice. (p. 53)

Therefore, the type of multicultural education sought involves a *critical* project that "draws upon the literature and analytical methods of cultural studies to gain a deeper understanding of how race, class, and gender are represented in various social spheres" (Kincheloe & Steinberg, 1997) and examines and eventually undermines current power differentials toward the promotion of a more equitable, just, and caring society. This more critical brand of multiculturalism, then, creates the possibility for constructing a third space in our social studies curriculums—a space, like that between the Paul Brown and the Great American Ballpark Stadiums, in which concepts are interrogated, interpretation is broad and open, and justice is the goal.

The same type of clarification must be made for antiracist education. Seen as a more radical project than multiculturalism (particularly in Canada), antiracist education advocates also differ on the composition of their own agenda. Using Albert Memmi's (2000/1982) excellent definition of racism as

> a generalizing definition and valuation of differences, whether real or imaginary, to the advantage of the one defining and deploying them, and to the detriment of the one subjected to the act of definition, whose purpose is to justify hostility and assault, (p. 100)

the most appropriate antiracist education is one not solely focused on race. According to George Dei (1999), it is imperative that teachers understand that race and *difference* (gender, class, sexual orientation, etc.) frame the context for power and domination in society. Thus, in an antiracist educational practice Dei states,

> We should be skeptical of the neo-liberal language of "social justice" when presented in a way that fails to name race, racism, and antiracism in stark terms. The need to "teach tolerance" and the discourse of "social justice for all" should not mean a downplaying of the political implications of race and social difference. (p. 33)

In order to avoid any lack of clarity or criticalness, Paul Gilroy (1987; 1992) provides a particular conception of antiracism, which lends itself well to taking up the Freedom Center in a third space. According to Gilroy (1992), antiracist agendas are in trouble unless a univocal definition and strategy can be developed. Gilroy criticizes an antiracism that is solely focused on eliminating racism. Racism, in his opinion, is intricately linked to too many other issues (i.e., other issues of social difference). Gilroy (1987; 1992) critiques the dualist nature of many antiracist agendas as an either/or, victim/perpetrator binary. Instead of viewing oneself as a victim, one should see himself or herself as an active force combating racial (and other) subordination. Gilroy's antiracism, then, is one of agency and resistance, similar to both McLaren's and Sleeter's conceptions of multiculturalism in which students glean a more critical understanding of the past in order to see new, more ameliorative, possibilities for the present. Moreover, like multiculturalism this antiracist approach also demands greater attention to critique and activism. In the space created here race, racism, and power are laid bare, beckoning students to take them up, wrestle with them openly and honestly, and devise more hopeful possibilities for the future.

Moving forward with these definitions and my questions above, then, the Freedom Center offers a physical space and theoretical symbol from which to take up a more critical social studies curriculum. Considering that high school curriculums mandate coverage of both history and culture, the Freedom Center provides an authentic place of learning that can connect theoretical learning in the classroom with the world outside of school. In my home state of Kentucky, where rabid standardization has been fermenting for fifteen years, the Department of Education promotes two pivotal academic expectations (among a myriad of pivotal and not so pivotal others). Academic Expectation 2.16 states, "Students observe, analyze, and interpret human behaviors, social groupings, and institutions to better understand people and the relationships among individuals and among groups." Academic Expectation 2.20 states, "Students understand, analyze, and interpret historical events, conditions, trends, and issues to develop historical perspective."[4]

While these expectations are particular to the state of Kentucky, they most assuredly mirror similar standards in other states. In fact, the Freedom Center website at Northern Kentucky University provides an excellent teaching guide that connects curricular areas such as social studies, African American studies, English, and art to national standards such as National Standards for History-Historical Thinking, National Standards for History-Content, National Standards for Social Studies, National Geography Standards, and National Technology Standards. In order to remain as practical as possible, I am compelled to flesh out these standards, acknowledging the constraints placed upon teachers today. In addition, and more important, though, I also want to demonstrate the enormous flexibility we have, as public and organic intellectuals, to operate within these close quarters to exploit the gaps and fissures in the rock walls of standardization.

In light of these expectations, then, it is clear the Freedom Center can provide a provocative site and symbol for understanding, analyzing, and interpreting both the cultural and the historical. Moreover, in consideration of Bhabha's concept of cultural hybridity, the Freedom Center offers the possibility that a new negotiated understanding of culture and history may emerge, particularly as these relate to race and racism. Again, assuming a more critical perspective of multicultural and/or antiracist education is/are preferred and promoted in our social studies classrooms, lessons that involve theoretical study of the civil rights movement, for example, might be significantly enhanced by materials provided by, and visits to, the Freedom Center in order to glean a more historical understanding of where this struggle for rights began. As another example, lessons that investigate segregation or Jim Crow might be augmented by the Freedom Center's symbol as antidote to the culture of racism that has existed throughout this nation's history. The Freedom Center may also propel teachers/students toward other struggles for survival and renewal (e.g., indigenous Americans, antirenters in the 1630s and on, Catholic Irish in the early to mid 1800s, women throughout history, etc.).[5]

WHAT VISITORS MIGHT "SEE": POSSIBILITIES AND PROBLEMATICS

During my drive along I-75 to the newly opened Freedom Center, I was initially dismayed by its comparative size to the two stadiums that dwarf it; however, upon walking up to the Freedom Center, its magnitude and beauty are remarkable. The inside is open and spacious, clean and refined.

While walking through the Freedom Center, I was struck by the provocative nature of the photos, words, and artifacts in the exhibits. Yet I was overwhelmed by their mostly "liberal" feel. It is still a bit inexplicable, but I felt as if the Freedom Center was trying too hard to be palatable. It is not necessarily a soft sell, but it does not seem to challenge the status quo in a way I had hoped. I felt like it asks, Can we all agree that slavery was bad? and Aren't we glad that part of our society/history is behind us?

However, my mind was eased when I arrived at "The Struggle Continues" exhibit. As visitors enter this exhibit, they are first treated to and challenged by a video that documents the various forms of racism and oppression that still exist today. Past this small theater, visitors travel down a long, narrow, industrial-feeling hallway with life-size video images of oppression covering and moving along the walls. In addition to the images, several interactive computers exist, which provide a more in-depth look at continuing oppression and educational materials targeted at combating these issues.

For social studies classes with a multicultural/antiracist focus visiting the Freedom Center, six issues in particular are explored in this interactive exhibit: genocide, hunger, illiteracy, racism, slavery, and tyranny. Not only do they provide background information, but the exhibit also highlights an individual who has combated these issues. For example, in the illiteracy section, the interactive exhibit highlights Paulo Freire for his critical work in Brazil and abroad. Additionally, a portion of each section is dedicated to what we can do, providing information about texts, other museums, and websites.

Thinking back to my time as a community service club moderator when I was a high school teacher, my students could have really benefited from the resources provided by this exhibit. Each year, when we participated in the thirty-hour famine put on by World Vision, our experiences could have been significantly enhanced by a field trip to the Freedom Center and research on the materials/resources they provide.[6]

Thinking ahead to other possibilities, social studies curriculums that focus on civics and government might be nuanced and deepened by resources offered by the Freedom Center such as Amnesty International (www.amnesty.org) and Human Rights Watch (www.hrw.org). Additionally, students could explore and activate the suggestions contained in the What can you do? section: exercise your own freedoms, vote, educate yourself about your government, read the Constitution, join in political activities, and read reports from Human Rights Watch.

USING SERVICE LEARNING AS A TOOL
TO ACTIVATE WHAT IS LEARNED

In addition to the educational materials and field trips that the Freedom Center offers for theoretical study in our classrooms, it also provides a site that can expand what is gleaned from service learning experiences tethered to high school curriculums. While no univocal definition for service learning exists, several elements cut across its conceptualization in the literature: authentic curricula, reflection, and service to the community. Leonard Burns (1998) refers to service learning as a "structured learning experience." V. Ann Paulins (1999) argues that the purpose of service learning "is to increase learning capacity by allowing students to apply knowledge rather than simply receive information in a lecture setting" (p. 67). In the same way, Theresa Prosser and Jeri Levesque (1997) claim, "Service learning programs are designed to build, improve, or advance participants' ability to solve problems and assume the responsibilities of community membership" (p. 33). Steven Fisher (1997) suggests that service learning should "seek the common good" and create "critical citizens." Carolyn O'Grady (2000) posits, "In a service learning program, individuals engage in community activities in a context of rigorous academic experience. Service learning allows teachers to employ a variety of teaching strategies that emphasize student-centered, interactive, experiential education" (p. 7). Finally, Angela Barton (2000) argues that service learning incorporates "activities that combine classroom work with social action and service in order to promote development of students' subject matter knowledge, practical skills, social responsibility, and civic values" (p. 803).

Since multiple interpretations of service learning exist, it is crucial, then, to articulate what goals, purposes, procedures, and outcomes are advocated. Wanting to make the common elements listed above even more critical, I argue service learning should work toward *collaboration* with the community, the twinning of theory and practice, an understanding of social difference, and the development of a sense of social justice and caring. Building upon Steven Fisher's (1997) service learning for social justice, cultural studies (Hall, 1992; Hytten, 1997; Wright, 2001), the feminist ethic of care (Noddings, 1984; Thayer-Bacon, 2000), and the joint creation of a framework and theory for service learning, "critical service learning" (Masucci & Renner, 2000), I use in my university courses, I continue to seek more constructive, critical, democratic, and emancipatory possibilities for service work and activism for any classroom.

To this end, Seyla Benhabib (1992), in *Situating the Self*, provides crucial direction. In an effort to articulate structural notions of justice with individual notions of care, Benhabib offers the concept of the 'general and concrete other.' In its most basic sense, relating it to service learning work (Renner, 2002; 2004), this concept requires that we position our service in both a structural and individual context. Similar to the concept of 'praxis,' where action and reflection build off of and depend on one another, an understanding of the general and concrete other necessitates that our service work with concrete others (often different from ourselves based on race, class, gender, etc.) be buttressed with more general understandings of why they face the injustice they do.

Conversely, just as reflection without action is empty, simply understanding the structure is as meaningless. Action with concrete others is critical. Here, injustice bears a face, a name, and a story. Here, theory breathes. And, from here, armed with an understanding of the structure, work for justice begins. Extending Benhabib's concept and weaving in Arendt's "enlarged mentality" and Noddings' "preparedness to care," students are better prepared to engage with society in the future as democratic citizens. Based upon their service learning work at an individual level and their theoretical understanding of injustice at a structural level, students are equipped to more critically interact with future concrete others and become activists for justice.

In a further attempt to remain practical, I follow here with suggestions regarding how work for justice might begin. In Kentucky, for teachers activating these more critical service learning opportunities that focus on difference and injustice, one might cite Academic Expectation 2.17: "Students interact effectively and work cooperatively with the many diverse ethnic and cultural groups of our nation and world." As an example of a potential service learning partnership, teachers may elect to partner with a local social service agency that deals with issues such as illiteracy, homelessness, hunger, immigration, or domestic violence. While exploring the connectedness of various forms of social difference such as race, class, gender, sexual orientation, and nation and the likely consequence of injustice that socially emerges, teachers and students can look to the Freedom Center as reminder, physical symbol, and theoretical presence to amplify the experience in the community. Questions such as those posed earlier on the concrete slab at the groundbreaking ceremony might receive much more nuanced answers with an articulation of classroom study, service learning, and use of the Freedom Center.

Reflecting back to "The Struggle Continues" exhibit, critical service-learning possibilities certainly exist for the civics/government class confronting tyranny. Again, students could involve themselves in political campaigns and issues revolving around injustice, using the Freedom Center's suggestions as invaluable resources. In addition, this particular exhibit's suggestions for resources on illiteracy may also be very useful for a service learning partnership targeted at combating poor literacy rates in schools and/or communities. Researching information on and/or gleaning suggestions from the National Alliance of Urban Literacy Coalitions (www.naulo.org), the National Center for Family Literacy, and/or the United Nations Educational, Scientific, and Cultural Organization (www.unesco.org) could be quite useful to both the theoretical and practical components of a service learning experience. Additionally, students could research more on the possibilities and (more likely) problematics of the current No Child Left Behind legislation (www.ed.gov) in terms of combating illiteracy.

THE FREEDOM CENTER AS RESOURCE AND CULTURAL HYBRIDITY HARBINGER: NEW MEANINGS AND TRANSFORMATIVE RESISTANCE

Clearly, racism is alive and well in our society. Potentially, our only site to begin to undo its history and presence starts in our schools. Such resources as Cincinnati's new Freedom Center offer transformative possibilities and a liminal third space for our students to make new sense of race and racism. Together, perhaps their study; their collaboration with fellow students, the community, and socially and culturally different "others"; and their time spent visiting the Freedom Center both virtually and physically will enable them to negotiate new meanings for justice, care, and antiracism. Like the solidarity established with the construction of the Underground Railroad, the same type of resistive unity may conceivably emerge with the construction and use of Cincinnati's new Freedom Center.

Our future, our history, and our present are all a process of "becoming," *not* determined and most certainly open to interpretation. Perhaps the erection and compromise of this Freedom Center, both as symbol and building—amidst other buildings and symbols of greed, corruption, and racism—resurrects and promises, like a beacon, hope and compassion for a nation and world that so desperately needs it.

EPILOGUE

Looking out the front doors of the Freedom Center, across the suspension bridge, I watch the Ohio River flow westward and consider what this view must have been like 150 to 200 years before. Was there relief from this vantage point? Was there still a sense of struggle? Was there still a sense that racism would continue beyond the bondage of slavery? Today, as people walk out these doors and share my southward view, can they feel the palpable heat from the racial tension of the city behind them? What message did they derive from the Freedom Center? Thank goodness that portion of our history is behind us? The struggle continues? Stealing one last glimpse of the mighty Ohio spanned by one of the most spectacular icons of the Industrial Revolution, the John Roebling Suspension Bridge (which was the prototype for the celebrated Brooklyn Bridge), I grab my partner's hand and head for the car that will carry us south again, ready to carry on in the struggle, renewed, if even only for a moment, by the possibility of Cincinnati's new Freedom Center.

NOTES

1. www.freedomcenter.org.

2. For example, as of July 11, 2003, the Freedom Center had raised $92 million, which included government and private commitments, pledges, and in-kind contributions.

3. Of particular concern/note here is the cost of admission to the Freedom Center. Considering the rising cost of attending events at either one of the stadiums adjacent to it, the Freedom Center struck me as a bit expensive: Adults $12; Students with ID $10; Seniors $10; and Children $8.

4. www.kde.state.ky.us.

5. For an exciting and critical listing of possible multicultural lessons, see www.rethinkingschools.org, www.teachers.net, and http://www2.lhrich.org/pocantico/tubman/class.htm. I would like to thank my friend and colleague, Dr. Milton Brown, for his close examination of this paper after his visit to the Freedom Center and for his particular suggestions in this section.

6. Sites include the Center on Hunger and Poverty at Brandeis University (www.centeronhunger.org), Share our Strength (www.strength.org), and specific information on hunger in the United States (www.secondharvest.org/site_content.asp?s=42), Sudan (www.careusa.org/careswork/countryprofiles/98.asp), Haiti (www.careusa.org/newsroom/featurestories/2004/mar/03162004_haitiqa.asp), and North Korea (http://seedquest.org/spi). The Freedom Center staff was extremely helpful in providing this information.

REFERENCES

Anglen, R., Alltucker, K., Bonfield, T., & Horn, D. (2001, October 7). Riot costs add up. *The Cincinnati Enquirer*.

Barton, A. (2000). Crafting multicultural science education with preservice teachers through service learning. *Journal of Curriculum Studies, 32*(6), pp. 797–820.

Benhabib, S. (1992). *Situating the Self: Gender, community, and postmodernism*. New York: Routledge.

Bhaba, H. (1994). *The Location of Culture*. New York: Routledge.

Burns, L. (1998). Make sure it's service learning, not just community service. *The Education Digest, 64*, 38–41.

Burton, T. (2001, June 7–13). Getting whacked. *City Beat, 7*(29).

Dei, G. 1999. The denial of difference. Reframing anti-racist praxis. *Race, Ethnicity and Education 2*, 17–37.

Fisher, S. (1997, June 5). Opening Remarks to the Service Learning for Social Justice Conference in Appalachia.

Gilroy, P. (1992). The end of antiracism. In J. Donald & A. Rattansi, (Eds.), *"Race," Culture and Difference*. London: Sage.

Gilroy, P. (1987). *There ain't no black in the Union Jack: The cultural politics of race and nation*. Chicago: University of Chicago Press.

Giroux, H. (1994). Insurgent multiculturalism and the promise of pedagogy. In D. T. Goldberg (Ed.), *Multiculturalism: A critical reader*. Oxford: Blackwell.

Hall, S. (1992). Cultural studies and its theoretical legacies. In L. Grossberg, C. Nelson, & P. Treichler (Eds.), *Cultural Studies*, 277–294. New York: Routledge.

Hine, D., Hine, W., & Harrold, S. (2003). *The African-American odyssey*. (2nd ed.). UpperSaddle River, NJ: Prentice Hall.

Hytten, K. (1997). Cultural studies of education: Mapping the terrain. *Educational Foundations, 11*, 39–60.

Kincheloe, J., & Steinberg, S. (1997). *Changing Multiculturalism*. Buckingham: Open University Press.

Masucci, M., & Renner, A. (2000). Reading the lives of others: The Winton Homes Library Project—A cultural studies analysis of critical service-learning for education. *The High School Journal, 84*, 36–47.

McLaren, P. (1997). *Revolutionary multiculturalism: Pedagogies of dissent for the new millennium*. Boulder: Westview.

McLaren, P. (1994). White terror and oppositional agency: Towards a critical multiculturalism. In D. T. Goldberg (Ed.), *Multiculturalism: A critical reader*. Oxford: Blackwell.

Memmi, A. 2000/1982. Definition. *Racism*. Steve Martinot, Trans. Minneapolis: University of Minnesota Press.

Moloney, S. (2001, April 12). Justice Department to review shooting. *The Cincinnati Post*.

National Underground Railroad Freedom Center. *Heroes are everywhere. Stand up and be one*. Brochure produced in Cincinnati, OH.

Noddings, N. (1984). *Caring: A feminine approach to ethics and moral education*. Berkeley: University of California Press.

O'Grady, C. (2000). *Integrating service learning and multicultural education in colleges and universities*. Mahwah, NJ: LEA.

Osborne, K. (2001, May 1). City wrestles with race remedies. *The Cincinnati Post*.

Paulins, V. (1999). Service learning and civic responsibility: The consumer in American society. *Journal of Family and Consumer Sciences, 91*, 66–72.

Prosser, T., & Levesque, J. (1997). Supporting literacy through service learning. *The Reading Teacher, 51*, 32–38.

Renner, A. (2004). Caring solidarity: Evolving a theoretical and practical agenda for service-learning and pedagogy. *Kentucky Journal of Excellence*. Available from http://www.secc.kctcs.edu/kje/article_list.htm.

Renner, A. (2002). *Butterflies, boundaries, and breadfruit: The shared story of a service learning experience in Jamaica*. Unpublished dissertation. University of Tennessee, Knoxville.

Sleeter, C. (1996). *Multicultural education as social activism*. New York: State University of New York Press.

Thayer-Bacon, B. (2000). Caring reasoning. *Inquiry: Critical Thinking across the Disciplines, 3*(2), 22–34.

United States Department of the Interior. (n.d.). *Underground Railroad*. Brochure produced by the Network to Freedom National Park Service.

Wright, H. (2001, March). Toward cultural studies praxis: Blending service learning for social justice and cultural studies. Keynote address: Southeastern Association of Educational Studies Conference, Knoxville, TN.

CHAPTER ELEVEN

COME AND LISTEN TO A STORY

UNDERSTANDING THE APPALACHIAN HILLBILLY IN POPULAR CULTURE

MARY JEAN RONAN HERZOG

INTRODUCTION

The Appalachian region of the United States has increasingly become the focus of scholarly investigation. Studies of the region's econmics, history, literature, music, and culture blossomed in the 1970s and have continued to identify the region as inclusive of multiple identities and multiple meanings, both geographic and cultural (Billings, Norman, & Ledford, 1999; Eller, 1982; Lewis, 1999; Williamson, 1995). Appalachia has differing geographic and political boundaries depending on the source used to define it. The Appalachian Regional Commission (ARC) was formed in 1965 as a state and federal initiative after the region attracted the attention of the John F. Kennedy and Lyndon B. Johnson administrations (ARC, n.d.). The subsequent War on Poverty mandates initiated by Kennedy and carried out by Johnson found the region to be abundant in natural resources and lacking in industrial and agricultural opportunities. Politicans argued that these economic failings were the reason why poverty was so pervasive among the mountain people. Besides establishing ARC, the War on Poverty initiatives also included a highway program to reduce the geographic isolation of the Appalachian region and to promote the growth of industry. Today, ARC defines the geographic boundaries of the region from northern Alabama to upstate New York and divides the region into northern, central, and southern sections including sections of Georgia, Kentucky, Maryland, Mississippi, North Carolina, Ohio, South Carolina, Tennessee, Virginia, and West Virginia.

Clearly, the geographical region is a vast hybrid of cultures, traditions, and religions. There are sections that remain relatively isolated, such as the mining regions on the borders of Kentucky and Virginia, while there are other areas that are flocked to by tourists. Increasingly, Appalachia is a target destination for retirees and young urban professionals alike.

Early in the twenty-first century, at the height of the reality television rage, rural stereotypes were thrown into the entertainment formula. The recent reality television shows featuring "hillbillies" including Columbia Broadcasting System's (CBS) *New Beverly Hillbillies* and the National Broadcasting Company's (NBC) *High Life* and to a lesser extent cable's FOX Broadcasting Company's *Simple Life*, starring millionare playgirls Paris Hilton and Nicole Ritchie, set off a wave of protest from rural-minded people in the United States. The Center for Rural Strategies (n.d.) in Kentucky led a nationwide campaign against the networks with press conferences and full-page advertisements in national newspapers. The center's website posted over forty commentaries from notable protestors such as West Virginia Senator Robert Byrd and Arkansas Governor Mike Huckabee, who argued it was time to stop stereotyping rural Americans and noted that no other gendered, socioeconomic, ethnic, or racial group would be subjected to such overt and "politically incorrect" public bias and media bias in the twenty-first century. Major newspapers were also sympathetic to the rural cause; in a piece called "Victory for Reality," *The Cincinnati Enquirer* (2003) published the following:

> CBS planned a reality TV series featuring [a] real-life, low-income rural family. In so-called "hick-hunts," they were searching for the perfect stereotypical Appalachian family. They would move them into an opulent California mansion with luxuries and invite the nation to laugh as they bumbled their way through the day. But plenty of Kentuckians, Ohioans, and Appalachian people elsewhere weren't amused—or silent. In this day of hypersensitivity to diversity and political correctness, Appalachians have been a group that it is still socially acceptable to demean and joke about . . . But rural folks have spoken up and said "enough" to the Hollywood mockers. Good for them, and for all friends of rural America. (p. B12)

Likewise, the indignation over *The High Life* took the commonly accepted hillbilly stereotype to task. Kentucky Congressman Hal Rogers (n.d.) stated:

> It is incomprehensible that anyone would think it's acceptable to propel negative and erroneous stereotypes about the people of Appalachia. No one would dare propose creating a program focusing on stereotypes about African Americans, Muslims, or Jews. Why

then would it be okay to bash those of us living in rural America?
(*Rural Reality*, para 3)

This chapter begins with a discussion of how I approach multicultural education with my preservice teachers at Western Carolina University, located in the mountains of western North Carolina. My goal is to enable my students to think critically about the issues of the day and to face discomfiting questions of social justice that might challenge their own comfort. In this chapter, I debunk the myth of the hillbilly caricature with the aim of enabling my students to develop a more informed understanding of the complexity and diversity of the Appalachian region and its people and to enable them to challenge the easily accepted stereotypes that perpetuate these negative and demeaning images in their own classrooms by situating the problem of rural and Appalachian stereotypes in the context of critical multicultural education and civil rights pedagogy through a deconstruction of the Appalachian mountain hillbilly image. Such stereotypes have been absent from national discussions on diversity and multicultural education, yet they have been stigmatizing an entire region of the United States and its people. Teaching critical analysis of the broad issues in multicultural education is more effective if students learn to empathize as well as sympathize with the plights of the downtrodden, thus expanding their perspectives. In other words, if students can relate to some of the experiences of oppressed people, even on a minor scale, their understanding and empathy will be enhanced. If inclined toward an us-versus-them attitude, the deconstruction of stereotypes about their own community state, or region can help them develop more of an us-and-them perspective (Carnes, 1995).

My classes begin with an analysis of texts framed by scholarship in Appalachian studies—a hybridity of history, literature, and cultural studies of the program—and an analysis of *the* historical, mass media, and popular cultural accounts of the Appalachian region and its people. In order to reveal the stereotypically based undocumented assertions and gross generalizations of the region's people, we begin with a discussion of Harry Caudill, *Night Comes to the Cumberlands* (1963); Weller, *Yesterday's People* (1965); Bill Bryson, *A Walk in the Woods*, (1988); and James Dickey, *Deliverance* (1970), whereby images of Appalachian people in these various works range from barbarians to people living hopelessly in the past with the future passing by them. What follows is a detailed discussion of the "hillbilly" as a cultural pop icon and the information I draw from for transformational curriculum and pedagogy in my classes.

APPALACHIAN STUDIES

To begin, I draw from the field of Appalachian studies, which is a hybrid field of regional, interdisciplinary studies of history, literature, anthropology, religion, and cultural studies. Early accounts of the Appalachian region were often based on widely read but biased and undocumented assertions and generalizations. These include Toynbee, *A Study of History* (1942); Caudill, *Night Comes to the Cumberlands* (1963); and Weller, *Yesterday's People* (1965). Images of Appalachians in these works range from barbarians to apathetic people living in squalor barely subsisting, with little hope for the future.

On the one hand, Appalachian culture is viewed as backward, incestuous, isolated, and poverty-stricken as in Dickey's *Deliverance* (1970). Billings, Norman, and Ledford (1999) referred to this view as "a traumatized culture where withdrawal, depression, inertia, self-blame and resignation rule" (p. 6). On the other hand, Appalachian people have also been romanticized as "strong women, noble African Americans, and virtuous Indians . . . a fierce and solitary people" (p. 10).

Scholars from history, literature, and the social sciences have produced a large body of work on the Appalachian region that flourished in the late 1960s and early 1970s. This Appalachian studies movement has been an academic vehicle for critical analysis, examining and challenging both negative images and stereotypes and the overly romanticized visions of the region. Both the negative and the romanticized generalizations have contributed to a public image based on myth rather than on facts and reality. Appalachian scholars within the academy have addressed the issues and spoken publicly, but they have not had much influence on media representations. The campaign against *The New Beverly Hillbillies* was a new approach by an advocacy group outside academe (Center for Rural Strategies, n.d.).

Historians criticize the overgeneralizations about the region as an isolated "backwater" and point to biases and contradictions. For example, Ron Eller (1999) argues that the Appalachian region is the "most maligned" in the United States and that it is "still dressed in the garments of backwardness, violence, poverty and hopelessness . . . playing the role of the 'other America' " (pp. ix–xi). Eller, like other Appalachian scholars, has challenged stereotypical ideas of the region with historical works that call many of the prevailing images into question. Writing about *The Kentucky Cycle*, a Pulitzer–prize-winning play that spawned a round of criticism, Eller (1999) says,

> The "idea of Appalachia," perpetuated in contemporary work such as *The Kentucky Cycle*, not only masks the exploitation of land and people in the region, but it obscures the diversity of conditions, relationships, and cultures within Appalachian society itself—diversity of race, gender and class as well as diversity in religion, education and history. Appalachian scholars have come to recognize that there are many Appalachians, and applying generalizations often contradict local heritage and experiences. (pp. x–xi)

Billings, Norman, and Ledford (1999) continue this line of criticism about the popular image of the Appalachian region, arguing that the stereotypical perceptions ignore the reality of the diverse communities and cultures within.

Other historians criticize the overgeneralizations about the region as an isolated "backwater" and point to biases and contradictions as well. For example, Horace Kephart (1976), one of the forces behind the development of the Great Smoky Mountain National Park, began his now classic *Our Southern Highlanders* with this description: "The Southern Highlander [is] a tall, slouching figure in homespun, who carries a rifle as habitually as he does his hat, and who may tilt its muzzle toward a stranger" (p. 11). Kephart traveled to the region to escape his life in the Midwest where he was a librarian, alcoholic, and father of five or six children to find the "back of beyond" and to chronicle the life of the mountaineer. He noted:

> When I went south into the mountains I was seeking a Back of Beyond. This for more reasons than one. With an inborn taste for the wild and romantic, I yearned for a strange land and a people that had the charm of originality . . . in Far Appalachia. (1976, p. 29)

Ronald Lewis (1999) writes that the idea of "Appalachia" was "born in the fertile minds of late-nineteenth-century local color writers" such as John Fox, Jr., for whom, he said, it was a "willful creation and not merely the product of a literary imagination" (pp. 21–22). Appalachian scholar Darlene Wilson (1999) analyzed Fox's papers and works in terms of creating an "Appalachian otherness" and has shown that they were economically self-serving. According to Wilson (1999), the Fox family was involved in developing the coal industry in central Appalachia, and John Fox, Jr., worked as a publicist for them. Fox's fiction became accepted as the normal representation of the region, and over time, it became entrenched as if historically accurate. Fast forward 150 years, and the region is still subjected to the "idea of Appalachia as a homogeneous region physically, culturally and economically isolated from mainstream America" (Lewis, 1999, p. 22).

THE HILLBILLY AS A BEST SELLER

As an entrée to a study of stereotypes and negative images of rural people, my students read *A Walk in the Woods: Rediscovering America on the Appalachian Trail* by Bill Bryson (1998), a nationwide bestseller on the *New York Times* nonfiction list in spite of its inaccurate depictions. For example, Bryson describes the Appalachian Mountains as having woods that are full of "animal" and "human" perils such as: "[R]attlesnakes and water moccasins and nests of copperheads; bobcats, bears, coyotes, wolves, and wild boar; loony hillbillies destabilized by gross quantities of impure corn liquor and generations of profoundly unbiblical sex" (p. 10).

In reality the closest water moccasins live several hundred miles away in southern South Carolina, and the closest wolves dwell in Montana and northern Canada. Moreover, the corn liquor industry has been replaced by the production of marijuana and methedrine.

After reading A *Walk in the Woods*, my students write reactions on a survey designed to ascertain attitudes about rural issues. My students' reactions are almost always uniformly negative. For example, one student wrote, "This book only adds to the myth that everyone in the South is a hick. I have lived in these mountains for my entire life, and I am sick and tired of this image." The book is useful as a point of departure for discussions of negative stereotypes and issues of diversity. Once the students examine stereotypes of the Appalachian region, they are more apt to examine other racial, ethnic, regional, social class, and gendered stereotypes.

In spite of its inaccurate depictions the Christopher Lehmann-Haup review for the *New York Times* (1998) praised the book as a "perceptive look at the strange territory where forest and American culture collide." Lehmann-Haup especially liked Bryson's tales of the "trail's perils: its dangerous animals, killing diseases, and loony hillbillies." Amazon.Com (n.d.), describes A *Walk in the Woods* as "a near perfect way to spend an afternoon." Plus, of the 888 customer reviews on Amazon.Com only a small portion were critical, and of those most were offended at his abuse of nature, and only a couple readers objected to his liberal use of stereotypes of the people in the region.

THE HILLBILLY AND HOLLYWOOD

Willliamson (1995) argues that the hillbilly stereotype has been entertaining the public since the midnineteenth century. His analysis of the purpose and function of the hillbilly stereotype was published in the well-documented book *Hillbillyland: What the Movies Did to the Mountains and What the Mountains Did to the Movies*. He says we have an "ambiguous need for hillbillies . . . that begins with laughter and ends in pain" and that the hillbilly is "safely dismissible, a left-behind remnant, a symbolic non-adult and willful renegade from capitalism" (1995, p. ix).

The hillbilly image is, indeed, fraught with ambiguity. It is sometimes light-hearted, comical, and entertaining and at other times, dark, dangerous, and violent. One of the most tenacious and terrifying hillbilly images came from the movie version of the novel *Deliverance*, in which a violent mountain man is graphically shown sodomizing a city dweller from Atlanta in a backwoods bayou. Williamson (1995) notes that the book's and the movie's violence was meant to symbolize an urban plan to pollute and exploit the environment of the Appalachian region by raping the mountains and damming the rivers. Regardless of Dickey's (1970) intention to portray the evil's "progress" in America, the *Deliverance* mountain man became a cultural icon, and to hear dueling banjos evokes an image of a moralless Appalachian region beset with incestuous imbeciles, trash, and violence.

A more recent film, *Nell*, shot in the western North Carolina mountains, is the sentimental and romanticized story of a woman with a speech
impairment who is being raised without the benefit of modern civilization
(Lewis, 1999). *Nell* continued the Hollywood tradition of illustrating the
region as backward, isolated, and populated by people of lesser intelligence.

These popular images are so entrenched that they are resistant to change
both within and outside the region. The Appalachian hillbilly is glorified
within the region itself and sold on highway billboards and in small town
shops. The media, both national and local, continue to perpetuate the negative stereotypes and overgeneralizations about the region. Scholars debate
the impact of the hillbilly caricature, some claiming that it is an honorable
and wise character and others arguing it is a factor in the marginalization of
the region (Harkins, 2003; Lewis, 1999).

THE TOWN OF MURPHY, THE HILLBILLY FUGITIVE, AND THE POPULAR PRESS

A recent example of the popular media's portrayal of the Appalachian region—and one that my students can relate to since it occurred in the western counties of North Carolina—is illustrated by the search and capture of
fugitive Eric Rudolph, who was identified as a suspect in the bombing of an
Alabama abortion clinic and Olympic Park in Atlanta, Georgia. The search
began in 1998 and ended on June 3, 2003, in Murphy, North Carolina.

Rudolph, the subject of a manhunt by the Federal Bureau of Investigation (FBI), and on the "Ten Most Wanted" list, was thought to be hiding
in the North Carolina mountains. After five years in the woods, Rudolph
earned his nomenclature as a mountain man, but like a large percentage of
the population of western North Carolina, he was not a "local" from North
Carolina. Originally from Florida, he moved to Nantahala, North Carolina,
with his mother, four brothers, and one sister when he was fourteen, shortly
after his father died. He attended Nantahala High School, a small school
with a typical graduating class of twenty, but dropped out after ninth grade
when he started working as a carpenter. The high school is in Macon County,
the fastest growing county in the state, about one and a half hours from
Atlanta. Eventually Rudolph received a General Education Diploma and
briefly attended college at regional Western Carolina University. After serving in the U.S. Army from 1987 to 1989, he was allegedly discharged for
smoking marijuana and then returned to western North Carolina and re-
sumed carpentry. In 1996, Rudolph started using aliases.

In the summer of 1996 a bomb exploded at Olympic Park in Atlanta
during the summer Olympics, killing forty-four-year-old Alice Hawthorne
and injuring more than one hundred other people. In January 1998, Rudolph's
truck was identified fleeing the scene of a bomb explosion at the New Women

All Women Clinic in Birmingham, Alabama, where a guard was killed and a nurse was seriously injured. The search for him began. The FBI linked two other bombings from 1997 to him. In 1998, his truck was found in the Nantahala Gorge by FBI agents, and they concentrated their search in the western counties of North Carolina, with headquarters set up in Andrews, in Cherokee County, the western-most county in the state with borders on Tennessee and Georgia. Rudolph had been living in a trailer two miles from Murphy, North Carolina.

Throughout the five-year search for Rudolph, the region was described in stereotypical terms based not on facts but rather on unexamined generalizations. Rudolph was cast by the popular press as a skinny, long-haired mountain man, when in fact his weight was in normal range, his hair was short, and his mustache was trimmed when he was found. He told one of the jailers that eating spring lizards was a little like eating sushi. Moreover, the town of Murphy was consistently depicted as "backwater" by the popular press who ignored the journalistic opportunity to present a more complex and nuanced picture of the town and the surrounding region. Rather than seeking facts and information from a wide range and variety of sources, journalists seem content to base generalizations on comments from characters supporting their viewpoints.

Many of my students at Western Carolina University come from the small town of Murphy, which is home to about 1,500 residents and is the county seat of Cherokee County in the far southwest corner of North Carolina. Hardly a backwater that is cut off from the rest of the world, Cherokee is described as vacation place "where the forested mountains touch the sky, the lakes sparkle, and the air is crisp and clean, and the charm of small town America still exists" (Cherokee County Chamber of Commerce, n.d.). Murphy has a downtown with wide streets and busy stores, including antique stores and the Daily Grind Café frequented by reporters and gawkers ordering cappuccino in the first days after Rudolph's capture. Murphy has a stately courthouse made of blue marble from the nearby town of Marble and a distinctive Baptist Church at the end of Main Street. A victim of contemporary suburban sprawl, the town also contains the requisite gentrified fast-food joints such as Burger King and McDonald's, along with several convenience stores, such as Wal-Mart, a Mexican restaurant, and a Chinese restaurant, which stretch down the four-lane highway that surrounds the downtown area.

Murphy is closer to the capital cities of Tennessee, Georgia, and South Carolina than it is to Raleigh, the capital of North Carolina, about 360 miles away. The phrase *From Murphy to Manteo* is symbolic of the 550 mile distance from the western edge to the farthest eastern coastal town, from border to border. Yet Murphy is only about 100 miles from Asheville, 120 miles from Atlanta, and 60 miles from Chattanooga, Tennessee. In fact, the traveler driving to Atlanta runs the risk of hitting heavy traffic within forty or fifty miles. It is about half an hour's drive to the Olympic whitewater course on the Ocoee River. Although Murphy is far from some places, residents tire of hearing how remote it is. As one of my students from Murphy said, "They're always surprised to hear that someone from Murphy has never been to Asheville. So I like to ask, 'What? And you've never been to Murphy?' "

The North Carolina Rural Center reports that 54 percent of the county population was born in North Carolina. The media portrayals of the area focus on negative stereotypes. In an article in the *New Yorker* about Rudolph, Tony Horwitz (1999) claimed the people in the area distrust outsiders and the government, saying, "[T]his part of North Carolina, like much of southern Appalachia, has always been jealous of its privacy" (p. 46). His source is a ninety-two-year-old former logger and bootlegger whose colorful quotes make most people in Murphy cringe. My students, who are teachers and school administrators in Murphy and throughout the region, were not interviewed by Horwitz, and they often complain about how the media finds the most illiterate and conservative people when they want to do an interview about Appalachia. Horwitz interviewed a nationally known wilderness guide who lives in the area but did not include his comments in the article, as they did not fit Horwitz' preconceived ideas.

Horwitz did however, interview a couple named Mosteller and concluded that "like almost all his neighbors in the Nantahala . . . abortion and homosexuality are almost universally condemned" (p. 46). Horwitz said rightwing extremists such as Rudolph and his family friend, Tom Branham, who was arrested for illegal possession of explosives and firearms are, "startlingly common in the Nantahala" (p. 47). Apparently, he did not observe and interview the hordes of middle-class tourists and new residents who have recently flocked to the area to work and play in the Nantahala River. These immigrants to the area are clad in expensive "outdoor" wear sporting clothing from Birkenstock, L. L. Bean, Eddie Bauer, and Patagonia.

The media images of the region suffer from the same syndrome that afflicts most American news. Conclusions are drawn on scanty evidence, news stories quickly become sound bytes, and notable reporters exaggerate, plagiarize, and lie. The mountains are described as snake-infested. The mountain people are variously described and stereotyped as bible-belt religious fanatics and dumb, inbred hillbillies. The mountains are not "infested" with snakes; it is the rare hiker who is lucky enough to discover one on a trail. There are no more snakes in the North Carolina mountains than in the Ramapo Mountains twenty miles north of New York City.

Although Christianity is hegemonic in the southern Appalachian Mountain region, each county has a great diversity of Christian religions, including Assembly of God, Baptist, Church of Christ, Church of the Latter Day Saints (a.k.a. Mormons), Roman Catholic, Methodist, Presbyterian, and Unitarian. While there are people who describe themselves as "born again" or evangelical, the stereotype of the Bible-thumping fanatic is pervasive.

Bumiller (2003) reported in the *New York Times* that white, southern evangelicals accounted for about 40 percent of the votes that George W. Bush received in the 2000 presidential election.

IMPLICATIONS FOR CURRICULUM AND PEDAGOGY

In my experience at Western Carolina University, undergraduate, preservice teachers are often uncomfortable challenging and recognizing their white, patriarchal, middle-class norms. For them, teaching about multicultural issues is often associated with information about the plight of African Americans starting with slavery, the Civil War, Reconstruction, *Plessy versus Ferguson*, *Brown versus Board of Education*, the civil rights movement, and the black power movement. Clearly with the recent influx of immigrants from all over the world into our nation's schools it is necessary to broaden the discussion to other groups of people who are currently also disenfranchised and marginalized in the United States.

In order to enable my students to learn to think more critically about issues around culture and race, I start by encouraging them to look inward at themselves and their place in the world. I begin with having my students view the Southern Poverty Law Center's award winning film, *The Shadow of Hate* (2000). This film includes historical information on the treatment of several minority groups, including Indians, Irish-Catholics, Japanese, African Americans, and Jews. The film ends with a dramatic juxtaposition of two dangerous extremists: the former grand wizard of the Knights of the Ku Klux Klan, David Duke, and the Nation of Islam leader, Louis Farrakhan. Both men are leading two different hate rallies where mobs are shouting in a frenzied rage. While Duke and Farrakhan are at opposite ends of the political spectrum, students often comment about how similar they are in their actions and rhetoric.

The students are also surprised that although one man is white and the other black, they both personify racism, anti-Semitism, and bigotry. After viewing the film, we begin with a discussion of the *hillbilly* stereotype since the students are living in Appalachia, and this iconic symbol is local and particular to their personal situation in life. This relevancy provides the stimulus and framework for a change process to take place through discourse. As they begin to recognize how Appalachian culture is marginalized in American society, they begin to develop empathy for other groups who are also disenfranchised.

As noted earlier, my students also read *A Walk in the* Woods by Bill Bryson (1988), a nationwide bestseller on the *New York Times* nonfiction list, in spite of its inaccurate depictions. Next, we turn our attention to the popular press, where students critique the media's caricature of the hillbilly cultural subgroup as an ignorant, straw-chewing, suspender-wearing mountain person. My students react to the hillbilly archetype on a continuum that ranges from humor to anger to embarrassment to apathy to silence.

My students are also exposed to the failed CBS reality show *The New Beverly Hillbillies* that set off a wave of protest from rural people, and they read the Center for Rural Strategies' (n.d.) arguments against the show. The gist of the opposition was that it is time to stop stereotyping and insulting rural Americans and that the ridicule of rural people would never be acceptable if aimed at any other cultural or racial groups, particularly people of color.

CONCLUSION

Clearly, Appalachian people remain one of the few cultural groups for whom still demeaning images are generally accepted and not questioned in American society. While the mainstream media would never cast aspersions on blacks, Mexicans, Asians, or gay people, they often readily talk about rural or mountain people as "rednecks," "hillbillies," and "grits." In this chapter an examination of the hillbilly caricature in contemporary American culture from three perspectives provides the platform for the analysis of several recent incidents in popular culture that perpetuate the hillbilly stereotype. Unlike the early biased accounts of the mountaineer, the scholarly work in Appalachian studies blossomed in the 1970s' objectively documented histories of communities from West Virginia to North Georgia and contested commonly held biased viewpoints. The recent movement against *The New Beverly Hillbillies* put the issue in the public spotlight for examination in the context of rural America. Continued work in this area would be more powerful if academics working in teacher preparation programs and educational leadership enabled school personnel to develop a more informed and public understanding of the complex and diverse Appalachian region and its people by challenging the taken-for-granted stereotypes and cultural myths.

REFERENCES

Amazon.Com. (n.d.). Customer's reviews of *A walk in the woods*. Retrieved October 18, 2006, from http://www.amazon.com/gp/product/customerreviews/0767902513/ref=cm_cr_dp_2_1/102-1751480-4225710?ie=UTF8&customer-reviews.sort%5Fby=-SubmissionDate&n=283155.

Appalachian Regional Commission. (n.d.). *Appalachian regional development act of 1965*. Retrieved November 28, 2005 from www.arc.gov/index.do?nodeId=1244#2.

Billings, D., Norman, G., & Ledford, K. (Eds.). (1999). *Confronting Appalachian stereotypes*. Lexington: University Press of Kentucky.

Bryson, B. (1998). *A walk in the woods: Rediscovering America on the Appalachian Trail*. New York: Broadway Books.

Bumiller, E. (2003, October 26). Evangelicals sway White House on human rights issues abroad. *New York Times.*

Carnes, J. (1995). *Us and them.* Montgomery, AL: Southern Poverty Law Center.

Caudill, H. (1963), *Night comes to the Cumberlands.* Boston: Little, Brown.

Center for Rural Strategies. (n.d.). *Rural reality: Comments from the guest book.* Retrieved November 28, 2005, from www.ruralstrategies.org/default.html.

Cherokee Chamber of Commerce. (n.d.). *Cherokee County.* Retrieved November 28, 2005, from www.cherokeecoutychamber.com/chamber/vacation/.

Cincinnati Enquirer, The. (October 7, 2003). *Victory for reality.* Retrieved October 26, 2005, from www.enquirer.com/editions/2003/10/07/editorial_wwwed1b.html.

Dickey, J. (1970). *Deliverance.* New York: Dell.

Eller, R. (1999). Forward. In D. Billings, G. Norman, & K. Ledford (Eds.), *Confronting Appalachian Stereotypes* (pp. ix–xi). Lexington: University Press of Kentucky.

Eller, R. (1982). *Miners, millhands, and mountaineers.* Knoxville: University of Tennessee Press.

Harkins, A. (2003). *Hillbilly: A cultural history of an American icon.* New York: Oxford University Press.

Horwitz, T. (1999, March 15). Run, Rudolph, run. *The New Yorker.*

Huckabee, M. (n.d.). *Common decency.* Retrieved November 28, 2005 from www.ruralstrategies.org/campaign/huckabee.html.

Kephart, H. (1976). *Our southern highlanders: A narrative of adventure in the southern Appalachians and a study of life among the mountaineers.* Knoxville: University of Tennessee Press.

Lehmann-Haupt, C. (1998). Book review: A walk in the woods, rediscovering America on the Appalachian Trail. *New York Times* (May 21, 1998).

Lewis, R. (1999). Beyond isolation and homogeneity: Diversity and the history of Appalachia. In D. Billings, G. Norman, & K. Ledford (Eds.), *Confronting Appalachian stereotypes* (pp. 21–43). Lexington: University Press of Kentucky.

Rogers, H. (n.d.). Center for Rural Strategies. *Rural reality: NBC's the High Life.* Retrieved October 26, 2005 from www.ruralstrategies.org/default.html.

Rural Reality. (n.d.). *Congressman Rogers: NBC backs away from "hillbilly" reality program.* Retrieved October 26, 2005 from www.ruralstrategies.org/campaign/highlife.html.

Toynbee, A. (1942). *A study of history.* New York: Oxford University Press.

Weller, J. (1965). *Yesterday's people.* Lexington: University Press of Kentucky.

Williamson, J. W. (1995). *Hillbillyland: What the movies did to the mountains and what the mountains did to the movies.* Chapel Hill: University of North Carolina Press.

Wilson D. (1999). A judicious combination of incident and psychology: John Fox Jr. and the southern mountaineer motif. In D. Billings, G. Norman, & K. Ledford (Eds.), *Confronting Appalachian stereotypes* (pp. 98–118). Lexington: University Press of Kentucky.

CHAPTER TWELVE

STORIES OF WOMEN OF MIXED HERITAGE

THE IMPORTANCE OF CULTURE

SILVIA BETTEZ

"Mixed Race" Studies is one of the fastest growing, as well as one of the most
important and controversial areas in the field of "race" and ethnic relations.

—Jayne O. Ifekwunigwe, *Mixed Race Studies*

INTRODUCTION

The numbers of mixed-race[1] students attending schools in the United States
is growing exponentially. Miscegenation laws were repealed in 1967, and the
number of interracial marriages has doubled in the past twenty years, creating a "baby boom" of multiracial children (Downing, Nichols, & Webster,
2005). Even as there is growing scholarship that is dedicated to understanding and responding to issues of race and racism in the classroom (Delpit,
1995; Bigelow, et. al., 1994; Valenzuela, 1999; Tatum, 1995), the issues are
complex and often overwhelming for teachers. Mixed-race identification and
experiences add to the complexity of racial issues. Each year the number of
multiracial children and young adults attending school will increase; however, there is a marked absence of content and courses that address interracial issues (Shoem, 2005, p. 15).

Scholarship addressing interracial issues is increasing (Zack, 1995; Renn
2004; Ifekwunige, 2004), but the research related to the lives of multiracial

217

people is still relatively limited. This chapter provides information gathered from a qualitative study conducted with six young women at a southeastern university. My mixed-race identity and my passion to promote social justice led me to interview women of mixed heritage. The goal of this chapter is three-fold. First, it is my hope that through these women's stories, readers may gain new insights into ways to connect across lines of difference. Second, these stories may offer teachers increased understanding of the complexity of young, mixed-race women's lives. Third, this chapter offers suggestions for how teachers and parents might offer better support to mixed-race youth.

LITERATURE REVIEW

The complexity of teaching about mixed-race identity can be overwhelming. Mixed-race identity has a long and sordid history in the United States, and people of mixed heritage have been caught in the crossfire of political issues for centuries. Although there is much evidence to show that race is primarily a social construct (Spickard, 1992; Omi & Winant, 2001), the effects of it are still real in their consequences. Historically, mixed-race people, especially women, were placed at the heart of the eugenics movement. An examination of the "hybridity" literature reveals this.

The term *hybridity* stems from biology and the selective interbreeding of plants. However, in the mid 1800s humans entered the debate, as the term became associated with the eugenics movement. White colonialists wanted to promote the idea that human beings were of different species to justify slavery and exploitation of people of color. Mixed-race women came under scrutiny in the effort to show that they were infertile in order to prove that people of different "races" were also different species (Young, 1995).

Hybridity has always been entwined in racial debates and carries the history of racist politics. The hybrid (mixed-race person) signaled the potential demise of the "great white race." "Hybrids" simultaneously offered hope to people of color, because the hybrid existence, and specifically the fertility of the hybrid woman, proved that people of color were indeed people and not another species that could be exploited at will. At the same time, some mixed-race children were daily reminders for women of color of the sexual assault they had endured.

Today, people of mixed heritage are often hailed as the answer to the racial divides. Trueba (2004) argues that as interracial marriages increase and racial differences become increasingly blurred, racial conflict will decrease. Alternatively, some conservatives cite people of mixed heritage as proof that reparations for racial injustice, such as affirmative action programs, are no longer needed (Williams, 2006). At the same time, both white people and people of color have made arguments that mixed-race people will be the demise of cultural preservation. Racist whites argue that race mixing should not occur, naming miscegenation as the ultimate sin. Some people of color, after being subjected to years of assimilation and cultural genocide also view mixed-race people as a threat to cultural preservation and argue against interracial coupling.

It is in this tricky terrain of racial politics that the stories of people of mixed heritage are situated. Until recently, the mixed-race voice was virtually absent from research and literature; however, in the past ten to fifteen years there has been a burgeoning of writings about multiracial experiences. In her recent book (2004), Kristen Renn asserts that "the literature on multiraciality divides roughly into four categories: the history of mixed race people in the United States, theories about biracial identity and biracial individuals, popular literature about multiracial individuals, and models of bi/multiracial identity development" (p. 7). This information comes out of a variety of disciplines, including sociology, anthropology, psychology/counseling, ethnic studies, and education. Renn provides an excellent overview of the literature for those interested in further readings. It is important to mention, however, Maria P. P. Root, as one of the authors who began to bring to the fore research about people of mixed heritage with her groundbreaking anthology *Racially Mixed People in America* (1992), which represents authors from a wide range of academic disciplines. She published a second anthology in 1996.

The same year that Renn's book *Mixed Race Students in College* was published, Jayne O. Ifekwunigwe (2004) published *"Mixed Race" Studies: A Reader*, establishing scholarship on multiraciality as a field. Downing, Nichols, and Webster (2005) stamped the field with a full-length resource guide on the history and literature of interracial issues. Their book provides a detailed overview of the literature, historical texts, and movies that represent interracial couples and mixed-race people and is a great resource for teachers who wish to address multiracial issues as it includes an annotated bibliography of books for children and young adults (2005).

Although the research and literature are growing, there are still relatively few studies that center the voices of mixed-race young women. Furthermore, there are only a handful of resources that speak directly to educators.

PARTICIPANT SELECTION

The federal government defines five racial categories: American Indian or Alaska Native, Asian, Black or African American, Native Hawaiian or Other Pacific Islander, and White.[2] In addition, the government recognizes one ethnicity: Hispanic or Latino. To use the term *mixed race* to describe my project would have technically excluded Latinos. Although by government delineation Latino is not considered a race, Latinos often view themselves and are treated as peoples from a distinct racial category; as such, I wanted to include mixed Latinos. My desire was to find people of mixed heritage/

ethnicity/race who are at least part "of color." Participant selection for this project focused on a large public southeastern institution. I created a flier that asked the question, "Are you a Woman of Mixed Heritage?" The fliers were sent to all of the campus listserves for students of color as well as the Campus Y listserve. The response was immediate: the day the fliers were posted through listserves, I began to receive emails from women interested in participating. I responded to everyone who expressed interest.[3] The voices of six women are included in this chapter: Annie, Bobbie, Martha, Brianna, Alexis, and Dalia.[4]

PARTICIPANTS' BACKGROUND

It seems best to let the participants describe themselves in their own words. The descriptions that follow are excerpted from their interviews and email correspondences.

ANNIE

I'm nineteen. I am a sophomore. I'm from a big city in North Carolina but not the biggest big city. My mom is Filipino. My dad is Caucasian, white, Scotch-Irish, but you know, it's not as big of a identity factor. And my mom is actually, I tell people she's a mail order bride, but, uhm, it's not strictly true. My dad was using a pen pal service in the eighties that was like, you know, like you were writing, like everyone had the intent of looking for someone, and it was called, I think *Wild Flowers*, the magazine. It featured women from Malaysia and the Philippines and India. And I remember when I was eight or nine, I discovered what was left of his research, which was a shoebox full of pictures of different women. I knew how my parents got together, but I had never been able to put any kind of concrete thing behind the details. I knew that they had gotten together that way, but I had never found the pictures of the other women's faces. I'm an only child, and my parents tried to have more children, but my mom wasn't able to for some reason after I was born. So I was it, and it's funny because I was kind of an accident, unexpected. They didn't have any furniture when I was born because they were very poor economically. They didn't have much financial security. So basically my dad got a house, and we still live in that same house to this day, and it's devoid of furniture so there are a lot of baby pictures of me running around in different rooms and having no problem of Mom being worried about me falling cuz there was nothing to hit. My dad when my mom first came was working as an accountant in a small accounting firm that was owned by another person. My mom enabled him to start his own business, and my mom does all the like unappreciated, secretary stuff for him, basically for free. So, uhm, so now he owns his own business. My mom came to the States having trained to be a teacher and finished her education here to become a teacher. I was in preschool while she was doing this, so I have memories of her picking me up in the middle of the day when classes were done. But then she realized she didn't like children and decided not to become a teacher and continued to work as a waitress as she had been since I was two. So basically my mom took care of me during the day, and my dad took care of me at night. So sometimes I didn't really ever see them together. When I was in fifth grade my mom got a job at Wachovia, and she's still there today.

BOBBIE

I'm twenty-three. I'm a senior. I grew up in a small farming community in Western North Carolina. And my mom's from Philadelphia and she's African American, and my dad is from Atlanta; he's white. There's some Native American blood back in there too, but I mostly identify as black and white. My parents met when they were up at school in New England. Got married, lived up in Philly for a few years. My dad missed the South, but my mom wasn't trying to move all the way down to Atlanta, so they found a happy medium and moved into this community that some of their college friends live in. And it's a pretty amazing place. It's just this small really tight community, faith based, and mostly one extended family, but it is predominately, you know, just a white community. I lived there my entire life. So just being at home and you know just being around the farm just with white people all the time, but then I went to a school, elementary school that was pretty diverse in Greyville, and I think that was a great experience. My mom purposefully sent me there. My mom, like, is a storyteller and works mostly with African American folklore and stuff like and is in a storytelling group with two other African American storytellers and does a lot of African American theater. She is like one of the only black actresses in the mountains of North Carolina. That aspect of the culture, more traditional African American culture, I was definitely exposed to, the sort of things that maybe in the white world would be considered like high culture like arts and you know older music and you know things like this. African American culture like that I was really exposed to and involved in. But African American culture as it is now I wasn't really exposed to. Like hip-hop I didn't get into until much later when my brother went off to college and started getting into it, uhm, like you know, or like styles or movies and things like this. People still get mad at me because I didn't see *The Color Purple*, and I didn't watch *Fresh Prince*.

MARTHA

I am a twenty-seven-year-old PhD student. I was born and raised in Tempe, Arizona. My background is I was born and raised in a working-class community in Arizona. My parents live there, and my father is an editor, a managing editor for a newspaper there, and my mom has always been a homemaker. My mom is white. I guess German would be her ancestry. My dad had a family of eleven and my mom had a family of three. She has only sisters. My father would identify himself as, I guess, Mexican American. It's interesting. He's kind of sensitive. When we were kids, and when they ask you what your race is, he would say, "the human race." He didn't like those labels put on him. So my parents met at college and my dad stayed in his hometown, and my mom went away to college but not because she was interested in college but because she said that's what everybody did, uhm, which is pretty opposite my father, which is that the only reason he got to go to college is because he had an English teacher that really saw his potential and nurtured it and pushed him to go to college. So the interesting part of all of this—so my mom's white, and my dad's Latino; my brother and I are both adopted. The interesting thing about that is my parents were foster parents before they had children and they adopted me. It turns out that my biological mother is white, with actually Irish ancestry. And my biological father on my birth certificate it says, uhm, I guess I'm to assume that he's Mexican, uhm, this is 1976, and his race says Chicano on it, which is a sign of the times. I essentially am biologically also what I am adoptively, if that's such a word.

BRIANNA

I'm twenty years old. I was originally born in Mississippi. I lived in Durham all my life. I was adopted as a newborn child. My birth mother was 100 percent Native American, and I was adopted off the Choctaw reservation. It's believed that my father is predominantly African American, but on both sides there's some I suppose European blood accounting for my little freckles I get in the sun. Uhm, my dad is Jewish. He's from Minnesota I guess he's Russian and Polish Jewish. And my mom is Irish Catholic from New York. They moved down here twenty-two years ago. My dad was a cultural anthropologist at Penn, I believe, and then he went to teach in Boston. He stopped teaching when he came down here. And my mom has always been in public relations communications kind of thing. They always made sure that I was culturally aware of all of my backgrounds, whether it's my Jewish background from being adopted, or they would always take me to powwows ever since I was one or two years old to see the background of my Native American heritage.

ALEXIS

I'm twenty-two years old, and I currently work on campus. I graduated in May 03. And from October 2003 to this October has been the busiest year of my life. I got married. I bought a house. I got a new car. I have become the chapter advisor for my sorority. It has been the busiest year. About me in general—my mom is Mexican American. She was born in Illinois, and my great-grandparents came from Mexico, and my dad is African American. He was raised in the Bronx. But then they got divorced when I was two. And then my mom got remarried to my stepdad who is white, and that was when I was four. And that's really who raised me, my mom and my stepdad. Uhm, but then they got divorced when I was a junior here. Like if somebody would have walked me down the aisle, it would have been him, that is where all the relationship, the father figure, all those things. My biological dad was in and out of my life. My mom and stepdad have a child, my little sister, Tammy, and she's a freshman. Usually when people ask if I have siblings, I say yes, Tammy, because I grew up with her, and I was there when she was born and everything; Tammy, she's my heart. I was actually born in Sing, Korea, and then was raised mainly in North Carolina. Both of my parents are retired army, so [I've lived in] different parts of North Carolina.

DALIA

I'm twenty years old. My father is Cameroonian from Cameroon, West Africa. My mother is Russian. Uhm, I was born in Russia and then I moved to Cameroon when I was four, I think, and went to kindergarten and first grade there. And then we moved to Canada when I was six, and I lived in Canada until the tenth grade, but somewhere in between for two years of middle school I went back to Cameroon to go to boarding school. So, like, it's been very interesting. In tenth grade we moved to Georgia, so now my parents live in Savannah. It's been wow! I mean I like it—I really—it's like a weird combination, but I've loved like all of it. And I've been lucky because my mom since I was born in Russia and my mom and grandma raised me and both of them only spoke Russian, Russian became my first language. And I've been exposed to a lot of languages and cultures, and my parents really made sure that I was grounded in both parts of my heritage. He's a doctor. She's a nurse.

There is a wide range of ethnic and racial diversities represented in this group of six women. There is, however, much less diversity in terms of education levels and socioeconomic status. Annie, Bobbie, Brianna, and Dalia are all undergraduates. Alexis has her B.A., and Martha is in the process of getting her PhD. They were all raised in middle-class families. All of the women have English as their only language except Dalia, who has Russian as her first language, although she speaks fluent English as well. Two of the women, Brianna and Martha, are adopted. Except for Alexis, all of the women's parents have stayed together. Annie, Bobbie, and Martha have light skin, and each of them recognizes that others may perceive them as white. Alexis and Dalia are most often perceived as black by others, based on skin tone. Brianna believes she looks mixed and is indeed perceived most often as such, passing for a multitude of ethnicities and races. The descriptions above are snapshots of these women, backdrops to the stories included in this chapter.

AUDIENCE AND RESEARCHER SUBJECTIVITY

This chapter is written for anyone with an interest in social justice. In a United States culture divided by false dichotomies such as black and white, women of mixed heritage are forced to carve out new social spaces for themselves as multiracial people *or* make the choice to claim only part of their heritage. Social justice is about promoting a society with equity among its members. "Social justice involves social actors who have a sense of their own agency as well as a sense of social responsibility toward and with others and the society as a whole" (Bell, 1997, p. 1). The stories of these women are stories of navigating a sense of agency. Sometimes they display a keen sense of social responsibility; sometimes they display a disheartening lack of such responsibility. All of them inform the reader about new ways to conceive of race, identity, and belonging.

This work connects to the core of who I am. Being a mestiza, the daughter of a Latina mother and a white father, has been a source of strength *and* struggle throughout my life. As I delve deeper into social justice work and my place in it, my sense of self as a person who literally embodies the oppressed and the oppressor is called into question. My desire to understand how women of mixed heritage negotiate their identities stems directly from my desire to better understand myself and my place in this world.

I approach this project as an insider and as an outsider. Like my participants, I am a middle-class, formally educated woman of mixed heritage. However, since women of mixed heritage can embody and represent an infinite number of racial and ethnic mixtures, I am also an outsider in relation to many of my participants and the stories of their lives. This combination of being both a part of and different from the participants places me in a unique position to delve into the complexity of issues identified by the participants.

METHODS

The population that I chose to work with put a limit on the kinds of methods I could use. Unlike other ethnographic projects in which a researcher can go into a community or group and observe, I had no such community with which to work. There are no established groups for people of mixed heritage near the area in which I live or at any of the local college campuses. As a result, my primary method of data collection was interviews. I conducted individual interviews (1–1.5 hours) with each of my six participants. At the end of each interview, I invited the participant to call or email me if she thought of something further that she wanted to share. Three of the participants sent emails after the individual interviews in which they added new information to their previously told stories. There also were some correspondence emails before the interviews that served as documents for this chapter. One woman sent me a copy of a poem and a performance piece she wrote about being a mixed-race woman. Two of the women brought pictures of friends and family to their interviews.[5] Document review was therefore a secondary method of data collection.

I had no specific research question going into this study other than: What are the life stories of women of mixed heritage? There were no preset questions for the individual interviews. I started each interview with the statement, "Tell me about yourself." As the participants talked I asked further questions based on what they shared. Those questions were often statements such as, "Tell me more about your family" and "Tell me more about your friends" or simply "Tell me more about that."

All of the women were invited to participate in a two-hour focus group. All six expressed interest, but Dalia had to leave town on an emergency. The other five women participated in the first focus group. I had one prepared question and two prepared requests for the focus group: (1) How do you identify yourself? (2) Tell me about the challenges of being mixed, and (3) Talk to me about the benefits of being mixed. However, the women were informed that they could talk about whatever they wished. It was a lively, interactive group. My facilitation role was minimal as the participants shared stories and asked many probing questions of each other. We were in the middle of telling stories related to the second question when we ran out of time. I asked the women if they would be willing to participate in a second focus group, and they all agreed. Brianna did not attend, but the other four women participated in a second two-hour focus group. They were asked to bring any topic ideas, stories, and questions they desired to the second group, and several of them did. Again the group was primarily led by them; I played a small role, occasionally sharing stories of my own that related to theirs rather than acting as "the researcher."

I transcribed all of the interviews and focus group discussions. Once that was complete, I coded the transcripts and documents and grouped them by emergent themes. Every piece of information in the data was encapsulated in a code and subsequent theme.

THE DATA: WHAT THE WOMEN SHARED

The women were quite candid in sharing very personal stories of their lives. Within the individual interviews, focus groups, and documents, several themes emerged, which I arranged into the following categories: (1) Self-Definition, including its relation to perceptions by others; (2) Fitting in and Not Fitting in; (3) Racial Prejudice; (4) Privilege; and (5) Dating, Marriage, and Offspring. This chapter addresses the first two themes. Although all the themes have relevance to these women's lives, the first two themes help set the stage for educators to understand how to best assist mixed-race young women. In this chapter I will present the data, provide an interpretation, and end with some specific suggestions for educators and parents on dealing with mixed race issues.

SELF-DEFINITION

Earlier, the women *described* themselves; however, there are varying ways the women *define* themselves in relation to race/ethnicity. All of the women described themselves through their parents. Instead of saying, "I am . . ." They would say, "My mother is . . . and my father is . . . ," adding in information about adoptive parents or stepparents as their particular situation warranted. For several of these women, how they defined themselves varied both situationally and over time. These women sometimes identified with all of their heritages and other times with only one heritage. The self-identifications sometimes came about as a result of others' perceptions of them but other times ran contrary to others' perceptions. They were also strategic in relation to schooling and associated benefits.

Of all the women, Brianna most strongly identified with the term *mixed* rather than her specific heritages, perhaps owing to being biologically Choctaw and African American while being raised by a Polish Jewish father and Irish Catholic mother. Of all the participants, she was most often asked the question, "What are you?" by others (at least twice a day) to which she typically responded, "I'm mixed." However, on forms for school and the census, she identified herself as Native American. She says:

> I put Native-American on the school things, but like I'm mixed, but for, I guess for statistics reasons, there's no Native Americans, so I'll add to the statistics a little bit. I don't know if now you can put two races on the census, or the things. I know you can on the census, but even then like if you put you're two or more races, you're just a blank because it doesn't really say anything. You're just two or more races or something. So I think, well, I might as well put Native American because that's one thing. I usually do Native American because they are such a minority that I just want one more to be counted.

Brianna is the recipient of a Native American scholarship, which she feels she should not be excluded from just because she is adopted. Aside from representing Native Americans on official forms, however, she says, "Day to day I'm just mixed."

Alexis on the other hand feels very strongly about identifying with both heritages and never says or marks otherwise when given the choice. She says,

> It's never sometimes one, sometimes the other. It's always mixed, or I might say I'm Mexican and African American. But it's never

like I'm black or I'm Mexican. It never has been. Even though I am African American and Mexican biologically at the same time I was raised a lot of the time in a military community where you're just people.

Alexis tells the story of getting forms in school that mark her as black only, and she changes them, then getting them back, and they say Hispanic, so she changes them again, but they never get it right. She complains that even the forms that do have a space for bi/multiracial never have a line long enough to list who she is. Although she strongly identifies as mixed, people who do not know her, she says, assume she is black, and sometimes when she tells people that she is mixed, they do not believe her.

Bobbie's sense of identity changed over time. She explains,

I used to just put African-American, and I think I even had a logic worked out like that, like since my mom's black like if I'd been born 150 years ago I'd a been a slave regardless of what my father was— so. But now I always say mixed because I feel like it's disrespectful to my father and that side of who I am to say anything else.

She says that she is perceived in different ways by different people: "I think most white people would be like, oh you know, she's just tan. Most black people or other minorities are like, 'she's something.' "

Annie's sense of her racial self also changed over time. She says, "Nowadays I just tell people I'm mixed, that my mom is Filipino and my dad is white." She used to perceive herself as white, in large part because that is how her parents perceived her. Her mom marked her race as white when she entered school. After our individual interview, Annie talked with her mom about this and discovered that her mom did this because she had to mark what was on her birth certificate, and the only options on the certificate were "white" and "black." However, her parents marked her ethnicity as Filipino when they wanted her to get into a magnet school in sixth grade, knowing that would give her an advantage. Still, her mom admitted that she used to perceive Annie as white but now perceives her as mixed. Her father is very threatened by Annie's new interest in exploring her Filipino heritage and seeking out cultural diversity; he "reminds" her often that she is white. Most people that do not know her also perceive her as white but sometimes after they had known her a little bit will ask, "What ethnicity are you? Cuz there's something."

Dalia, who has the strongest connection to both her parents' *cultures* says,

I always avoid the term *African American*. I always told people that I'm mixed, I'm Russian and Cameroonian because I didn't identify with being African American, and I also didn't really identify with like the issues that came around that.

However, her sense of racial identity has been changing; she says, "since I've gotten to college I've identified more with the African American community because I don't have a choice because in America you're black." She explains that she has learned from "radical" friends that if she is going to be discriminated against, it will be because she is black. Although she identifies with the African American community more, she still feels she brings an "outsider's" perspective to it. She also identifies as Black for her university scholarship, which she feels she deserves because "everyone's perception" of her is black. Although she admits that in winter, when her tan fades, people will ask her if she is mixed.

Martha's ethnic/racial self-identification remains constant in different situations and over time; she identifies as Latina. The term may change— sometimes it is *Hispanic*—but she always has identified as such. She says she never put much thought into it. Her last name made her Latina, but she adds, "If somebody asks me, I don't deny that the white side exists." She says that other people "never really know what to make of me," but she feels other Latinos are often "surprised" to find that she is Latina. She describes herself as being raised in a mostly white culture, but in the past several years of her life she has been making a conscious effort to connect with other Latinos and her "brown" side.

These women's stories demonstrate that racial identification can be fluid and is impacted by the perceptions of others. In some cases, they try to match these perceptions, and in other cases, they try to counteract them. Racial identification is also determined by perceived opportunities, such as scholarships. Only Martha and Alexis have identified racially the same way throughout their lives; interestingly, their self-identifications counteract the perceptions of others. Annie, Bobbie, and Dalia have changed their racial identifications over time. Annie and Bobbie now identify more often as mixed, and Dalia identifies less often as mixed and more often as African American. Brianna maintains her identity as a mixed woman, although she claims an identity on paper as Native American. All of the women have had their self-identifications challenged in some way, either by family, friends, or strangers.

FITTING IN AND NOT FITTING IN

This is the most widely discussed topic that runs through the women's stories. The notion of fitting in was a central theme as the women talked about their family, their friends, and school. As mixed-race women, they were sometimes placed in situations where they were forced, against their wishes, to choose one ethnic/racial identity over another. Other times their ability to choose varying identities helped grant them access to people, places, and opportunities that might have been denied them had they occupied a monoracial identity.

FAMILY

Estrangement from extended family was a strong common denominator among this group of women, although there were a variety of causes for the estrangement. Dalia is the only woman who experienced no estrangement from any of her family members. She is close to both parents and both sides of her family. Bobbie was estranged from her dad's side of the family because they were not happy about his marriage to an African American woman. As a result she did not get to know that side of the family well. Alexis was estranged from her mom's side of the family because they disapproved of her marrying an African American man. Consequently, they did not acknowledge Alexis for the first two years of her life. Martha was estranged from her dad's side of the family because, as she said, he had many black marks against him,

> My dad married outside of his race, which was seen as black mark number one. He married a woman who would not convert to Catholicism, which is black mark number two. And the most important key factor was that they couldn't have children that were their own.

As a result, although her dad's family was only a few hours away, Martha and her parents rarely spent time with them, and she missed out on most of his big family's gatherings. Annie was estranged from both sides of her extended family. Her mom's family was too far away to visit frequently. She visited her grandmother in the Philippines once as a child when she was nine and then visited her grandmother and other family members in Hawaii when she was in tenth grade. Annie was also estranged from her dad's family. Annie says her dad's family accepted her mom and treated her well, but her dad had a "falling out" with them and his siblings, so Annie rarely saw them. Brianna was not close to her grandparents on her mom's side because they "weren't too happy about [her parents] having a nonwhite child or even adopting." Although the estrangement from extended family happened for different reasons and to varying degrees, it impacted the women's ability to learn about the culture of that side of their family and often highlighted the fact that they were different somehow from other family members.

Most of the women shared stories of feeling close to or different from their cousins and/or siblings. Annie, Martha, and Brianna all talk about being different from their cousins. Martha talks about an incident in which she was visiting her Grandma Garcia, and her brother came in crying because one of the cousins was telling the other cousins that they didn't have to play with him because he wasn't their real cousin. Martha adds that none of her other cousins were mixed. Annie says,

> Like I know my mom's family loves me, but I don't know if they necessarily look at me as anything. They look at me as, oh her dad's white, you know. Like, it's always a reminder because I don't look like any of my cousins.

Annie also describes a recent experience of going to visit an estranged cousin on her dad's side and quickly realizing that her cultural ways of being were different from those of her cousin's family. They also made assumptions about her based on her mom being Filipino (for example, that she ate rice for breakfast). Brianna, although she is different from her cousins on her dad's side, does not *feel* different because she has several cousins who are mixed and adopted thus providing a point of connection for her. She says, "The Jewish family, they never like treated me as different. Like, it's just I was just part of the family always." Dalia says that because her mom earned the respect of her dad's family in Cameroon and because she knew Russian (the language of her mom's family), she says, "I never really felt awkward. I never really felt like I was treated differently by family or by the community as a whole."

Bobbie and Alexis made no mention of cousins, but they both talk about the importance of their siblings in their lives. Bobbie felt strongly that she did not want to be associated with the "tragic mulatto" stereotype; therefore, it mattered to whom she disclosed her conflicting feelings. Her siblings provided an outlet for her. She says, "When I am with my siblings I am not having to choose." Alexis also felt very close to her sister and noted how a person once commented that she and her sister were "each other's people," meaning mixed people. This closeness transcended their differences and the challenges they faced from others who would not believe they are sisters since Alexis "looks black" and Tammy has a white father. Alexis proudly tells stories of her sister defending black people when classmates make derogatory comments remarking to them: "My sister is black." Dalia did not discuss being either close to or distant from her brothers. Martha felt very different from her brother because although Martha's brother looks darker than she does, he considers himself white and makes derogatory comments against people of color. As a result they argue often, and she does not connect with him.

Two of the women shared stories about being made to feel different from their families by outsiders. Alexis shared three stories of people not believing that Alexis is her mom's child. She also told a story of people disbelieving that she is related to her sister, Tammy. This story, she said, is the most painful:

> We were at the mall at one of the kiosks, and we were going to
> get ice cream, and my sister ordered, and my dad ordered, and
> then I went to order, and the man was like, "I'm helping this
> family right now." He thought that I was like butting in or some-
> thing. And my mom was just like, "She IS a part of this family."
> And he was very apologetic, and you know I don't think he meant
> anything by it but still the way he snapped at me in the first place
> and what he insinuated.

Most often the challenges are directed at Alexis' mom or her sister, but
sometimes, as in the story above, they are directed at her. Brianna also
shares stories of people making assumptions about her relationship with her
parents. Interestingly, for her, sometimes when she was out with only one
parent, they assumed that she was the biological child of that parent.
When she was with her mom, "the white ladies would look at her like
really unhappy [because she had] a little brown child next to her." Other
times she would be with her mom, and people, gas station clerks for instance, would ask her if her father was African, which would make her
mom very mad. Brianna also tells stories of having a phobia of Burger King
because "all the black ladies would come up to me and touch my hair."
Surprisingly, the other women did not share stories of being perceived as
different from their parents.

Two of the women, Martha and Annie, tell stories of their white
parent feeling threatened by the ways in which they are exploring their
identities of color and becoming more involved with communities of color.
Martha's mom asks her why she is not learning about her (white) culture.
These are Martha's thoughts in response:

> I've been learning about her culture my whole life, and now is a
> different point in my life, but I also wonder why does it threaten her
> so much? Why, does it make her think that I'm going to love her
> less because she is white, you know?

However, Martha's father is "living vicariously" through Martha, reading all
of her papers and enjoying learning more about Latino issues, although they
both keep this from her mom. Annie says to Martha,

> I can really relate to what you were saying about your mom feeling
> threatened because I could use almost the exact same terminology
> with my dad. And he hasn't spoken to me about it, but he speaks
> to my mom, things like, "Make sure she doesn't forget where she
> comes from."

Her dad was disappointed when Annie decided to live in the multicultural dorm and told her she was going to be with a "bunch of weirdoes." He uses her mom as an intermediary, so her (Filipino) mom ends up telling Annie not to forget that she is white.

All of these stories—of estrangement from family, feelings of difference or connection with siblings and cousins, and being made to feel different by outsiders, dealing with a threatened parent—reveal the intricacies of fitting in and not fitting as mixed, and adopted, women within their own families.

FRIENDS

On the whole, the women had diverse groups of friends. They discussed varying degrees of feeling like they fit in or did not fit in within their different communities of friends. For some of the women the ethnic and racial makeup of their groups of friends changed over time either because they consciously chose to change them or because of the circumstances they were in.

For Alexis, there appears to be no conscious thought about who makes up her groups of friends. When she was young and was in Germany most of her friends were black, but her best friend was white. When she returned to the states she recognized a girl she had been in school with before, and she says,

> She and I got to be friends again and I kinda got pulled into her circle of friends who were all white, and all of my friendships since then have kind of perpetuated off of that. Most of my friends now are white, short of my [multicultural] sorority.

Alexis is very much into promoting multiculturalism and as a part of a military family sees herself as "American." She did not discuss feeling more or less comfortable around different groups of friends. She and her (white) husband are friends with another interracial couple, and her husband says that she "acts crazy" around the black woman of the couple.

Dalia has friends who are black and friends who are white. She says she knows other biracial people have felt uncomfortable in certain groups, but she has never felt "not black enough." She attributes this to the way her parents raised her: "I was always very grounded and very secure in who I was, so I didn't need to see that around me." As a result there may have been discrimination against her, but she chose not to see it. She says,

> I've always been really comfortable, and I've always picked friends, no matter what race they are that are comfortable with me, that I'm comfortable with, so I kind of like—I have a security blanket that protects me from that.

As a result she feels "equally comfortable around an entire group of white students and an entire group of black students just depending on the actual group." She has a "good base" of white friends and some Hispanic friends, but her core group of friends and her best friend are black. Her social activities and group activities tend to be with black people.

Bobbie also has a group of white friends and a group of black friends. However, in contrast to Dalia's experience, she says,

> I don't think I really see myself fitting in either of those sort of paradigms or worlds perfectly, and there are times where uhm you know where I fall more on one side or the other. And I hate that it definitely does feel like two worlds in a lot of ways.

She is very involved in a black spoken word group, and most of her friends from church are black. However, most of her friends from other avenues of her life and all of her housemates have been white. She works hard to keep her two communities separate and worries about how they will treat each other and view her if they are brought together. She says,

> I worry that like if I bring those communities together that for the black people they will just be like—they will just sort of like be patronizing the white people. Just being nice, when really they will go back and be like whatever, "Those crazy people." Like I was saying, "They don't get me, they don't know what's going on, but let me just go and play nice with them." So like—and then for the white people that will be like maybe the same idea of kind of like dabbling, like, "Oh, now I get to go meet all of Bobbie's black friends." Like okay, great, you know like, and if I choose to submit myself to either of those sentiments you know like where I'm that person that you know, I'm your black friend, or I'm the, "You know, you don't get me either." Like, that's fine, like I can submit myself to that, but it's different, if I'm like you know, bringing other people into the mix and sort of setting up the game for somebody else to play. You know?

This sense of responsibility to keep the two communities separate caused tension for Bobbie. During the time I was interviewing her she started to relax about maintaining such separateness and began to introduce some of her white and black friends when they came to see her perform spoken word.

Martha also thought very consciously about who her friends were and how she fit in with them or not. Growing up and through high school most of her friends were white. When Martha went to college she began to seek out friendships with people of color. She became friends with a few Latinos. After she graduated she worked in college admissions and had a circle of

African American friends. She continues to seek out Latino friends, but this causes some conflict because, as she says, "a lot of my Latino friends, they want me to not like white people." This causes conflict, not only because she continues to have white friends but because it calls into question her identity. She says, "I'm like what does that say about me? I'm white, I'm white too. I'm white too. So should I have like hatred for myself, you know? Should I hate myself?" Because of her cultural background she says she feels at home with white people, but she is actively trying to connect with people of color.

Annie has also actively started seeking out diverse friends in college. In high school her two closest friends were white. One of her close friends was mixed white and Filipino, but he considered himself white. She had a close black friend, but due to her dad's racism she had to hide that friendship. Now her friends are a diverse and "interesting lot." She says that she has many friends of color—black, Indian, Chinese, and so on—but she says, "I have to admit that my friends of color were usually unusual characters." She explains that they are into anime (Japanese animation), poetry, and philosophy. What makes her stand out, she says, is that she is mixed:

> I guess I had this idealized picture of me and my friends, and I was trying to place them ethnically and then figure out where do I place myself, so I'm like the token mixed heritage child within my friends.

Brianna wishes very much that she had more mixed friends. Although she has a diverse group of friends, she feels different because she is mixed.

> I have some mixed friends. It's one thing I wish I had more of because there's not many here. Like at my high school there was like five mixed people. It's just really hard, you can't go around asking people cuz, it's kinda—I know how it feels.

She says she is selective of her white friends: "I just have to make sure that people are okay with someone being mixed." She describes her white friends as "more conscious" because they are foreign or more ethnic, like Italian, and they are "like totally into like all black culture, all black culture, they don't even look at a white guy ever." She has two best friends, one is Persian and one is Puerto Rican. She feels like she has been questioned the most by African American people, who say things like, "Why does your hair look like that?" She tends to be friends with people "from the North whether they are white or black." She feels she has a "unique experience" as someone who is mixed and "wanted to start a multiracial group on campus when [she] stops having so much work to do."

All of the women negotiate their racial/ethnic identities through their friends. Dalia feels most secure in a variety of groups, but she is leaning toward the black community. Alexis also feels secure in her identity, but she is leaning toward the white community. Bobbie and Martha juggle their two separate communities of friends. Annie tries to figure out how she fits in as a "mixed heritage child" within her diverse group of friends while hiding her friendships with people of color from her racist white dad. Brianna surrounds herself with a diverse group of friends but still longs to find other mixed friends.

School

One of the striking things about this group of women and school is that all of the women talked about being in AP and/or honors classes and therefore, for most of them, being separated from other people of color.

Alexis says, "I was always in the honors classes and the AP classes, and there were like not nearly as many black people in those classes. There would be like two out of the thirty of us, or two out of twenty-five." Bobbie says that there was definitely an African American presence, but not in her classes. She says, "There was like one or two other black girls in some of my classes, none of my AP classes, and you know, just being in AP and honors track I was not with any other minorities." Martha states that even though her high school was 60 percent Latino, only one other Latina was in her classes: "We were the only two in the top twenty-five percent." Annie and Brianna both attended magnet schools housed within a public school. Brianna says, "It was a magnet school, which is basically a code word for white people bussed in." The white people were in the upper division classes, and black people remained at "the bottom of the classes." Annie says that there were lots of Latinos and African Americans in her school, "But racially, the IB [International Baccalaureate] class at our school was, uhm, mostly white, some Asian, and my graduating class had no African American students in the IB program." Brianna adds that although the school was 50 percent black and 50 percent white she felt she did not fit in because "there were only about 5 mixed people" and being mixed in the South was looked down upon. Dalia also attended an IB program in Savannah. In fact, her father had their house built within that district specifically so Dalia and her brothers could attend school there. As a result her IB program had a greater number of African Americans—nine black people and three white people. However, Dalia was not close to anyone in her high school. All of the women, with the exception of Dalia, discussed the difficulty in making friends with people of color because of being segregated in their upper-level classes.

Alexis, Bobbie, and Brianna all talked about how they appreciated being in diverse schools earlier in their lives. Alexis was in a diverse middle and high school before her parents moved. She experienced culture shock and could not make friends in the new school. She had her parents drive her back to her old town every weekend. Even though her old friends had not been black, she could not adjust to the homogeny of the new school. Still, although she thinks of it as an awful experience socially, she says,

In retrospect, when I graduated my senior year I realized that it was the best thing that my parents could have done for me. I mean Dover high school is like the second high school in the state, and I know that I got a better education there than I would have gotten in Forestview.

Bobbie's mom put her in an "alternative" grade school so that she would experience "not only the ethnic/racial but also religious and just sort of like worldview diversity." Bobbie loved that school and is grateful she had that experience. Brianna attended Montessori school for three years but says it had a huge impact on her because it was "extremely diverse" and "very different from public school." About her Montessori experience, she says that "it always seems like it was my whole childhood because there are so many things that I remember from there, and like I am still in contact with a lot of those people." Although their experiences in diverse communities where they felt like they fit in were transient, they had a lasting, positive impact on their lives.

FORCED TO CHOOSE

As mixed-race women, they were at times put in situations where they were forced to choose one part of their heritage over the other. These challenges arose from institutional structures, friends, and even family members. Martha sums up the dilemma when she says,

> People still expect you to choose. People expect you to choose. I'm mixed is not really an acceptable term. So also, I'm brown or I'm white is also not an acceptable answer because they're like, well you're not all brown, or you're not all white.

This dilemma is reflected in experiences with both her friends and family. Martha is consciously connecting with other Latinos, but that places her in a dilemma when they want her to "hate white people." Martha also finds herself at times caught between her parents, balancing her dad's delight in her Latino studies and her mom's fear of being excluded. Annie similarly ends up in that struggle between her parents as her dad tries to force her to define herself as white. Bobbie tells a story of being in a group for black students in which a prospective student identified herself as mixed and asked if there was a community for mixed people. One student responded by saying, "You needed to choose just white or black and then just deal with it." Bobbie's response to his comment is, "I don't think I'm down with that. I think that I am down with choosing who you are in terms of other things and how you want to define yourself." However, Bobbie, because her white community and black community are separate, every day has to choose the community in which she is going to spend time. Dalia does not name this so much as a dilemma, but she does say that a friend explained to her: "You have to identify with the struggle of the black community because you're automatically placed into that category and you're automatically associated with the struggle, and you have to take that on." As a result, although she says she does not feel discriminated against, she increasingly claims an African American identity rather than always explaining that she is Cameroonian and Russian.

Alexis, Brianna, and Annie talk about the frustration of dealing with forms that identify them as one race. Brianna tells a story of doing an online work application, and the computer would not let her check a second box. Annie tells a story of trying to get her race changed on school forms. She says,

> I remember going up to a teacher on those testing days when they ask you, "Is all the information correct?" and saying, "I'm not—I don't identify with this. Can I change it?" And they'd always tell me, "I'll get back to you," and it never happening.

Alexis tells a similar story of getting forms back in school that marked her identity wrong.

> I put on the form black and Hispanic, and I get the form back, and [it] just says black. So I fix it and write Hispanic and black and then I get it back the next time, and it just says Hispanic. So I'm like okay you need to like make your line longer or something.

All of these women tell stories of being forced to choose one race/ethnicity over another by friends, family, and institutions. The interpersonal interactions perhaps have the strongest impact, but the forms are representative of a larger society that erases mixed-race identities. There is no area of life—with friends, with family, with community structures such as school—that these women do not have to negotiate how they fit in as multiracial individuals.

ACCESS

The flip side to being forced to choose is having access to multiple spaces by virtue of being mixed. Although all of the women expressed hardships that resulted by virtue of being mixed, they also expressed benefits.

Alexis brought up the benefit of the variety of food in a focus group, and all the women concurred. Alexis also discussed the benefit of having the opportunity to educate white people about black people. Martha and Bobbie agreed that it is a privilege, as well as a burden, to have the opportunity to educate white people about people of color. Annie says that because she is mixed she feels included in more things than she would be if she were solely white. Brianna also emphasizes the possibilities of fitting in with different people when she says,

> But then again I would never want to change who I am just cuz I feel like I am so knowledgeable for a lot of cultures. I feel like I'm knowledgeable; I can relate to a lot of people if they want to relate to me.

Martha also touts the benefits of being mixed. She says,

> I love the fact that—I mean food is one element, but I do like the idea, I like the exposure of going to my mom's side of the family and going to my dad's side of the family, it's just an interesting thing that I get to do that not everybody else gets the opportunity to do.

Although there are some downsides and challenges to being mixed, Martha concludes, "I have nothing to complain about . . . I think that we've seen the tensions and contradictions of privilege. It's kind of like we get to code switch. Not everybody gets to code switch." Martha's Latino friends remind her that there are spaces of power in which she will be listened to where other Latinos may not be heard. Dalia also loves the benefits of how she grew up. She says, "I think being mixed has been really helpful to me. Because I've been mixed, I've been exposed, and not just because I've been mixed, but because I grew up in different countries, because my parents speak different languages." Bobbie sums up the sentiment in this statement:

> I think there's just an accessibility that comes with being mixed, just on the political and social level, and on the personal level that I really appreciate. You know, I think that like the kind of conversations that we're having, or the realizations that we come to, or the struggles that we face are like our privileges as well as burdens in a lot of ways and we're privileged to have been given opportunities to see into these things, uhm, and then to be able to actually navigate them as well. Because I think there are a lot of people on either side of the—of an ethnic/racial fence that might start to see some of those things but then not really be able to do much about it, even in their own personal lives.

INTERPRETATION

These stories provide a sense of belonging everywhere yet nowhere simultaneously. The racial/ethnic/family mixtures of these women provide them with lives of privilege and burden. Outside forces constantly challenge them to define and redefine themselves, forcing them to prove their worth in certain spaces. They battle pressures to erase, deny, or ignore parts of their heritage in order to fit in. Other times they are able to occupy spaces and benefit from privileges that some people may say they do not deserve precisely because they have the option of emphasizing one part of their racial/ethnic identities.

Listening to these stories, a connection to specific cultures and/or desire to connect to specific cultures appeared to be a determining factor in how the women defined themselves. Brianna, who had the least connection to the cultures of her races, identified most strongly with the term *mixed*. Her stories demonstrate that, for her, finding a sense of belonging was most closely linked to being with other mixed people. Annie and Martha "pass" for white and were raised in predominately white culture; however, both women have a strong desire to make a connection with their respective Filipino and Latino heritages as well as other people of color. That desire is turned into action as both women consciously work to better understand their cultures and those of other people of color. They have a unique position, as biracial women, of doing so while dealing with the insecurities of a threatened white parent whom they love and do not want to hurt. Bobbie has switched from identifying as African American to identifying as both black and white because she wants to consciously connect to her father and the "amazing" white, tight-knit community she grew up in as well as her African American culture. Dalia always identified as Cameroonian and Russian because she very strongly identifies with both those cultures, although she began to increasingly identify with the African American community and culture. Alexis is perhaps the anomaly because she strongly identifies as "Mexican and African American," although she is not strongly connected to either of those cultures. Instead it appears to be her desire to promote a general "multiculturalism" that drives her racial identification.

Dalia comes across as the woman who felt the most secure in herself and most comfortable in the spaces she inhabits. She is also the woman who feels most strongly and intimately connected to both her cultures. Her sense of connection to her extended families, their cultures, and their languages helps her feel grounded in every situation. In contrast, Annie struggles with her sense of self as her Filipino mother's daughter:

> I used to think, I guess that I was more white than anything else . . . but I don't think that's true really, because you can't be, I simply am who I am, and, just because I haven't like experienced living for extended periods of time in the Philippines or something and just because I don't speak my mom's native dialect.

Annie's lack of connection to her mother's culture calls her self-identity into question. Martha also struggles with her identity as a Latina because of her lack of connection to Latino culture and her father's family growing up. This makes her feel "less than" others and leaves her wondering if she "will ever be brown enough." Bobbie also struggles with her sense of self and belonging because she was raised in a white community and exposed only to "high" African American culture through her mom's storytelling work, which makes it difficult for her to connect with many aspects of the African American community. Brianna, as an adopted child raised in Jewish culture, finds solace only with other mixed people who identify as "mixed" rather than with people who reflect her races and cultures. She describes a sense of loneliness as she says, "I mean I have been at a disadvantage that I haven't been able to like be around more mixed people, but . . . I've learned more I guess . . . just about like going through things being by myself." Although her parents took her to powwows when she was young, they did not teach her about Choctaw culture or people. As an adult she went to visit her birthmother and was surprised to find that she did not look Native American to her, "not like the people you see on Northern Exposure" she said. As a result of that feeling of disconnection from that culture she now identifies less as Native American and says, "That hasn't been my favorite side." Alexis appears to identify most with military culture "where you're just people." This is reflected in her desire to promote multiculturalism without a focus on the specific cultures represented. How much the women felt a part of their families' cultures appears to be a key factor in these women's sense of belonging and sense of self.

CONCLUSION

This chapter points to the importance of maintaining cultural identity. It has been proposed that people of mixed heritage are the answer to the racial divide, with the argument being that the more mixed we become, the less racial division there will be. These women's stories argue against this logic. With the exception of Alexis, the women who had the least connection to their cultures had the most concern about the races and ethnicities of the people in their lives. In some ways racial lines became more prominent and caused more angst. Dalia, who had strong cultural ties to both her heritages, felt the least threatened by the challenges of others, trusting that her perspective was a valuable perspective even if it was different from those around her.

At the end of the second focus group, I asked the women if there was anything they would say to parents with mixed-race children or teachers who wanted to better serve mixed-race students. These were their suggestions:

> Teachers need to stop telling kids that they are something other than what the child (and the child's parents) perceives herself to be. (Alexis)

> Parents need to recognize both sides. It is good to be exposed to both sides of the family. If that isn't possible then it is important to pass

along the missing culture in concrete ways, "cultural event kind of ways." (Martha)

Pass your languages along to your children. (Annie and then all of them)

Parents need to know that if they are patient with their kids, things will be okay. Kids may rebel against one parent or be mad about the way they were raised. (Bobbie)

Know that being mixed adds this whole other like political social element to just the throes of adolescence, and so it just compounds all of it, or the identity crisis that so many people face when they hit college. It becomes this whole race thing, which is really scary. (Bobbie)

Don't emphasize too much that life for a mixed child will be hard. It may be, but it may not be, at least for a while, so you don't want to send your child to school saying, "Tough life out there cuz you're mixed so be ready for it." (Alexis)

Kids are resilient, you know. You probably will screw them up and they'll be in therapy, but do the best you can, and they'll be fine. (Martha)

There will be consequences for those choices that you make that you need to think about balancing. For example, if you want to raise your kids in the suburbs because you feel like it's a safer lifestyle, realize what the consequences are of what the neighborhood is going to look like and think about what you have to do to balance that out. (Martha)

Many of these suggestions stress the importance of passing along both parents' cultures to children of mixed heritage regardless of how they look or to what privileges they may have access. For the interracial family, passing along culture is made complicated by racism within the family and estrangement from parents and/or extended family members. Adoption can add to the complexity. However, with effort, parents and teachers can assist mixed-race youth in attaining cultural knowledge that reflects their multiracial origins. Passing along culture in the form of visits with extended family, participating in cultural events, and teaching languages may be key to improving the ability of mixed-race women to successfully maintain a strong sense of self as they navigate relationships with their families, friends, community organizations, and public institutions. Teachers can assist parents in the effort by acknowledging the mixed-race identities of the students in their classrooms and working to have the cultures of their students represented in their classrooms through visuals, readings, and class discussions on diversity. The stories and suggestions of these women demonstrate examples of working to claim agency while acknowledging a sense of responsibility to their families, their friends, and their cultural communities. As such, they provide insight into new ways we can promote social justice.

NOTES

1. The terms mixed race, people/women of mixed heritage, multiracial, biracial, and interracial will be used interchangeably in this chapter.

2. According to U.S. Office of Management and Budget Directive 15 (1997).

3. This chapter is a pilot project for a dissertation project I intend to conduct on the same research topic. When potential participants expressed difficulty in participating this semester with this project, I asked them if they would be willing to participate in my doctoral research in the near future.

4. To protect participants' confidentiality, pseudonyms are used throughout this chapter for people and places.

5. All of the women were invited to bring "pictures, drawings, writings, or anything else that might help you tell your story" to the individual interviews.

REFERENCES

Bell, L. A. (1997). Theoretical foundations for social justice education. In M. Adams, L. A. Bell, & P. Griffin (Eds.), Teaching for diversity and social justice (pp. 1–15). New York & London: Routledge.

Bigelow, B., Christensen, L., Karp, S., Miner, B., & Peterson, B. (1994). Rethinking our classrooms: Teaching for equity and justice. Milwaukee: Rethinking Schools Ltd.

Delpit, L. (1995). Other people's children: Cultural conflict in the classroom. New York: New Press.

Downing, K., Nichols, D., & Webster, K. (Eds.). (2005). Multiracial America: A resource guide on the history and literature of interracial issues. Lanham, Maryland: Scarecrow.

Ifekwunigwe, J. O. (Ed.). (2004). "Mixed race" studies: A reader. London: Routledge.

Omi, M., & Winant, H. (2001). Racial formations. In P. S. Rothenberg (Ed.), Race, class, and gender in the United States: An integrated study (5th ed., pp. 11–20). New York: Worth.

Renn, K. A. (2004). Mixed race students in college: The ecology of race, identity, and community on campus. New York: State University of New York Press.

Root, M. P. P. (1992). Racially mixed people in America. Newbury Park, CA: Sage.

Root, M. P. P. (1996). The multiracial experience: Racial borders as the new frontier. Thousand Oaks, CA: Sage.

Schoem, D. (2005). Teaching an interracial issues course. In K. Downing, D. Nichols, & K. Webster (Eds.), Multiracial America: A resource guide on the history and literature of interracial issues (pp. 13–22). Lanham, MD: Scarecrow.

Spickard, P. R. (1992). The illogic of American racial categories. In M. P. P. Root (Ed.), Racially mixed people in America (pp. 12–23). Newbury Park, CA: Sage.

Tatum, B. D. (1995). "Why are all the black kids sitting together in the cafeteria?" and other conversations about race. New York: Basic Books.

Trueba, E. H. T. (2004). The New Americans: Immigrants and transnationals at work. Lanham: Rowman & Littlefield.

Young, R. J. C. (1995). Colonial desire: Hybridity in theory, culture and race. London: Routledge.

Valenzuela, A. (1999). *Subtractive schooling: U.S.-Mexican youth and the politics of caring.* Albany: State University of New York Press.

Williams, K. (2006). *Mark one or more: Civil rights in multiracial America.* Ann Arbor: University of Michigan Press.

Zack, N. (Ed.). (1995). *American mixed race: The culture of microdiversity.* Lanham, MD: Rowman & Littlefield.

CHAPTER THIRTEEN

I CAN RELATE TO THIS! "LEVELING UP"

MATHEMATICS CURRICULUM AND INSTRUCTION
THROUGH PERSONAL RELEVANCE
AND MEANINGFUL CONNECTIONS

LAURA B. KENT AND TERRI CARON

INTRODUCTION

Mathematics curricula and pedagogical techniques have evolved immensely over the last two decades. The formation of national standards to guide curriculum development vastly changed the expectations for teaching and learning mathematics (National Council of Teachers of Mathematics [NCTM], 1989; 2000). This was done largely in response to the "poor performance" in higher level mathematics of United States students compared to students in other countries as documented by the Third International Mathematics and Science Study (TIMSS) (U.S Office of Education, 1996). Historically labeled as "gatekeeper" content into higher education and more formidable careers, mathematics was presented as abstract and devoid of meaning for the majority of students. Only those students fortunate enough to be able learn effectively through "transmission" models of instruction were rewarded with entrance into advanced mathematics classes.

The research and curriculum development projects of the 1990s as well as advances in technology launched more innovative approaches to mathematics teaching and learning through increased emphasis on problem solving and construction of knowledge (e.g., National Science Foundation [NSF] funded curriculum projects such as *Mathematics in Context*). This has led to increased performance of students across the country on mathematics standardized tests, particularly in elementary and middle schools. However, the gap between middle-class white students and working-class poor and students of color continues to exist at all levels.

In this chapter, we propose the adaptation of mathematics curricula to meet the diverse needs and interests of students and gain access to significant mathematics. We draw on two theoretical perspectives related to mathematics teaching and learning. The first is Freudenthal's (1983) phenomenological approach that emphasizes the study of mathematics through students' lived experiences. The second is Ladson-Billings' (1995; 1997) ideas of "culturally relevant pedagogy" in which teachers are expected to understand and respect the culture of diverse student populations and utilize techniques such as scaffolding to bridge their experiences with mathematics content. We argue that the merging of these two perspectives has the potential to improve all students' interest and learning in mathematics and transform teachers' thinking and enactment of curricular materials at all levels.

Our experiences as white females teaching in schools with predominately African American students have influenced our perspective on constructing and adapting curriculum materials that honor the potential of our students through relevance and access to significant mathematics. We take a somewhat different stance from some of the recent discussion of culturally relevant mathematics curricula that emphasizes issues of social justice and equity (Murtada-Watts & D'Ambrosio, 1997). This is not to say that we do not acknowledge the importance of critically examining the political nature of education. However, our focus is on domain-specific thinking and bridging students' informal knowledge of mathematics content with formal notations and procedures to improve their opportunities to enter and succeed in courses that traditionally serve as gatekeepers to advanced degrees in mathematics, science, and engineering fields. This may include but is not limited to the use of contexts that may be interpreted through political lenses.

We further advocate our approach as an opportunity to "level up" the mathematics curriculum for all students by encouraging teachers to use students' interests as a foundation for engaging and learning the content. It could be argued that such techniques would "dummy down" the mathematics curriculum. Prior to the development of national standards for mathematics teaching and learning, there was a tradition of keeping mathematics concepts and procedures abstract and obscure so that only those who can "master" such ideas can succeed and progress in the field (NCTM, 1989, 2000). We dispel this type of thinking by carefully outlining trajectories for how to explicitly connect students' understandings to these concepts and provide suggestions to help teachers critically examine the textbooks they are using to construct more authentic mathematics examples in their lessons.

"REAL-WORLD" MATHEMATICS

In the past couple of decades, researchers and mathematics educators began to examine the types of mathematics that children use outside of formal classroom instruction (Mukhapadhyay, Resnick, & Schauble, 1990). These authors showed a disconnect between the mathematics that children used to solve "real-world" problems, primarily number sense strategies, and symbolic and rote strategies taught in schools. For example, children who were not exposed to formal schooling were found to be able to use numbers flexibly to solve problems involving integers to keep track of earning and owing money in selling of items on the street but could not solve the same types of problems when written symbolically (1990). At the same time, studies of students' mathematical problem solving abilities in the United States showed that while they may have mastered computational procedures, they were unable to apply them to "real-world" situations (Carpenter, 1983). This led to the creation of new curriculum standards that would emphasize more connections between school mathematics and real-world mathematics (NCTM, 1989).

These studies and new standards were the impetus for a closer examination of how teachers might find ways to utilize students' informal methods for solving problems in their own instruction (Carpenter, et al., 1999). These cognitive-based approaches were also beginning to provide frameworks of students' problem-solving trajectories to connect what students already know to what was expected in the way of formal mathematics procedures and conventions. Much of this data was gathered through the use of interviews with students to assess their thinking prior to and following formal instruction. The results indicated that students are capable of constructing a variety of algorithms to solve problems involving whole numbers, some of which mirrored the foundation of standard algorithms, and moreover, that emphasis on standard algorithms could actually be detrimental to student understanding of mathematics (Kamii & Dominick, 1998).

While much has been written with respect to whole number concepts, there still exists wide speculation about whether it is possible to detail students' thinking and learning trajectories in more complex mathematics domains. Some of the classroom-based studies related to Realistic Mathematics Education (RME) (RME attempts to bridge starting points to more formal mathematics and will be explained in the next section of this chapter) ideas and curriculum materials have shown some promising results with respect to identifying tools that students effectively use as intermediaries between their informal strategies and standard mathematical algorithms (Streefland, 1991; Gravemeijer, 1994; Brinker, 1996, 1998; Kent, 2000). For example, in Brinker's (1996) study in a combined fourth- and fifth-grade class, students invented procedures for multiplying and dividing fractions and mixed numbers using ratio tables—in effect, mirroring the distributive property in several cases.

"MATHEMATIZING" REALITY

The premise of Freudenthal's (1983) phenomenological approach to mathematics teaching and learning is that any significant mathematics should be grounded in the reality of students and serve as a starting point for instruction. From these ideas emerged a broader approach called "Realistic Mathematics Education" (RME) that attempts to bridge these starting points to more formal mathematics (e.g. Gravemeijer, 1994). What differentiates this approach from generic recommendations for using real-life examples to capture students' attention in mathematics (e.g. NCTM, 2000) are the domain-specific tasks and trajectories. For example, Streefland's (1991) research outlines a trajectory for learning formal fraction concepts and procedures through the initial task of "fair-sharing."

In the 1990s the National Science Foundation funded a research and curriculum development project that included the collaboration between the Freudenthal Institute in Utrecht, the Netherlands, and the University of Wisconsin-Madison to develop a comprehensive curriculum, *Mathematics in Context* (Encyclopedia Britannica, 1997–98) or MiC, that would simultaneously capture the essence of RME and the NCTM *Standards* (1989; 2001) recommendations with a focus on open-ended tasks and mathematical problem solving. MiC is a comprehensive middle grades mathematics curriculum that emphasizes problem posing to elicit certain learning trajectories through carefully selected contexts.

An important component of any tasks or curricula reflective of RME is the potential for horizontal and vertical mathematization (Treffers, 1991). With horizontal mathematization, students have the opportunity to use features of the context to solve problems, such as dividing up objects in different ways to solve problems within the fair-share context. With vertical mathematization, meaningful representations are adapted to bridge students' informal strategies involving semantic features of the context, with more formal mathematical symbols and procedures, as was the case with the table arrangements and ratio table for fraction problems (Streefland, 1991; 1993).

The nature of the cognitive analysis of domain-specific learning is such that the most fully developed topics are whole numbers and rational numbers from the elementary mathematics curriculum (e.g. CGI and others). In other words, fairly detailed trajectories of students' thinking and progression through the topic have been identified. Not surprising that more complex topics in mathematics, such as functions, have yet to evolve in terms of the identification of learning trajectories. Fortunately, as RME evolves from print curricula such as MiC, upper-level mathematics content is continuing to undergo examination for ways to better connect students' informal understandings to more formal mathematics (Case, 2005).

CULTURALLY "REALISTIC" MATHEMATICS CURRICULUM

There are many ways to think about culturally relevant curriculum. Some have argued for the construction of curriculum materials that challenge the status quo and provide opportunities for students to use these to critically examine the political and social order of our society. Others have advocated pedagogical approaches that emphasize ways to merge cultural relevance with aspects of the NCTM standards recommendations (Gutstein, et al., 1997). Common to both approaches are helping students develop a critical stance toward the use of mathematics in the world.

Ladson-Billings (1997) offered some possible principles to guide curriculum and instruction in mathematics classes based on her study of successful teachers of African American students. Her outline of several heuristics that may guide teachers toward the enactment of a more culturally relevant curriculum in mathematics includes the following:

1. Students treated as competent are likely to demonstrate competence;

2. Providing instructional scaffolding for students allows students to move from what they know to what they do not know;

3. The major focus of the classroom must be instructional;

4. Real education is about extending students' thinking and abilities beyond what they already know; and

5. Effective pedagogical practice involves in-depth knowledge of students as well as of subject matter. (Ladson-Billings, 1997, pp. 703–04)

While we maintain that all of these heuristics are equally important in "leveling-up" students' achievement in mathematics, we will focus this chapter on exploring domain-specific methods for addressing the second heuristic since this is a natural tenet of RME as well.

"KID-RELEVANT" CONTEXTS

In this section, we highlight various contexts that we have found not only to engage kids in mathematics but also to build on their informal knowledge and connect their strategies to more formal procedures. In addition to culturally relevant contexts, we coin the phrase *kid relevant* to emphasize contexts that appeal to many kids and illustrate the use of intermediary representations to bridge their understandings to significant mathematical ideas in the spirit of RME.

INTEGERS

Building off of the work of Mukhapadayay and colleagues (1990) and RME, Kent (1999) implemented an instructional unit in a fifth-grade class that emphasized connecting students' informal knowledge of integers within the context of assets and debits to more formal methods for adding and subtracting integers. The students were considered below grade level in their mathematics performance. However, they were able to work effectively with integers presented in context. Therefore, the goal was to provide opportunities to bridge the gap between their mental calculations with integers and calculations that involved notations for integers.

The two representations that were the most effective intermediary tools that students used were a ladder that was partially below water and partially above water to place 0 and numbers above ("dry") and below ("wet") 0 and numbers with arrows to represent the four directions within the context of a game. For example, when students were asked to calculate the distance from "dry 2" to "wet 2," they responded, "4" which is the equivalent of $2- (-2) = 4$. Similarly, within the context of moving the marker on the game board, students were able to recognize that a move of $4 \rightarrow$ combined with $6\leftarrow$ resulted in a move of $2\leftarrow$ because as one student stated, "west had the biggest number" (Kent, 1999, p. 65). In conventional symbols this computation equates to the sentence, $4 + (-6) = -2$. Eventually, the contextualized notations for positive and negative numbers were replaced by the conventions "+" and "–" for working with integers. The intermediary models served as tools to "level up" their informal methods for working with integer concepts to formal symbols and conventions for integer computations.

Other kid-relevant contexts that have been found to be useful for bridging students' informal knowledge of fractions with more formal procedures include recipes and jumping situations. With recipe problems, students use ratio tables as intermediary models between invented strategies for solving fraction problems and more standardized computational procedures such as the distributive property (Brinker, 1998). With jumping situations, students used linear models to represent and solve linear equations (Kent, 2001).

The opportunity exists in mathematics curriculum development to locate the intersection between kid-relevant contexts and culturally realistic contexts that both honors the culture of diverse populations of students and "levels up" their understanding of significant mathematics concepts. The following example from Caron (2006) highlights her study in which she adapted curriculum materials from the Interactive Mathematics Program to her high school mathematics course populated primarily with low-achieving African American students.

FUNCTIONS

The concept of 'functions' is fundamental to higher-level mathematics courses. Yet most students' understanding of functions is limited because it is typically presented in its most abstract form. However, two of the most important aspects of functions, arbitrariness and "univalence" (Even, 1993), are not difficult to represent in situations that are personally meaningful to students. The following input-output tables provide both numerical and nonnumerical examples of these two aspects of functions.

Table 1

In	Out
rap	a
reggae	e
country	o
jazz	a
classical	
hip hop	

Table 2

In	Out
5	11
7	15
2	5
1	3
8	
10	

At first glance, they may appear to be completely unrelated. However, both represent functions, an important concept in mathematics in which a special relationship exists between the input and output objects. The goal in each situation is to define this relationship or determine "the rule." For mathematicians, the table on the right would perhaps be easier to define since the prerequisite knowledge is based on understanding of number relationships; that is, the output number is found by doubling and adding one to the input number, so the output for 8 would be 17 ($2 \times 8 + 1$). A rule for the table on the left is that the letter in the output column is the second letter of the word in the input column.

Both examples capture the essence of the modern definition of functions, that is, arbitrary relationships with a unique correspondence, also known as "univalence" (Even, 1993). However, we would assert that the nonnumerical example has broader reach because it does not require students to have mastered prerequisite math skills in order to interpret and gain access to the underlying concept. In other words, the nature of the nonnumerical example suggests that functions can be arbitrary. Common sense would dictate that there cannot be two different second letters in any of the words—reggae having both an "e" and an "a" as outputs for the second letter of the input word.

ACCOUNTABILITY AND STUDENT PERFORMANCE

In the era of high-stakes testing and accountability legislation (e.g. No Child Left Behind Act or NCLB, 1992), teachers may be reluctant to veer too far from state standards in their curriculum planning and instruction. Yet there still exist widespread gaps between whites and minorities in performance in mathematics areas (e.g. Haycock, 2001). The major thrust of NCLB is that "all students will be given the opportunity to achieve" (George, 2002, p. 20). Many traditional methods of mathematics instruction, particularly those that emphasize teaching concepts as isolated skills devoid of meaningful contexts have failed to motivate and improve students' performance in higher level mathematics, in many cases, serving as a gatekeeper to careers in science and engineering.

We argue that methods specifically designed to help improve minority students' performance in mathematics should be implemented and that it is the responsibility of the teachers of these students to become familiar and make use of students' cultural experiences and background to bridge their understanding of significant mathematics concepts. However, this knowledge alone does not guarantee improved performance. Much additional content-specific research is needed to help teachers understand the most productive ways to build on their students' understanding of the world through their own experiences and connect it to the mathematics standards.

The examples presented in this chapter are but a few of the multitude of possible opportunities for students to define learning trajectories that bridge their informal knowledge of the world with formal mathematics. Identification of intermediary models to help students make meaningful connections to mathematical ideas devoid of context appears to be a critical aspect of the learning trajectories. As Ladson-Billings (1997) notes, "Real education is about extending students' thinking and abilities beyond what they already know" (p. 704). Within RME, the mathematics should eventually become the context for learning. The combination of these approaches has the potential to "level up" all students' understanding and performance in school mathematics.

REFERENCES

Brinker, L. (1998). Using recipes and ratio tables to build on students' understanding of fractions. *Teaching children mathematics*. National Council of Teachers of Mathematics: Reston, VA, 5 (4), 218–224.

Brinker, L. (1996). *Using structured representations to solve fraction problems: A discussion of seven students' strategies*. Paper presented at the annual meeting of the American Educational Research Association Annual Meeting, March 1997, Chicago, IL.

Caron, T. (2006). *Building upon students' intuitive knowledge of function concepts utilizing culturally sensitive pedagogy: A classroom-based approach*. Unpublished doctoral dissertation, University of South Carolina.

Carpenter, T. P. (1983). Results of the Third NAEP Mathematics Assessment: Secondary School. *Mathematics Teacher*, 76(9), 652–659.

Carpenter, T. P., Fennema, E., Franke, M. L., Levi, L., & Empson, S. B. (1999). *Children's mathematics: Cognitively guided instruction*. Heinemann: Portsmouth, NH.

Case, R. (2005). Report from the Netherlands: The Dutch revolution in secondary school mathematics. *Mathematics Teacher*, 98(6), 374–384.

Even, R. (1993). Subject-matter knowledge and pedagogical content knowledge: prospective secondary teachers and the function concept. *Journal for research in mathematics education*, 24(2), 94–116.

Freudenthal, H. (1983). *Didactical phenomenology of mathematical structures*. Dordrecht: Reidel.

George, P. (2002). *No child left behind: Implications for middle level leaders*. Westerville, OH: National Middle School Association.

Gravemeijer, K. (1994). Educational development and developmental research in mathematics education. *Journal for Research in Mathematics Education*, 25, 443–471.

Gutstein, E., Lipman, P., Hernandez, P., & de los Reyes, R. (1997). Culturally relevant mathematics teaching in a Mexican American context. *Journal for Research in Mathematics Education*, 28(6), 709–737.

Haycock, K. (2001). Closing the achievement gap. *Educational Leadership*, 58(6).

Kamii, C., & Dominick, A. (1998). The harmful effects of algorithms in grades 1–4. In L. J. Morrow & M. J. Kenney (Eds.), *The teaching and learning of algorithms in school mathematics: 1998 Yearbook* (pp. 130–140). Reston, VA: National Council of Teachers of Mathematics.

Kent, L. B. (2001). Contextualized models for slope and linear equations. International Group for the Psychology of Mathematics Education Annual Meeting, July 2001, Utrecht, the Netherlands.

Kent, L. B. (2000). Integers and meaningful contexts: A direct connection. *Mathematics teaching in the middle school*. National Council of Teachers of Mathematics: Reston, VA, vol. 62–66.

Kent, L. B., Arnosky, J., & McMonagle, J. (2002). Using representational contexts to support students' multiplicative reasoning. In B. Litwiller (Ed.), *Making sense of fractions, ratios, and proportions: 2002 NCTM Yearbook* (pp. 145–152). Reston, VA: National Council of Teachers of Mathematics.

Ladson-Billings, G. (1997). It doesn't add up: African-American students' mathematics achievement. *Journal for research in mathematics education*, 28(6), 697–708.

Ladson-Billings, G. (1995). Toward a theory of culturally relevant teaching. *American education research journal*, 33, 465–491.

Mukhapadhyay, S., Resnick, L. B., & Schauble, L. (1990). Social sense-making in mathematics: Children's ideas of negative numbers. Paper presented at the Psychology of Mathematics Education Conference, Mexico, July, 1990.

Murtada-Watts, K., & D'Ambrosio, B. S. (1997). A convergence of transformative multicultural and mathematics instruction? Dilemmas of group deliberations for curriculum change. *Journal for Research in Mathematics Education*, 28(6), 767–782.

National Council of Teachers of Mathematics. (2000). *Principles and standards for school mathematics*. Reston, VA: National Council of Teachers of Mathematics.

National Council of Teachers of Mathematics. (1989). *Curriculum and evaluation standards*. Reston, VA: National Council of Teachers of Mathematics.

Rodriguez, A. J., & Kitchen, R. S. (2005). *Preparing mathematics and science teachers for diverse classrooms: Promising strategies for transformative pedagogy*. Mahwah, NJ: Erlbaum.

Streefland, L. (1991). *Fractions in realistic mathematics education: A paradigm of developmental research*. Netherlands: Kluwer.

Treffers, A. (1991). Didactical background of a mathematics program for primary education. In L. Streefland (Ed.), *Realistic mathematics education in primary school: On the occasion of the opening of the Freudenthal Institute*. Culemborg: Technipress.

United States Office of Education. (1996). Pursuing excellence: Initial findings from the Third International Mathematics and Science Study. Washington, DC: Office of Educational Research and Improvement.

CONTRIBUTORS

BENJAMIN BAEZ is a professor of higher education at Florida International University. His work in the area of historically black institutions and the status of minorities in the profession is internationally recognized.

SILVIA CRISTINA BETTEZ is a doctoral candidate in the School of Education at the University of North Carolina at Chapel Hill. She is biracial and bicultural; her mother is Colombian, and her father is French-Canadian. Her personal background and professional interest in the intersections of race, class, and gender led her to conduct research on the experiences of mixed-race women. Her other academic areas of interest include critical multicultural education, qualitative methods, and feminist gender studies.

DENNIS CARLSON is a professor in the Department of Education and the Center for Education and Cultural Studies at Miami University. He is the author of *Teachers and Crisis: Urban School Reform and Teachers' Work Culture* (1992), *Making Progress: Education and Culture and Culture in New Times* (1997), and *Leaving Safe Harbors: Toward a New Progressivism in American Education and Public Life*. He has also coedited a number of books in education, including *Keeping the Promise: Essays on Leadership, Democracy, and Education* (With C. P. Gause, 2007), and has published articles in major educational journals.

TERRI CARON is a high school mathematics teacher who recently completed her dissertation on students' intuitive understandings of function concepts through the use of culturally sensitive contexts. She was the recipient of the Fulbright Scholarship in 2004 and studied mathematics instructional strategies in Japan. She visited mathematics classes in Philadelphia public schools and adapted innovative curriculum materials based on the Interactive Mathematics Curriculum to enhance low-performing students' achievement in mathematics. She has served as a mentor to numerous student teachers in mathematics over the last five years. Currently, she serves as a mathematics curriculum supervisor in Asheville, North Carolina.

KATHERINE CHADDOCK is a professor of the higher education administration in the College of Education at the University of South Carolina. She is the

255

author or coauthor of five books and many articles on various aspects of American educational history and culture, particularly focusing on early twentieth-century educational innovations and experiments. Chaddock serves on the editorial boards of the *History of Higher Education Annual* and the *ASHE-ERIC Reader in Higher Education History*, and she is associate editor for the *South Carolina Encyclopedia*.

JENNIFER ESPOSITO is an assistant professor of educational policy studies at Georgia State University where she teaches qualitative research methods. Her research interests include popular culture as a site of education, urban education and race, gender, class and sexuality performativity. She has published in *Cultural Studies*, *Critical* Methodologies, *Educational Studies*, and *Teacher Education Quarterly*.

SUELLYN HENKE is associate professor and chair of the Department of Education at Albion College. Her areas of interest include secondary education, curriculum theory, and socio-cultural foundations of education. She has published an article in *Cultural Studies*, *Critical Methodologies*, as well as a chapter in *Promises to Keep: Cultural Studies, Democratic Education and Public Life*.

MARY JEAN RONAN HERZOG is a professor at Western Carolina University in the Department of Educational Leadership and Foundations. Her research interests include rural education, teaching methods, and democracy in education. Herzog is program coordinator for the M.A.T. degree and specializes in teaching qualitative research methods and curriculum foundations.

RHONDA B. JEFFRIES is an associate professor of curriculum studies in the Department of Instruction and Teacher Education at the University of South Carolina. Jeffries has taught in the areas of cultural foundations, urban and community education, curriculum studies, and qualitative research methods. Her research interests include understanding the educational experiences of marginalized people, and her work often examines educational phenomena through a performance theory lens. She is the author of *Performance Traditions among African American Teachers* and is coeditor of *Black Women in the Field: Experiences Understanding Ourselves and Others through Qualitative Research*.

LAURA B. KENT is an associate professor of secondary mathematics education in the Department of Curriculum and Instruction, College of Education, at the University of Arkansas. Her interests include students' mathematical thinking and the role of context and classroom discourse in facilitating understanding of mathematics. She has worked on several Nation Science Foundation (NSF)–funded projects and coauthored articles in leading mathematics education journals as well as the middle school textbook *Mathematics in Context: A Connected Curriculum for Grades 5–8*, published by Encyclopedia Britannica. She is currently researching the impact of professional development on student achievement in the state of Arkansas.

PEPI LEISTYNA has a masters and doctorate from Harvard University. He is an associate professor of applied linguistics graduate studies at the University of Massachusetts Boston, where he coordinates the research program and teaches courses in cultural studies, media literacy, and language acquisition. Speaking internationally on issues of democracy, public education, and social justice, Leistyna has published articles in various scholarly journals. His books include *Breaking Free: The Transformative Power of Critical Pedagogy; Presence of Mind: Education and the Politics of Deception; Defining and Designing Multiculturalism; Cultural Studies: From Theory to Action;* and *Corpus Analysis: Language Structure and Language Use.* His forthcoming book is entitled *Laughing Matters: Entertainment Television's Mockery of the Working Class.* His recent documentary film with the Media Education Foundation is *Class Dismissed: How TV Frames the Working Class.* He is a research fellow for the Education Policy Research Unit, associate editor of The Journal of English Linguistics, and vice president of curriculum development for ACME: Action Coalition for Media Literacy. He is also on the editorial board of the following journals: *Simile: Studies in Media and Information Literacy Education; Situations: Project of the Radical Imagination; Public Resistance; Radical Teacher; The Journal for Critical Education Policy Studies;* and *Taboo: The Journal of Culture and Education.*

RICHARD R. LUSSIER is a teacher and administrator at Ridge View High School in Richland School District Two, Columbia, South Carolina. He holds an Ed.D. in curriculum and instruction from the University of South Carolina and continues to write concerning multicultural curricular issues in secondary schools.

TAMARA POWELL is associate director of the extended graduate campus in the Graduate School at the University of South Carolina who recently completed her dissertation, "Communities in Collaboration: A Struggle to Increase Literacy in South Carolina." Powell is a former public school English teacher and administrator with research interests in southern history, library history, equity and parity in public education, and professional development for educators. She holds an Ed.D. in curriculum and instruction.

ADAM RENNER is an associate professor and graduate chair at Bellarmine University. He teaches courses on social difference and social justice. His research interests also include pedagogy and service learning. He has published articles in *The High School Journal, Educational Studies,* the *Kentucky Journal of Excellence, The Rouge Forum, Rethinking Schools, EcoJustice Education, The Journal of Curriculum Theorizing,* and *The International Journal of*

Learning. He also writes a column at www.pucknation.com, called "The Hopeful Struggle." He lives with his partner in Louisville, Kentucky.

SUSAN SCHRAMM-PATE is a former public school art teacher in Ohio and associate professor of curriculum studies in the Department of Instruction and Teacher Education at the University of South Carolina. Her teaching concentration and research interests revolve around gender studies, historiography, cultural studies, and integrated arts-based curriculum. Her books include *Transforming the Curriculum: Thinking outside the Box* and *A Separate Sisterhood: Women Who Shaped Southern Educational Reform in the Progressive Era,* coauthored with Katherine Reynolds Chaddock. Her research appears in *Southern Studies: An Interdisciplinary Journal of the South, High School Journal, Journal of Curriculum Theorizing, International Journal of Educational Research, Journal of Communications and Minority Issues, Art Education Journal,* and *Journal of Secondary Education.*

NAME INDEX

SUBJECT INDEX

Ability grouping, 17
Abolitionism, 92
Abolitionist, 32
Acceptance, 53, 167–172
Affective, 105
Affirmative Action legislation, 27
Aiken Negro School, 89
American Missionary Association, 46
Amnesty International, 198
Anglo-Saxon, 165, 170
Anthropology, 130, 20, 219, 222
Anti-communist loyalty program, 143
Antiracist, 4, 9, 58, 195–198
Appalachian Regional Commission
    (ARC), 205, 215
Appalachian Studies Movement, 208
Archetype, 9, 136–139, 150, 215
Assimilation, 219

Baugknight Negro School, 88
Benedict College, 81
Berry College, 44
Bias, 34, 206–209, 215
Bigotry, 23, 149, 162, 214
Black History Month, 21, 168
Blackface minstrelsy, 9, 150–155, 160–
    163
Brown vs. Topeka Board of Education,
    162
Busing, 26, 170

Canon, 37, 119, 148
Capitalism, 57, 74, 99, 148, 166, 191,
    210
Carnegie, 51
Catholic church, 168
Christian Marxist, 61
Cinco de Mayo, 168, 185

Citizen rights, 17, 14, 27
Civil Rights Act, 156
Civil rights pedagogy, 2, 4–5, 207
Class, 60, 72, 94, 120, 122–123, 125,
    136–137, 144, 149, 162, 221, 242,
    255–256
Cognitive, 110, 247–249
Cold War, 64, 167
Collaboration, 137, 199, 201, 251
Colonialism, 147
Color blind, 17, 27–28
Commodity, 99
Communism, 31, 108, 167
Confederate, 8–9, 147–151, 153, 156,
    162, 164–166, 169, 171, 173, 175,
    177–179, 186–187
Confederate Memorial Day, 166, 176,
    186–188
Cotton production, 78
Critical legal studies, 21
Critical multiculturalism, 5, 8
Critical pedagogy, 5, 8, 69, 72, 113,
    189, 257
Critical Race Theory, 29, 31
Critical reader, 147
Critical service learning, 197–198, 203
Critical Theory, 72
Cross cultural mentoring, 136–137,
    144–145
Cultural capital, 89, 92
Cultural criticism, 99, 195
Cultural genocide, 219
Cultural hybridity, 8, 148, 150, 162,
    191, 197, 201
Cultural inhibition, 36, 40, 47
Cultural preservation, 218–219
Cultural studies, 2, 5, 8, 10, 147–148,
    150, 162, 199, 207, 254–258

267